Air Transport

Studies in Transport History

Series Editor: John Armstrong

Air Transport

Edited by

PETER J. LYTH

Routledge
Taylor & Francis Group

LONDON AND NEW YORK

First published 1996 by Ashgate Publishing

2 Park Square, Milton Park, Abingdon, Oxon OX14 4RN
711 Third Avenue, New York, NY 10017, USA

Routledge is an imprint of the Taylor & Francis Group, an informa business

First issued in paperback 2016

British Library Cataloguing in Publication Data
Air Transport
    (Studies in Transport History)
    1. Aeronautics, commercial—Great Britain—History—20th
    century. 2. Airlines—Great Britain—History—20th century.
    I. Lyth, Peter J.
    387.7'0941

Library of Congress Cataloging-in-Publication Data
Air transport/edited by Peter J. Lyth
        p. cm. (Studies in Transport History).
    ISBN 1-85928-309-8 (cloth)
    1. Aeronautics, commercial—Great Britain—History—20th century.
    2. Aeronautics, commercial—United States—History—20th century.
    I. Lyth, Peter J. II. Series.
HE9843.A3A36 1996
387'.087'0941'0904—dc20   96-22319
                                                      CIP

ISBN 978-1-85928-309-7 (hbk)
ISBN 978-1-138-27245-3 (pbk)

Transferred to Digital Printing in 2014

Contents

Studies in Transport History

Series Editor's Preface

The idea for this series originated in a meeting of the Editorial Board of *The Journal of Transport History*. As part of the celebrations to mark the fortieth anniversary of the founding of the journal, a classified index of the articles appearing in each of the series was compiled by Julie Stevenson and published in the September 1993 number of the journal. This exercise revealed the wealth of material that lay in the journal but which was largely forgotten and relatively inaccessible, unless a full run of the journal was close to hand. The index took the first step in making it simpler to determine what was in the journal. The Editorial Board decided it should continue this process by making the best of the essays more readily available.

Hence it is proposed to issue a series of volumes, each containing a number of articles reprinted from *The Journal of Transport History*, dealing with a particular mode of transport. As initially planned there are eight volumes in this series, each covering one form of transport and edited by a different member of the Editorial Board. Each volume contains about ten articles, reprinted from *The Journal of Transport History*. The articles have been selected because they were seminal at the date of their publication and have stood the test of time. Hence they are still important contributions to the state of our knowledge on the topic.

Each volume also contains an introduction by the editor of the volume, which seeks to contextualise the articles selected; that is, to show how each contribution fitted into the state of knowledge at the time of its publication, to explain its importance, to indicate any more-recent literature on the topic that might moderate its findings, and suggest how the debate has moved since the initial publication. Each article retains its original pagination, as in the journal. This will allow citations to be made to the original source.

Thus this series aims to make easily available the most important essays which have appeared in *The Journal of Transport History* over the last forty years, collected together on a thematic basis. It is hoped that this will encourage and provoke further research into transport history, in order to carry the debates into the twenty-first century.

John Armstrong
1996

Thames Valley University

Introduction: aspects of commercial air transport history

PETER J. LYTH

'The airlines, as they changed the shape of the world, were also locked into the ambitions of nations. They provide a kind of visual projection of changes on earth - the shifting political balances of power and wealth, the swings of economic beliefs, the technological developments coming up against political deadlocks and reactions'.[1]

In its 75 year history the airline industry has developed from a technological curiosity and an adventure for the social élite, into the leading long-distance transport mode. Air travel has shrunk the globe and transformed the way we perceive its dimensions and, in doing so, it has become big business. In 1929, a decade after the first commercial air services began in Europe, world scheduled passenger traffic was a mere half million, and even in 1949 less than 30 million people flew on scheduled services. In 1990 total scheduled passenger traffic amounted to 1.16 billion - a fifth of the world's population.[2]

The history of the airline history seems to have a number of distinguishing features. First, until recently at least, the air transport and aircraft manufacturing industries have been concentrated in Europe and North America. This is not to ignore the important contributions that airlines have made to the development of regions with poor surface communications in Asia, South America, Australia and Africa, but rather to recognise the fact that air transport is dependent on a costly form of technology which has been largely restricted to advanced industrial economies.

Secondly, air transport has grown, and spectacularly so since 1950, because its costs and prices have risen more slowly than income levels, and this is mainly due to more efficient production and technology. However, the industry's very dependence on modern technology has caused it to be subjected to an extraordinary degree of old-fashioned government control.

The third feature of its history therefore is that it has had a political and strategic importance independent of its commercial possibilities. Indeed one influential commentator has gone as far as to claim that the evolution of international air transport 'is less a function of aviation technology or conventional commercial traffic than an expression of political forces in specific historical periods. It has been the politics of expansionism, war preparation, diplomacy, economic doctrine, or other conditions not intrinsically related to air transport itself that have defined the development of international civil aviation'.[3]

It might be argued that the State has always taken a strong interest in national transport systems and, just as European governments, with the exception of Britain, became involved in railway construction in the second half of the nineteenth century, so they assumed ownership of the national airline in the inter-war period. However whereas in the first case government participation can be seen as a contribution to the modernisation of the economy, in the second it was for prestige and, to some extent, strategic reasons. Air transport did not make much money for anyone in its first thirty years; the fact that in Europe direct state involvement continued for a further thirty, proves how important for national prestige has been the survival of the flag-carrier.

In the last twenty years the deep involvement of governments in international civil aviation has been questioned and, since the deregulation of the American domestic airline industry in 1978, increasingly challenged. A slow process of disengagement has begun which signifies that the industry has become mature and financially autonomous. In Europe prestige and strategic considerations are giving way to purely economic criteria in the formation of air transport policy, although some fierce opponents of liberalisation and deregulation remain, particularly among those countries whose flag-carriers are comparatively weak international airlines, or compelled for social or political reasons to fly loss-making routes.

Britain's attitude to liberalisation, or 'open skies', has not surprisingly changed over the years according to the relative strength of its air transport industry and the composition and commercial success of its flag-carrier. In the wake of the Second World War when its industry was weak and vulnerable to American domination, British policy towards international civil aviation was restrictive and aimed at achieving the maximum protection for the nationalised airlines British Overseas Airways Corporation (BOAC) and British European Airways (BEA). By the 1980s, and especially after the privatisation of the modern British Airways, British policy was less concerned with protection and more with the encouragement of competition in the industry. At least, as a recent addition to the literature has shown, this was true in so far as Britain's approach towards Europe was concerned; in its dealings with the United States it has remained fairly uncompromising in its efforts to limit competition from American carriers, particularly where vital 'fifth freedom' rights have been at stake.[4]

The vicissitudes of British policy towards air transport since 1919 reflect the changing course of the debate on its place in the national economy. Was it to be a comprehensive public service like the Post Office or the telephones? Or was it just another business sector to be exploited in the most profitable manner? The British Government has treated it as various combinations of these two extremes, with a propensity to draw a line between internal services (public service) and international operations (profit-seeking business). What is clear is that uncertainty over the question has been at the root of policy inconsistencies since the earliest days and is one of the reasons why fashions in airline ownership have swung from private to public and back again to private.[5]

The twelve articles in this volume, themselves the product of changing fashions in scholarship over a forty-year period, form an interesting and informative mosaic of civil aviation history. No apology is made for the fact that they concentrate largely on Britain, since Britain, if not the largest, has none the less been one of the key players in the historical development of the air transport and aircraft manufacturing industries. The eighty years which the articles cover can usefully be divided into five sections.

I

The early days of air transport were characterised by brave souls and primitive technology. Indeed the first generation of aviators seems to have been celebrated precisely because their craft were crude and unreliable; as Peter Fritzsche has noted in a telling phrase, 'virtue gathered only where technology failed'.[6] In Britain, France, Germany and Holland the first airlines began carrying passengers soon after the end of the First World War. In the United States passenger services came only in the later 1920s, the first domestic air routes being for mail only. For the few intrepid passengers, conditions were spartan in the tiny, unheated cabins of what were little more than converted bombers. For the pilots it was a hazardous job with only the most rudimentary navigation and landing aids. For the airline entrepreneurs themselves there was little reward for their pioneer efforts and a fair likelihood of crash landing in bankruptcy. Some of the early airlines, like Junkers, Farman and Handley Page, were part of aircraft manufacturing companies which used the transport undertakings to showcase their creations. Other famous plane builders like de Havilland and Fokker concentrated on construction.

One of the first aircraft manufacturers in Britain was the north London company of Claude Grahame-White. As A. D. George shows, the firm began building military aircraft for the Government with the outbreak of the First World War, but like many of the early aircraft builders its existence was precarious; while its neighbour Handley Page was able to make the switch to civilian transport types after the end of hostilities, Grahame-White fell victim to its dependence on government contracts. The most valuable part of the undertaking seems to have been its premises at Hendon which passed to the Royal Air Force on the company's dissolution and is now near the site of the present-day RAF Museum.

The early airlines in Britain faired little better. In his two articles on British civil aviation between 1919 and 1924, E. Birkhead highlights the confusion in government policy towards air transport and the inadequacy of its various subsidy schemes. Although it was comparatively easy to establish an airline, it was much more difficult to survive at a time when air transport was fundamentally unprofitable. Indeed the lack of profits makes one wonder what it was that motivated the early entrants in the first place. In the case of Daimler Airway the introduction of a new subsidy scheme in the spring of 1922 seems to have been one factor, although as Birkhead explains, the heavy competition on the short service to Paris and the totally uneconomic nature of the aircraft, meant that the chances of achieving unsubsidised operations at that stage were virtually nil. The fact that Daimler earned £114,000 in its two-year history, of which no less than 80 per cent was in the form of government subsidy - and even then it lost money overall - must have had a salutary effect on other intending airline entrepreneurs and probably influenced the outlook of its managing director (Colonel Frank Searle) and general manager (George Woods-Humphery) when they moved to Imperial Airways in 1924.

Britain's first scheduled passenger air service, provided by Air Transport and Travel (AT&T) in 1919, was from London to Paris. It had the obvious advantage of a sea crossing and was about the right distance for the aircraft of the time, ie. 200 miles, but the traffic potential of the two capitals was never realised and high fares made air travel a poor alternative to first class rail travel. Moreover demand was highly seasonal and practically dried up in the winter months - a feature that was to plague short-haul airlines for many years to come. Even after the introduction of the 'permanent subsidy scheme' in March 1922 and the doubling of passenger traffic in the following year, airlines still could not make a profit.[7]

The basic problems of low traffic volume and high unit costs seemed intractable. The aircraft were so expensive to operate that they would have had difficulty breaking even with passenger load factors of 100 per cent, as it was the airlines were lucky to take off with their planes half-full. In his second article Birkhead notes the paradox that although the operations of airlines like Daimler, Instone and Handley Page were too small to cover their fixed costs, none the less the available traffic did not justify the size they had reached. In his breakdown of Daimler's costs he shows what a high proportion of the total was spent on advertising: at 13.7 per cent it was over six times greater than that spent by BEA forty years later. The reason, of course, was the pressing need to get people to fly - in 1922 air travel was a complete novelty and demand had to be created from scratch.

With competition not working and no prospect of unsubsidised air travel in sight, the Government appointed a committee in January 1923 under the chairmanship of Sir Herbert Hambling to look into the future of British civil aviation and advise on the best method of securing its future. The Hambling Committee's report concluded that the benefits of competition under the prevailing circumstances in the air transport market were 'illusory' and it recommended that all British private airlines be merged to form a single monopoly or 'chosen instrument'.[8] The committee's advice was followed and in March 1924 a new company called Imperial Airways was founded.

II

The formation of 'chosen instruments' to guide the national air transport effort was a common development in Europe in the industry's first fifteen years. Besides Imperial Airways (1924), the Belgian airline SABENA was formed in 1923, Deutsche Lufthansa in 1926, Swissair in 1931 and Air France in 1933; the Dutch carrier KLM takes the honour of being the first, having begun operations in 1920. Even in the United States, where an oligopolistic structure was adopted for the development of the domestic market, international air services were entrusted to the chosen instrument Pan American Airways after its formation in 1929.

The chosen instruments had a number of things in common. They enjoyed monopoly rights, at least at the outset, combined with an exclusive claim on government subsidy; indeed the concept of the chosen instrument is synonymous with subsidy and their creation amounts to a recognition by governments that air transport would not survive without financial support from the state. The chosen instrument was also an overt means for projecting national prestige and an expression of nationalist competition in the inter-war years. As a consequence, much of the effort and resources expended on them went into developing air communications with colonial possessions. For Britain's aptly-named

Imperial Airways this meant building up services to India, South Africa and eventually Australia. For the French it meant air links to West Africa and Indochina, for the Dutch, the East Indies, Surinam and Curaçao, and for the Belgians, the Congo. For the Germans, without any formal colonies since the Treaty of Versailles, routes to South America and the Far East acted as a substitute.

There was another, more practical reason why the new national flag-carriers devoted themselves, with such jingoistic acclaim, to forging links to far-flung colonies and dominions. It was already obvious that air transport showed itself to maximum advantage over long distances and where geographical obstacles had to be crossed; in other words the benefits of air travel were more obvious on a flight from London to Karachi than one to Paris or Amsterdam, and competition from surface transport was much less intense. For Imperial Airways, which although a subsidised monopoly was nevertheless a privately owned airline, the chances of achieving profitability and rewarding its shareholders were much greater operating over the great expanses of Africa and southern Asia than the short stages between European capitals.

As A. J. Quin-Harkin stresses in his reminiscences, Imperial Airways, under the management of Woods-Humphery, was successful in achieving profitability within three years and paid annual dividends of up to 6 per cent after 1927. This was an extraordinary achievement given the inherently unprofitable nature of the industry, but it also begs the question of whether one can speak of a company being truly 'profitable' when it is receiving, in incremental payments, up to £1 million in government subsidy. And this was one of the issues taken up by parliamentary critics at the time of the Cadman Report on British civil aviation in 1938: was it not wrong for taxpayers' money to be redistributed by Imperial Airways to its shareholders in the form of private dividends?

It is likely that Imperial Airways would have been able to rebut its critics in the 1930s and point convincingly to a subsidy-free future, had there not been two further areas of complaint against the airline, both of which brought into question its success as a promoter of national prestige. First, its British aircraft were noticeably outdated, particularly in comparison with the new Douglas and Lockheed models used by other European flag-carriers such as KLM and Swissair. Quin-Harkin rightly praises the achievement of Imperial Airways in establishing one of the longest route networks in the world, and the success of the Empire Mail Scheme and the creditable performance of the Short Empire flying boats in the latter half of the 1930s is beyond question. However the Handley Page HP42, a lumbering four-engined biplane designed in 1929 and the mainstay of Imperial's fleet throughout the 1930s, was barely 20 m.p.h. faster than the HP 0/400 bomber of the First World War. It was infinitely more luxurious of course, and may have offered the 'safety, regularity, comfort and silence' that Quin-Harkin claims for it, but it was years behind the level of aeronautical technology being achieved in the United States and Germany at the time. As one writer on the industry has put it, 'both in terms of type and quantity of aircraft ordered, Imperial Airways was not able to offer the stimulus to the British aircraft industry that would enable its many gifted designers to produce path-breaking large civil airliners'.[9]

The second major criticism being levelled against Imperial Airways by the mid-1930s was that, in its devotion to the task of establishing colonial air routes, it was seriously neglecting Europe and simply not 'showing the flag' at many of the major airports on the Continent. This was undoubtedly true but probably inevitable given its limited size and resources, and the fact that its long-haul colonial routes were more likely to yield a satisfactory return for its investors than competing on the crowded airways of Europe. However the Cadman committee, whose report came out in March 1938, seems to have taken a harsh view of Imperial's failure in Europe and accused its manager, Woods-Humphery, of taking 'a commercial view of his responsibilities that was too narrow'.[10] Within fifteen years of Imperial's creation as a monopoly chosen instrument, British air transport was ready for competition again, this time from an airline which was willing to carry the flag back to Europe in modern aircraft.

British Airways Ltd was formed from a merger of three British independent airlines and began operating passenger services to northern Europe in 1936. When the Government favoured it with a mail contract and a subsidy for the route from London through Amsterdam to Hamburg, Copenhagen and Malmo, it was in effect giving Britain its second chosen instrument. As R. Higham points out, it was a condition of the subsidy that British Airways used 200 m.p.h. aircraft - fast by the standards of the day and certainly faster than any available British types. This led to its decision to acquire American Lockheed Electras, the first time that a subsidised British airline had been allowed to buy foreign aircraft. There were rumblings in Parliament when Neville Chamberlain went to Munich to see Hitler in a British Airways Electra in 1938, but the precedent had been set and in the post-war period the purchase by the British flag-carrier of American equipment became a more frequent necessity.

One of the independent airlines which was eventually absorbed into the British Airways group was Highland Airways, a regional carrier offering air services in the north of Scotland. Highland was the creation of Edmund Fresson, one of the first generation of pioneer British airline entrepreneurs.[11] As A. J. Robertson shows in his polished article, Fresson was a capable businessmen and a skilled pilot - which he needed to be as his aircraft 'flew over some of the most daunting and forbidding country in Europe'. Domestic airlines in Britain started later than the international carriers and, competing with an extensive rail network, had a long climb to get themselves established. Where they did achieve a measure of success was in areas where geography presented serious obstacles to surface transport and particularly where a sea crossing was involved. The chief attraction for passengers of Highland Airways was the dramatic reduction in the time required to cross the turbulent Pentland Firth from mainland Scotland to the Orkney Islands. A further characteristic of outlying air transport services like Highland's, which it shared with similiar 'outback' airlines in Australia, Canada and South America, was the broad range of passengers it carried: according to Robertson the typical Highland Airways passenger list included businessmen, politicians, admirals *en route* to Scapa Flow, tourists, crofters with their produce and 'fisher lassies'!

III

The Second World War revolutionised air transport. It hastened the development of the world's most prestigous and profitable long-haul route - the North Atlantic. It brought forth new radio and navigational aids, as well as bigger four-engined aircraft like the Douglas DC4 and Lockheed Constellation with higher wing loadings, more powerful engines, nose-wheel undercarriages, and pressurised cabins (Constellation).[12] These innovations meant that more passengers could be carried further and, for the first time, on a commercial basis. Not only aeronautical technology received new impetus from the war; the air-consciousness of the Western world was transformed by the Blitz and Pearl Harbor. The experience of aircraft and flying was widened beyond the confines of a small social élite to form the basis of a future mass transport system. As Roger Bilstein notes, even Hollywood got in the act: Michael Curtiz's 1942 film *Casablanca* recognized that the age of the train, and of farewells in steamy stations, had given way to the age of the plane when Humphery Bogart watched Ingrid Bergman disappearing into the clouds in an Air France Lockheed Electra.[13]

International civil aviation in the post-war era was obviously going to be more important, but just how was it to be organised? During the 1930s aviation in Europe and America had taken very different courses. Over the vast distances of the United States air transport had developed swiftly within a structure of regulated competition, halving the journey times between major cities. In Europe aviation had received less help from geography and more competition from the railways; and air transport had been entrusted to monopolies. When an international assembly of nations gathered in Chicago in late 1944 to work out a governing regime for post-war civil aviation, the gap between a dominant United States and an exhausted Britain could hardly have been greater. The Americans had an overwhelming technological and commercial lead which they were anxious to extend around the world. They wanted freedom to carry all the international traffic they could, the British by contrast wanted a breathing space to rebuild their air transport industry and produce their own aircraft; in the meantime they wanted tight control of rates, rights and routes.[14]

The Chicago conference failed to produce any multilateral agreement on these issues and they were carried over to the Anglo-American bilateral negotiations at Bermuda in 1946, the results of which set a model for the rest of the post-war world to follow. D. Mackenzie demonstrates that Britain's bargaining position at Bermuda was weakened by its desperate need for American financial aid after the end of the war. However, Bermuda was not a total defeat for the British, for although they were forced to give way on capacity and frequencies, including the granting of generous Fifth Freedom rights on the North Atlantic, the strict control of international air fares by the International Air Transport Association (IATA) was accepted by the United States. The striking thing about the Bermuda agreement, considering the extent to which its outcome was determined by factors within the wider context of Anglo-American relations at the time, is how long it lasted as a regulatory basis for international air transport. It was only in 1977 that its provisions were renegotiated, at Britain's request, in what became known as the *Bermuda 2* agreement.[15]

Britain's preparations for post-war civil aviation focused on the development of a number of new airliners in the Brabazon Programme and the drawing up of plans for new chosen carriers. In the wake of the 1938 Cadman Report the decision had been taken by the Conservative Government to combine Imperial Airways and British Airways to form a new nationalised airline: BOAC. However, by the time it was ready to begin flying in the spring of 1940, the skies over Britain were already full of combat aircraft and for the rest of the war BOAC's operations were determined by military rather than commercial considerations. P. J. Lyth traces the origins of the post-war arrangements of the coalition government that were formulated during 1944-45. The idea for three separate airlines, with different spheres of operation, was mooted in the plan of the first Minister of Civil Aviation Lord Swinton; with the Labour victory in the summer of 1945 the plan was adopted with the elements of private ownership favoured by Swinton replaced with total nationalisation.[16] The 1946 Civil Aviation Act marked one more shift in Britain's policy on civil aviation: after subsidised private monopoly (Imperial Airways, 1924), subsidised private duopoly (the addition of British Airways, 1936) and state-owned monopoly (BOAC, 1939), there was now to be three nationalised 'instruments'. In fact the number was quickly reduced to two after the ill-fated British South American Airways was taken over by BOAC in 1949.

The other airline created in the 1946 legislation was BEA. It is typical of the zig-zag course of British policy-making that the privately owned British Airways, subsidised after 1936 and on course to become a second chosen instrument the equal of Imperial Airways, disappeared in the merger that created BOAC and yet reappeared only six years later as the publicly owned BEA. BEA's history between 1946 and its merger with BOAC in 1974 was largely successful, indeed probably more so than BOAC's. Above all it had greater luck in aircraft procurement: while its big sister was floundering in the wake of the 1954 Comet crashes, BEA was introducing the turbo-prop Vickers Viscount, the most successful British airliner ever built. Unfortunately BEA's happy experience with the Viscount, which like the Comet had been conceived in the wartime Brabazon Programme, was not to be repeated when the airline ordered its second generation aircraft in the late 1950s. As Lyth argues in his contribution to this volume, the reason for the relative lack of commercial success with the Vanguard and the Trident lies in the 'over-tailored' specifications which BEA forced on its suppliers, a phenonomen which in itself was the result of BEA's singular creation as a short-haul carrier in Europe.

BOAC's chequered history and the enormous amount of money that it had cost the taxpayer by 1960, can be attributed partly to weak management, but mainly to the lack of clear direction from the Government. Not only was it required to operate costly and unproven British aircraft (Comet, Britannia, VC10 and finally Concorde), but it was also compelled to fly uneconomic routes for prestige reasons - a relic of policy from the 1930s - as well as subsidise colonial and Commonwealth airlines on the grounds that they would feed traffic into BOAC's main trunk routes. Only in 1964, after a major shake-up in the corporations's management, did the new chairman, Sir Giles Guthrie, obtain not only a government write-off of BOAC's massive debt, but also a written undertaking that the airline would in future be run as a commercial enterprise, with any deviation from this policy, on grounds of national interest, requiring a specific directive from the responsible Minister.

IV

Broadly speaking, up until the 1970s the performance of international scheduled airlines was subject to a number of distinct market features which had grown out of the settlements reached at Chicago and Bermuda, that is, restriction of competition to the two relevant flag-carriers, fare levels determined by IATA, low seating density and flights scheduled at frequent intervals throughout the year. The result was not especially good economics, and capacity tended to run in advance of demand, but this hardly mattered since nearly all flag-carriers were state-owned and their losses were covered by the taxpayer. Average passenger load factors were low but the impact of this on revenue was eased by pooling agreements between rival carriers. In general the system worked well and provided a strong element of stability during the growth years of the industry in the 1950s and 1960s. Working through IATA, the scheduled carriers were able to expand and democratise the market for air travel, using periodic fare reductions to increase the flow of traffic.

However, the greatest impetus to the popularisation of air transport in Europe came from outside the scheduled system altogether, from the rapid growth in the 1960s of non-scheduled airlines specialising in Inclusive Tours. This was a sector of the industry, led by British independent airlines, which exploited the general rise in living standards to create a major portion of the modern leisure air business.[17] As the two articles by B. K. Humphreys make clear, these independent operators came from modest beginnings in the postwar Labour administration. Initially they were the product of ex-servicemen and cheap war surplus machines, typically Douglas Dakota C-47s, the military version of the DC3. At first the shortage of capacity at BOAC, and particularly BEA, led to agreements whereby they performed services on behalf of the new corporations, and quite a few of them were saved from impending bankruptcy in 1948 by participation in the Berlin Air Lift. For a number of years the British independents led a precarious existence, although a few became larger and more established, eg. Airwork, Skyways and Hunting. The return to Conservative government in 1951 did not in itself improve their situation greatly, despite the expectation among many of them that more competition to the nationalised air corporations would be allowed. Instead, what revived their fortunes was the Korean War and the bright idea of someone in Whitehall that troops could be more swiftly conveyed to international troublespots and Britain's remaining colonial garrisons by air than by sea.

Air trooping contracts kept British independents airborne in the 1950s; as Humphreys puts it, it was their 'bread and butter'. Trooping was easy: the contracts were large, the costs were low and the load factor was guaranteed to be 100 per cent. Moreover it was the one area of the air transport business from which the air corporations were specifically excluded, making it in effect a means by which the Government could provide private airlines with an indirect subsidy. Although BOAC and BEA had an unassailable monopoloy on scheduled passenger traffic, new investment flowed steadily into the independent air transport sector from British shipping interests who were anxious to diversify and were preparing for the day when the government was ready for more competition in the air. By the early 1960s the number of independent airlines had shrunk and British United Airways and Cunard Eagle had emerged as major players. While trooping had contracted along with the closure of Britain's overseas bases, a whole new tourist industry was growing in its place around the Inclusive Tour operations of charter airlines such as Britannia Airways.

The formation of British Caledonian (BCal) from the merger of Caledonian Airways and British United Airways in 1970, created a competitive airline of sufficient size to compete with BOAC, ready to fly scheduled services as a 'second force' in line with recommendation of the Edwards Report of 1969. With the addition of Freddie Laker's Skytrain in 1977, the new British Airways, which had been formed from the merger of BOAC and BEA in 1974, found itself in a considerably more competitive environment. British air transport policy had evolved from the era of prestige and 'chosen instrument' monopolies to an acceptance of greater competition and the recognition that the old regulated system could no longer continue in the face of mounting consumer protest about the high cost of air travel in Europe compared to deregulated America.[18]

V

In 1919 an Airco DH-4 of AT&T with a single Rolls-Royce Eagle engine carried two passengers at about 100 m.p.h. and took well over two hours to travel from London to Paris. Fifty years later a Hawker Siddley Trident of BEA with three Rolls-Royce Spey engines carried 100 passengers at 600 m.p.h. and took fifty minutes for the trip. Aircraft speed had increased sixfold over half a century, but the time taken to cover the distance on this blue-riband route had only been cut by a factor of three. Moreover by the time the passenger had travelled from city centre to airport and back again, the journey time in 1969 showed little improvement over 1919. A critical weakness in air transport had revealed itself: over very short stages flying with conventional fixed-wing aircraft did not offer much, if any, advantage over surface transport. Air transport is optimised over long distances - George Woods-Humphery of Imperial Airways understood this in the 1920s - but does that mean that the short intercity journeys that are typical of the Europe network should be left to the train and car?

One solution is the helicopter. Sikorsky's first successful machine flew in 1939 and was quickly improved during the Second World War. After 1945 the Americans addressed themselves to the question of how the helicopter could be used for civilian purposes and, as A. G. Peters and D. F. Wood describe, helicopter airlines were established to provide shuttle services around the airports of four metropoli: Los Angeles, New York, Chicago and San Franciso. It seems in retrospect however that helicopter airlines were a false trail as far as regular passenger services were concerned. They had difficulty surviving without subsidy and relied to a large extent on carrying mail for the US Post Office. Their chief advantage over fixed-wing airlines was their ability to deliver passengers to city centres, often onto the roof of major down-town buildings like the Los Angeles Post Office, or the Pan American Building in New York.

But the economics of helicopter operation were always against them: their costs were really too high for commercial operation and they simply could not carry enough passengers to make themselves an indispensable element of mass transport around and between large cities. Moreover, they exploited the fact that major cities like Chicago and New York had more than one airport and needed shuttle communications between them; when the airlines chose to cut back on the use of Chicago's Midway airport and concentrate operations at O'Hare, the helicopter services of Chicago Helicopter Airways declined in importance.

In two of the cases studied by Peters and Wood, namely New York and San Franciso, helicopter services were able to exploit the obstacle that waterways presented to surface communications between local airports, that is, between Idlewild, La Guardia and New Jersey, and between San Franciso and Oakland. One could imagine that Edmund Fresson might have used helicopters to cross the sea to the Orkney Islands had they been available when he founded Highland Airways in 1933; he would certainly have had less difficulty setting up the necessary airfields in the wilds of northern Scotland. In fact the first regular helicopter service in Britain was operated for a few months during 1950 - 51 by BEA between Liverpool and Cardiff with Sikorski S-51s, the model which Los Angeles Airways used in its pioneer days. The chief executive of BEA at the time, (Sir) Peter Masefield, was keen on helicopters and looked to them as the solution to rapid inter-city travel in the future.[19] In the early 1950s BEA launched various experimental helicopter schemes, and from July 1955 until May 1956 ran a scheduled passenger service between Heathrow Airport and its Southbank terminal adjoining Waterloo station. However, like the airport shuttle services in the United States, it proved unsustainable.[20]

Helicopters have enjoyed a successful history in military roles and they are also well suited to perfoming rescue and emergency missions, but for regular commercial services their noise and technical complexity has proved to be a major drawback, while their passenger-mile costs have remained much higher than equivalent fixed-wing aircraft. Another factor which was not foreseen in the 1950s, particularly in Britain, was the tremendous growth in private car ownership which turned out to be the transport mode of choice on the short city-to-city routes that were envisaged for the helicopter. By 1963 *The Economist* was lamenting the disappearance of the only cross-Channel helicopter service (of the Belgian carrier SABENA) and the fact that BEA's solitary helicopter route, from Lands End to the Scilly Islands, could not survive without a government subsidy.[21]

Many helicopter services were started to provide passenger shuttles between airports and city centres. Airports themselves however have changed dramatically in size and function and new urban rapid transit systems, with capacities infinitely greater than the helicopter, now connect them to city centres. As P. W. Brooks's description of developments in and around London shows, airports have come a long way in the course of the airline industry's seventy-five year history. Hendon, Heston and Hounslow Heath, Cricklewood and Croydon, Northolt and Heathrow, Gatwick and Stansted; London seems to have tried every possible location, the chief determining factor being space for longer runways and expanded terminal buildings as aircraft got bigger and traffic heavier. When Heathrow opened for business in 1946, there was one runway and a few hastily erected tents for waiting passengers. Today, like its rivals at Frankfurt and Amsterdam, London's premier airport looks like a giant shopping mall with air transport attached. In the last twenty years the European airport has in many places evolved from a lacklustre branch of government to a full-blown private business which can be profitable even when the air transport industry is depressed and its customers - the airlines - are losing money. One of the reasons is that airports enjoy scale economies to a far greater degree than airlines and are able to spread their costs further as aircraft and passenger numbers rise. As one authority put it recently 'the more congested, crowded and uncomfortable an airport, the more likely it is to be highly profitable'. [22]

As airports are privatised and diversify beyond the simple task of handling passengers, they have opened up a profitable new sector of the travel business. However, ultimately they may also present one of the most significant limits to growth in the air transport industry. Unlike land-based transport modes using road or track, airports represent one of the main areas of fixed investment in civil aviation, but also are a potential bottleneck. Already in Europe there is strong indication that people are not willing to tolerate the expansion of airports beyond a certain size, particularly if they happen to live near them. Nor do they seem to want new ones built. Environmental concerns are obviously important here and it would seem to be in this direction that limits to growth and the technical challenges of the future will lie.

Notes

1 A. Sampson, *Empires of the Sky: The Politics, Contests and Cartels of World Airlines* (London, 1984), p. 19.

2 ICAO, *Development of Civil Air Transport* (Montreal, 1971), p. 3; *Civil Aviation Statistics of the World* (Montreal, 1978), p. 19; *Scheduled Air Traffic Digest and Bulletins*.

3 B. Gidwitz, *The Politics of International Air Transport* (Lexington, Mass., 1980), p. 73.

4 See A. Dobson, *Flying in the Face of Competition. The Policies and Diplomacy of Airline Regulatory Reform in Britain, the USA and the European Community 1968-1994* (Aldershot, 1995).

5 For the background on the decision to nationalise the British flag-carrier, see Peter J. Lyth, 'The changing role of government in British civil air transport, 1919 to 1949', in R. Millward and J. Singleton (eds), *The Political Economy of Nationalisation in Britain, 1920-1950* (Cambridge, 1994), pp. 65-87.

6 P. Fritzsche, *A Nation of Fliers. German Aviation and the Popular Imagination* (Cambridge, Mass., 1992), p. 51.

7 The number of passengers carried between Britain and the Continent on British aircraft rose from 1,155 in the year ended March 1920, to 5,692 in the year ended March

1922 and 10,066 in the years ended March 1923; *Annual Report on the Progress of Civil Aviation, 1922-1923*, Air Ministry Directorate of Civil Aviation (London, 1923), p. 27.

8 *Report on Government Financial Assistance to Civil Air Transport Companies* (the Hambling Report), Cmd. 1811 (London, 1923), quoted in Sir Henry Self, 'The status of civil aviation in 1946', *Flight Magazine*, 3 October 1946.

9 P. Fearon, 'The British airframe industry and the state 1918-1935', *Economic History Review*, vol. XXVII (1974), pp. 249-51.

10 *Report of the Committee of Inquiry in Civil Aviation* (the Cadman Report), Air Ministry, Cmd. 5685 (London, 1938), p. 15. For a full account of Imperial Airways' history see R. Higham, *Britain's Imperial Air Routes, 1918 to 1939* (London, 1960).

11 A brief biography of Fresson's career can be found in R. E. G. Davies, *Rebels and Reformers of the Airways* (Washington, DC, 1987), pp. 215-27.

12 For the technical development of modern aircraft see P. W. Brooks, *The Modern Airliner: Its Origins and Development*, 2nd edition (Kansas, 1982). Also valuable is R. Miller and D. Sawers, *The Technical Development of Modern Aviation* (1968).

13 R. E. Bilstein, 'Travel by air: the American context', *Archiv für Sozialgeschichte*, vol. XXXIII (1993), p. 275.

14 H. Stannard, 'Civil aviation: an historical survey', *International Affairs*, vol. XXI, no. 4 (1945), pp. 497-505.

15 For the details for Bermuda 2, see Dobson, *Flying in the Face*, pp. 119-45.

16 See also B. K. Humphreys, *Nationalization*, in this volume.

17 See P. J. Lyth and M. L. J. Dierikx, 'From privilege to popularity: the growth of leisure air travel', *Journal of Transport History*, vol.XV, no. 2 (1994), pp. 97-116.

18 S. Wheatcroft and G. Lipman, *Air Transport in a Competitive European Market: Problems, Prospects & Stategies*, Economist Intelligence Unit, Travel and Tourism Report, no. 3 (1986).

19 Masefield, P. G. (Sir), 'Some economic factors in air transport operations, *Journal of Institute of Transport* (1951), p. 90.

20 C. Woodley, *Golden Age: British Civil Aviation 1945-1965* (Shrewsbury, 1992), p. 35.

21 'What happened to helicopters?', *The Economist*, 18 May 1963, pp. 682-3.

22 R. Doganis, *The Airport Business* (London, 1992), p. 4.

1 Aviation and the state: the Graham-White Aviation Company, 1912–23

A. D. GEORGE

In the main exhibition hall of the RAF Museum at Hendon is displayed a Hawker Hart biplane in the yellow livery of a flying training unit. This aircraft was flown by volunteer pupils of the Civil Air Guard in the late 1930s, the formation of which was part of general defence preparations at that time. The revival of procurement for the Air Ministry after 1934 was the salvation of many struggling aircraft firms. Lean times had of course followed the cancellations of contracts and the collapse of orders in 1919 when little thought seems to have been given to a possible future emergency. The purpose of this article is to examine the effects of state intervention in the aircraft industry during and after the First World War on the fortunes of one of the private entrepreneurs, namely Claude Grahame-White (G-W) of Hendon, sometime proprietor of the London aerodrome, pioneer aviator, populariser of aviation as a spectacle for the masses, and founder of one of the earliest planned manufacturing concerns in the new industry.

When the Hendon factory was being laid out in 1912, the nominal capital of the Grahame-White Aviation Co. Ltd was £200,000 though only 1,600 5s shares seem to have been taken up and G-W made up the subscription to £56,500 from his own resources.[1] (It will be seen that this was to prove totally inadequate for the equipping of an extensive production facility on the scale required by wartime production.) Although the business (like that of Henry Royce) was originally started with a small amount of cash (£400 in the case of G-W), he was under no illusion that something of the order of £1 million in government subsidies would be required to launch the aviation business in Britain and campaigned to that effect. Nevertheless a considerable amount of development was achieved at Hendon in the early days with limited resources in terms of hangars,[2] workshops equipped with wood working and metal working machines, plant, engines and planes. However, since it was all something of a gamble,[3] G-W wisely arranged that his service agreement as managing director would be limited to a term of ten years.

Starting with a few designs of his own for training and pleasure flying machines, and assisted by unspecified amounts from the Dunlop Rubber Co. as sponsor, G-W built up the factory as well as the aerodrome business and was rewarded soon after the outbreak of the war with contracts to produce quantities of BE2Cs for the Admiralty, Avro 504s, Farman biplane trainers and others. It would seem that the labour force was recruited and plant and equipment for these contracts were built up with financial assistance from the Ministry of Munitions,[4] and partly from overdrafts. Producing for the Services was not, however, by any means without its problems as the 1915 correspondence files indicate.[5] There were difficulties in meeting contract dates for the Admiralty and War Office, a shortage of drawings and specifications, frequent changes in design and amendments, and an inability to obtain steel tubing. A government inspector moreover had criticised the standard of workmanship and the congestion in the workshops and the Ministry refused to authorise further capital expenditure. For his part G-W complained of the difficulty of obtaining payment for work done and the need for further bank borrowing to the tune of £20,000.[6] The headed notepaper announced the company as aeronautical engineering contractors to the Admiralty and the War Office and it may be assumed that this was the sole source of orders. Additional land was still being acquired in 1917 and some capital transferred to revenue but the directors' report for the meeting of the 31 July 1917 does indicate a considerable increase in the turnover and valuation of the company.[7] However, G-W was conscious of the need to inject new blood or new capital or both, and was making overtures to the motor magnate S. F. Edge to join the Board.

By September 1917 the total realised from the sale of planes and engines had risen from £159,617 to £402,445. This had given a (gross) profit of £89,213, the value of plant and machinery (including stock in hand) had risen to £147,000 and total assets to £323,108.[8] By this time the Ministry of Munitions had taken over the functions of the procurement of aircraft for the Armed Services and was itself arranging to build three National Aircraft Factories as well as building and leasing workshops to the Airco and Handley Page companies.

G-W saw the opportunity of a further injection of capital and expansion and concluded an agreement with the Ministry[9] for a maximum loan of £320,000 to be used for capital works or the settlement of accounts. The Ministry usually drove a hard bargain and placed restrictions upon the companies it supported. In this case, as long as the balance of the loan remained unpaid, (*a*) no further capital commitments would be permitted; (*b*) no additional executive staff were to be appointed without prior consent and no top salary increases were to be paid; and (*c*) the Ministry reserved the right of access to the books.

The 1917–18 bomber offensive and boom in aircraft orders was, of course, short lived. Even by Armistice Day there was not enough work in hand for the four principal aircraft manufacturers in the North London area. The V 1500

Handley Page contract was cancelled and the Ministry divested itself of the Cricklewood factories. The giant Airco firm was soon to be sold to BSA as an asset-stripping exercise, with thousands paid off. In the case of the Grahame-White company the Ministry dithered. First of all the firm was invited to retool for the production of 500 Sopwith Snipes. Then this order was cancelled. Next instructions were given to produce another 500 Avros for stock, but this was aborted. Now there was simply not enough work for the metalworking shops. Between 800 and 1,000 men were idle (out of a total work-force of 3,000) and the company was told to pay them off. Many were laid off, including the wood-workers, fitters and erectors, but the remainder were in an ugly mood and this sudden collapse in demand placed G-W and his co-directors in a difficult position. How could they repay the outstanding £200,000 on the loan if there was no work to tide them over, especially since not all the payments for contracts had been received? There were no reserves of capital and there was the unsettled question of compensation from the War Commission for the use of the aero-drome. In desperation G-W wrote a long plea[10] to the Minister of Supply, Winston Churchill, with whom he was on personal terms and whom he had shown round the factory in April 1915. It was very much a final appeal. G-W genuinely feared liquidation because of the outstanding government loans; he feared for the future of his work-force and he urged the government to do something to ease the transition from war to peace.

In fact the plea fell on deaf ears, but whether out of a feeling of responsibility to the work-force or a desire to meet his liabilities, G-W called an extraordinary general meeting at which the word 'Aviation' was dropped from the name of the company and the directors authorised to turn over the factory to the production of furniture and car bodies. As the end of his contract approached G-W grew weary of the struggle and began to make preparations to sell up and withdraw from the scene. The bank's advice had been that he should drop manufacture, sell or lease the premises, and convert his land to real estate — a course that one day both his neighbours Handley Page and De Havilland would adopt during the recession in the late 1920s and early 1930s. The first move was a letter from his solicitor, Abrahams,[11] arranging a lease of the famous clubhouse. By December 1922, however, negotiations were in hand[12] for the complete sale of the pre-mises, properties, plant and assets (excluding the stock-in-trade) at a price of £75,000 to a Mr Tilden-Smith whose business address was Lombard Street. Apparently, Tilden-Smith had the idea of turning the aerodrome into a horse-racing course and selling the buildings not required for use to the London hospi-tals. The London offices and showrooms of the company were to be excluded from the sale, but the purchaser was to be required to discharge G-W's other liabilities. Writing to his uncle, Lord Barnby,[13] G-W feared liquidation if the sale did not go through. He still hoped for £50,000 from the Government by way of compensation for impressment of the airfield and to maintain a presence on the site at Hendon in the shape of the free use of a shed and its equipment for twelve months. His intention was to realise some £115,000 from the sale and, after meeting his personal liabilities, to have £90,000 clear to provide a reasonable income. Doubts remained, however, since in a further letter[14] he envisaged an alternative scheme of leasing the accommodation to the Civil Aviation Department for a rent of £10,000 per annum. There might also have been something to be gained from the impending extension of the London Underground for which the railway company would require land.

Unfortunately the sale fell through. The evidence seems to suggest[15] that Tilden-Smith had objected to G-W wanting it both ways and that an adjustment of the sale price based on a valuation of the retained stock would be necessary. Apparently the purchaser was against anything being excluded,[16] G-W's legal advisors seemed to believe that the government would wish to secure Hendon for aviation and a later letter shows G-W was having second thoughts about the sale,[17] and so it turned out. Soon after the Treasury appointed a receiver who took possession of Hendon, presumably because of the outstanding loan and the inability of the firm to meet its creditors. Indeed, as Wallace states,[18] it was impossible for G-W to put up the £120,000 owed to the Air Ministry. After protracted negotiations in which G-W threatened to bring an action against the Treasury civil servants because of their inadequate offer of £250,000 for the aerodrome and factory coupled with a write-off of other claims, the matter was eventually settled out of court, but only after G-W and his allies had threatened to use the front page of the *Daily Mail* to blacken the reputation of the government. All claims were waived and G-W received the impressive sum of £800,000. Clearly, this much inflated figure contained elements of compensation for the impressment or seizure of the aerodrome (twice), a reward for past services to aviation and the war effort, and a recognition of the site's future potential and value to the state.[19] All manufacture ceased and by 1925 the Royal Air Force had moved into the aerodrome and hangars and henceforth staged its military pageants and displays on Empire Air Days, where the fashionable classes of London had once thrilled to the exploits of Claude Grahame-White and his fellow pioneers.[20,21]

Notes

1 Grahame-White (G-W) archives, RAF Museum, Hendon, file B.771, undated letter and annexe referring to the position in October 1912.

2 A total of twenty were already occupied, twelve new ones 50 ft × 50 ft were under construction and twenty further planned to be let at a proposed rent of £110 p.a., an estimated yield of £2250 p.a.

3 Although a promising venture at the time since £10,000 had been taken in gate money in the season just ended plus £750 from passenger flights. Running expenses had been £2000. The statement of assets for

1st October 1912 is as follows: fixed capital investment, £18,500; stock and spares, £11,700; with sundries bringing the total to £31,000.

4 G. Wallace, *Claude Grahame-White* (1960), pp. 224–7 states that in 1922 the figure of £120,000 was quoted as being owed to the Air Ministry.

5 G-W archives file B.777, managing director's report for July 1915.

6 B.777, managing director's notes dated 13 July 1915.

7 B.779. The base line selected was 30 September

1916 with certain adjustments made for stock in hand and work in progress on 18 March 1918. The report declares a dividend of 8 per cent and a net profit of £11,225. The value of plant and machinery was £71,675 with £50,175 of work in progress. Both G-W and the Admiralty had made additional loans totalling £60,000. Reference to the financial statement indicates that the salaries of the secretary and managing director totalled £3,325, the school of flying continued to bring in some £11,000 in tuition fees including surprisingly those from civilian pupils and that £5000 was raised from the hire of planes.

8 B.779. Summary of accounts, September 1917.

9 B.782. Agreement dated 1 March 1918. The loan was to be granted at bank rate plus 1 per cent and one method of repayment would be by the deduction of 15 per cent from all invoices to the Ministry for work done. The time allowed for repayment would be extended to three years from the end of hostilities but while any balance was outstanding, the company would lose the benefit of any depreciation allowance from the Inland Revenue.

10 B.783 Letter dated 23 November 1918.

11 B.789. Letter dated 10 June 1922. Some land it seems which belonged to G-W personally and not the company and other property belonging to the Air Council was sold for housing.

12 B.789. Copy agreement dated 31 December 1922.

13 B.790. Letter dated 28 November 1922.

14 B.790. Letter dated 7 December 1922.

15 B.790 G-W's notes 8 January 1923.

16 B.790. MA to G-W 9 January 1923.

17 B.790 G-W to MA 10 January 1923.

18 Wallace, *Claude Grahame-White*, pp. 224-7.

19 Regrettably the official Air Ministry documents dealing with the sale appear not to have survived.

20 See C. R. Smith, *Flying at Hendon* — a Pictorial Record (1974).

21 The subsequent history of the site is covered in *The Royal Air Force Museum 1972-75* and in an article in *Flypast* (September 1985).

2 The Daimler Airway: April 1922–March 1924

E. BIRKHEAD

THE history of organized air transport in this country begins with the airlines that preceded Imperial Airways. Though not by any means the first of these, the Daimler Airway is a good example to take, because a full set of monthly accounts still exists from which a great deal of information can be extracted to supplement references in the journals and newspapers of the time. It is possible to trace in these accounts the actual effects of changes in government policy on the fortunes of one of the companies receiving grant.

On 1 April 1922 the first "permanent" subsidy scheme for British air transport companies came into operation. From 1919 until February 1921 the new industry had struggled into existence without direct financial aid from government. Only two companies, Handley Page and Instone, survived from this initial period[1] to be revived in March 1921, with a subsidy scheme hurriedly devised by the three-man "Cross-Channel Subsidies Committee" under Lord Londonderry. This arrangement, originally intended to last until October 1921, continued until 31 March 1922, by which time the Committee had produced the "permanent" scheme already referred to.

1 April 1922 was also the official first operating day of the Daimler Airway, a department of the London car hire firm which was, in turn, a member of the B.S.A. group of companies. The Company had been constituted with rights to fly commercial air services in June 1919. B.S.A. had bought up the parent company of Air Transport and Travel[2] in 1920, but had allowed the airline to continue operations for some months before deciding that the losses were too great to bear. The fact that the group had connections with the earliest air transport company was noted by speakers at the luncheon held to celebrate the beginning of Daimler's air activities in April 1922.[3] On this occasion also, the Secretary of State for Air, Captain the Rt Hon. F. E. Guest, said that Daimler was the first company "to have indicated an expectation of carrying on successful air travel without the aid of subsidy". The Managing Director of Daimler, Colonel Frank Searle,[4] endorsed this: he thought that the London to Paris service could be operated at a profit with the new subsidy and hoped to show, within a year, that it could be run entirely without subsidy.

This was contrary to existing experience. Handley Page had knowledge of unsubsidized operation and the manager of the only other operating company, S. Instone & Co. Ltd, had, over a year before, called commercial aviation "a financial failure".[5] The initial optimism was also to prove contrary to Daimler's own experience.

The new airline began scheduled operations with two return flights daily between Croydon and Le Bourget. On this route it was in direct competition with the two existing British companies as well as with two French companies. In addition to the passenger service, a regular daily newspaper flight to Paris was begun. Taking off at 5.30 a.m. or, as winter approached, as soon after dawn as possible, it arrived in Paris soon after 7.30 a.m. In its first month the new service carried only 50 passengers and just over one ton of freight and excess baggage. In the following months, however, traffic increased until August, when 496 passengers and over 13 tons of cargo were carried. In July, the Air Ministry noted this summer increase in traffic, which was common to all companies, but it also pointed out that the overall passenger load-factor was only 36 per cent. For cargo, it was only 47 per cent.[6] Modern short-haul airlines operate successfully on annual load-factors of about 60 per cent. Frederick Handley Page had said in 1920 that his aircraft could earn a profit with a 75 per cent load-factor.[7] There was certainly no hope in 1922 of earning a profit on the load-factors then being attained. Even with subsidies, profitability could not be assured.

It is hardly surprising that rumours were soon heard about a proposed amalgamation of the three British airlines. In discounting the idea, one of the aviation journals nevertheless commented that it was "well recognized, however, that there is not sufficient traffic on the London to Paris service to warrant the existence of three British services in addition to the two French concerns".[8] Daimler's experience bore this out: in its first six months, in the best period of the year for traffic, it carried 1,514 passengers, earning an income from flying operations of £10,292. Government subsidy and supplementary grants increased this to £18,992 which had to be set against a total expenditure of £42,350, thus yielding a loss in six months of £23,358.

The subsidy scheme had been worked out on an estimated doubling of traffic on the London to Paris route in 1922 as compared with 1921. On this basis it was agreed that each company should receive a periodic sum equal to 25 per cent of its gross takings with an additional £3 per passenger and 3d. per pound of freight. It very soon became clear, however, that the estimate on which the scheme was based had been far too optimistic. For the first two months, the traffic, though increasing for the normal summer period, was about the same as it had been in the comparable period of 1921. But it was shared among 50 per cent more aircraft, averaging twice as many journeys in the same time. There was, therefore, more than three times the 1921 capacity available[9] to carry much the same amount of traffic. The operating companies quickly found the position untenable. The Air Ministry had to make a number of supplementary grants each month, without which the figures for Daimler, as given above, would have been very much worse.

As a result of this unsatisfactory state of affairs, one of the first tasks of the new Director of Civil Aviation, Sir Sefton Brancker,[10] was to revise the scheme of subsidy. His "revised" scheme was put into operation on 1 October 1922, superseding the "permanent" scheme after only six months. The outstanding feature of the new plan was an end to the hopeless competition over the single route to Paris. Brancker saw the neces-

sity of developing a more widespread network of routes and of extending them over
greater distances in order more fully to utilize the speed advantage of the aeroplane. His
new scheme incorporated both these principles. Handley Page retained the Paris route
with the possibility of an extension to Basle; Instone took the Brussels route with a proposed extension to Cologne; Daimler were to fly from Croydon to Amsterdam with
extensions from each end to Manchester and Berlin.[11] For three weeks after the scheme
was launched Daimler continued to operate its newspaper flight to Paris, arranging for
Handley Page to use this machine as a "spare" whenever return traffic required it.
Daimler had maintained a Paris office, at 25 Rue Royale, and Handley Page were also
able to make use of this.

Already, during the summer of 1922, Daimler had been involved in negotiations
with three Continental airlines[12] about the organization of air services in northern
Europe. Under the new subsidy scheme and in co-operation with K.L.M., the British
company began flying to Holland on 9 October. At first the Dutch terminal was Rot-
terdam, but on 23 October the route was extended to Amsterdam. On the same day
the service to and from Manchester was begun. The Alexandra Park airfield in Manchester was used, and the service was timed to connect with the services from Croydon
to the Continent. The fare to Amsterdam was £4 and to Manchester it was £2 5s. In
December 1922 "season" tickets were introduced on the Manchester route. Costing
£100, they were available for twenty-five return or fifty single journeys.[13] Autumn
and early winter was not a good time to begin new routes. Even today air passenger
traffic has a pronounced summer maximum. This was even more marked in 1922 when
flying was much more subject to the dangers, discomforts, and delays of winter
weather. Bearing this in mind, however, the early results indicated a good beginning.
This was especially true of the new internal route which began by providing more
passengers than that to Amsterdam.

The extension of the Continental route to Berlin was long delayed by difficulties in
arranging international flying facilities in Germany. Eventually, however, in April
1923, agreements were reached, and a Daimler aircraft (G-EBBS) made the first London to Berlin flight on Monday, 30 April. The twice-weekly British service was in
addition to two other weekly scheduled flights by German aircraft. A difficulty in subsidy arrangements between the German airline and its government delayed the start by
three weeks. Even when it did begin, the German service was not very satisfactory,
largely because the aircraft used were unsuitable for the relatively long distances involved. It was said that they could hardly cover the whole distance between London
and Berlin, via Amsterdam and Hamburg, during daylight hours in early summer.
Daimler's D.H.34s were scheduled to complete the trip in about seven hours. The fare
over the whole route was £6 10s.—a figure apparently set low deliberately to attract
custom.

Traffic during the summer of 1923 was quite good, though the Manchester service, which had fallen away disappointingly during the winter, did not fully revive. During July and August the airline often had insufficient capacity to cope with the traffic offered. Bookings on the Berlin service were sometimes complete for a week in advance. The Manchester service was suspended over the Bank Holiday period to free an aircraft for the German route. At the end of August a third scheduled weekly return flight was instituted.

In September, however, two things happened which tended to accentuate the usual seasonal decline in traffic. On 10 September the fare to Berlin was raised to £8 2s. 6d. because, at the original low fare, traffic seemed to be outstripping capacity. It can hardly have been thought, however, that this would continue throughout the winter. More important than the fare increase was the crash, on 14 September, of a Daimler aircraft flying from London to Manchester. Forced down by bad weather, the aircraft crashed at Ivinghoe, in the northern Chilterns, killing all five people aboard. This was the Company's second fatal accident. Only a few days after commencing operations in April 1922, the newspaper flight collided with a French Farman "Goliath" with loss of life to all six persons involved.[14] It was this accident which resulted in several meetings between representatives of British and French airlines to draw up regulations for flying between London and Paris. The impact on public opinion of the second accident, however, was the greater because the career of the aircraft concerned, G-EBBS, had long been followed with admiring interest. It had been selected by the Director of Civil Aviation as an example of an aircraft operated intensively and with safety.[15] Its mounting total of mileage without accident was often reported and at the time of the crash it had flown 150,000 miles.

The slump in October, of passengers carried, was also contributed to by some inconsistency about the winter routes. The German route, having been shortened on 8 October by making Hamburg the terminus, was again extended to Berlin in November by using a shorter route. The Manchester route was suspended after the Ivinghoe crash, resumed on 1 November, and finally discontinued later in the month. It was started again only in the last month of the Company's existence, March 1924.

By the autumn of 1923 Daimler, like the other independent companies, was probably not very inclined to make strenuous efforts to improve its position. Its fate was already all but sealed. In February 1923, the Civil Air Subsidies Committee under Sir Herbert Hambling[16] had reported in favour of merging all existing British airlines into a single company which would have financial resources enough to plan for future expansion. During the debate on the Air Estimates on 14 March 1923, the Secretary of State for Air, Sir Samuel Hoare, had signified the government's acceptance of the recommendation, to take effect when the existing contracts with operating companies expired in March 1924. A few days later the Air Ministry had announced that it was prepared to receive proposals from "responsible persons" for the formation of an Air Transport Company on the lines suggested by the Hambling Report. Throughout the rest of 1923 the existing companies concerned themselves with their part in the impending merger. Originally they each submitted separate schemes but, in October, agreed to co-operate in a combined plan. By December, the Director of Civil Aviation was able to announce that arrangements for "The Million Pound Scheme", as it came to be called, were nearly complete. With its future cut off, Daimler, like the other companies, can hardly have felt impelled to great efforts.

The onset of winter, the fatal crash, fare increases, a fluctuating route policy, and the generally dispiriting effect of the coming merger are reflected in a disastrous falling-away in traffic on Daimler routes from October 1923. In December only 23 passengers were carried: in January only 9. This compared with 205 and 232 in the corresponding months of the previous year. The numbers increased slightly in the final two months but showed no real sign of recovery, and the Company ceased operations working at a very low pressure.

The independent airlines disappeared into the new Imperial Airways on 1 April 1924. Daimler made a noteworthy contribution of personnel to the new Company. Both its Managing Director, Colonel Frank Searle, and its Manager, Major G. Woods Humphery, passed into the same posts with Imperial Airways. During their time with the Daimler Airway both had earned high reputations. It was said of Searle that he "revolutionized" the organization of air transport, particularly by the intensity of his use of aircraft.[17] Four aircraft seems to have been the maximum number operated by Daimler at any one time, and new aircraft were taken only as replacements.

In two years these aircraft carried 5,796 passengers for various journeys and earned a total income of £113,939. The real commercial position of civil aviation at this time is revealed in the fact that £92,622 of this income was from government. In other words, an airline noted in its day for efficiency relied on subsidies and grants for over 80 per cent of its income. Despite this large subsidy, total expenditure over the two years amounted to £131,242, giving a total loss of £17,303. Bearing in mind the large losses of the first six months, this indicates a slight profit to the Company for the eighteen months under the "revised" scheme of subsidy. The monthly returns showed a profit between October 1922 and April 1923 (average £464), after which the loss appeared again. The position was retrieved by a government payment in October 1923, in compensation for losses under the "permanent" scheme and by final subsidy payments amounting to £12,666 in February and March 1924.

Among the items of expenditure in the Daimler accounts, advertising naturally figures most prominently during the first few months of operation when it was necessary to call attention to the new service. This contributed substantially to the large losses for these months. The most consistent item throughout the airline's career was that for wages and salaries, which varied only slightly with the level of activity. Fuel charges, of course, varied almost directly with the amount of flying done. In relation to the total bill, insurance was a constantly heavy item, generally increasing until the middle of 1923 and then remaining fairly steady until the fall away in the final months.

Financially, therefore, Daimler's venture into civil aviation hardly came up to expectations. The overall operating ratio, which indicates the relation between revenue and expenditure (100 per cent break even), was 115 per cent. This included income from government: excluding this, the figure would be 524 per cent! The reasons are not hard to find. Compared with a modern airline, the fixed capital involved was inconsiderable, yet the scale of operations was too small to cover even this. Four aircraft, even with a much higher load-factor, could hardly have earned income enough to cover all costs. The D.H.34s used earned a high reputation among their contemporaries, but they were not capable of earning a profit under the conditions then existing. It has been said that no such aircraft existed before 1926.[18] It was a considerable achievement to reach an average rate of 1,500 flying hours per annum with G-EBBS,[19] although this would be regarded as quite inadequate today, when B.O.A.C.'s fleet of medium-range Britannia 102s is giving an annual average utilization of 3,750 hours.[20] The achievement was in any case neutralized by low overall load-factors. Although it was sometimes noted that Daimler's passengers on the Amsterdam and Manchester routes included a proportionately larger business element than the Paris route attracted, numbers were not maintained during the bad-weather months.

Civil aviation had a long way to go when Imperial Airways took over before it could become profitable. It still needed an adequate aircraft, an adequate network of routes flown intensively enough to attract an adequate demand from the public. Such a position was not reached until after the second World War. The Daimler Airway and its contemporaries, however, brought the ideal a step nearer; it made its own particular contribution to the economical organization of civil air transport. It says much for the pioneering spirit of an independent firm that it could so determinedly maintain a conviction about the potentialities of a new mode of transport in the face of considerable financial loss.

NOTES

1. Air Transport of Travel and Air Post of Banks ceased operations at the end of 1920.
2. The Aircraft Manufacturing Company.   3. *Flight*, XIV (1922), 207–8.
4. Colonel Searle had already had experience in operating air services: he took over the management of Air Transport & Travel Ltd, when it passed into B.S.A. hands.
5. Proceedings of the Air Conference (1920, Cmd. 1157), 21.
6. *Flight*, XIV (1922), 517. Load-factor is the percentage relation of payload carried to capacity provided.
7. Cmd. 1157, 50. He evidently left depreciation out of account in arriving at this figure.
8. *Flight*, XIV (1922), 359.   9. *The Times*, 20 June 1922, 6.   10. Appointed 10 May 1922.
11. A new company, The British Marine Navigation Co., was to operate flying boats between Southampton and the Channel Isles.   12. K.L.M., Deutsche Luft Reederei, and Danske Luftfartselskab.
13. *Flight*, XIV (1922), 775.   14. *The Times*, 8 Apr. 1922, 12.
15. Proceedings of Third Air Conference, 1923. Report of Director of Civil Aviation (Cmd. 1848).
16. Report of Civil Air Subsidies Ctee. (1923, Cmd. 1811).   17. *Flight*, XV (1923), 150, 533.
18. A. J. Quin-Harkin, *Journ. Transport Hist.*, I (1953–4), 203–4.   19. Cmd. 1848, 17.
20. *Flight*, LXXIV (1958), 396.

3 The financial failure of British air transport companies, 1919–24

E. BIRKHEAD

Civil air transport is one of the "new" industries developed in the twentieth century and is without roots in the "steam and iron" technology of the nineteenth century. It is, indeed, wholly a product of the years since the first World War. Although experiments were made before 1914, no serious efforts to establish scheduled air services were possible with the level of knowledge then attained. By 1919 air transport was a technical possibility, but it was quickly shown to be still a most uneconomic business proposition. It is the purpose of this article to indicate to what extent it was uneconomic down to the formation of Imperial Airways in 1924 and to suggest reasons why it was so.

Civil flying in the United Kingdom was officially permitted after the war from 1 May 1919. A number of firms opened internal services during the summer months, but all were closed again in the autumn. Much more important was the inauguration of the routes to the Continent by Aircraft Transport & Travel, Ltd., and Handley Page Transport, Ltd. Both these companies were subsidiaries of aircraft constructing firms and both opened services to Paris, the former on 25 August and the latter on 2 September 1919. Services to Amsterdam and Brussels followed. During 1920 they were joined on the Paris route by a third British airline, S. Instone & Co. the shipowners, and for a few months by a fourth, Air Post of Banks. By the end of 1920 all four were in financial difficulties, and before the end of the year Aircraft Transport & Travel and Air Post of Banks had ceased to function. In February 1921 Handley Page Transport and Instone also suspended operations, and direct financial assistance from government was necessary to revive them. These two airlines received subsidy alone under a "temporary" scheme between February 1921 and March 1922, when a "permanent" scheme was introduced and the Daimler Airway joined in the competition on the only surviving route—that to Paris. A "revised" subsidy scheme covering several other routes was introduced in October 1922 and maintained until 31 March 1924. No effort will be made here to describe in detail the various subsidy schemes,[1] but it will become clear that financial assistance was necessary to the continued existence of British airlines after the crisis of the winter of 1920–21.

It is difficult to speak in exact terms about the economics of air transport in this period. Adequate and reliable statistics are scarce, and consistent figures, comparable over the whole period, are not generally available. It is, however, possible to illustrate the extent of the losses of the pioneer airlines. In the period before subsidy, August 1919 to March 1921, losses were such as to drive all four British airlines out of business—two permanently. Few figures have yet come to light to demonstrate these losses, but an ex-Aircraft Transport & Travel pilot has recently written: "This is certain: civil flying at this stage was the most unsound and uneconomic form of transport ever evolved".[2] That losses were substantial can, however, be inferred, if the subsidy adjustment is excluded from Table I covering both operating companies in the period of the "temporary" subsidy scheme, between 19 March 1921 and 31 March 1922.[3]

TABLE I

The "Temporary" Subsidy Scheme: Handley Page Transport and the Instone Airline,
March 1921 – March 1922

Expenditure	£	£
Operating Costs: Flying charges (Fuel, aircrew pay, wireless)	23,939	
Operating Costs: Non-flying charges (Repairs, maintenance, insurance, salaries, wages, etc.)	59,822	
Overhead Charges	36,732	
Total Expenditure		120,493
Revenue	£	£
Passengers and Freight	38,211	
Less agents' commission and car hire to aerodrome	9,888	
	28,323	
Miscellaneous Revenue	1,101	
Total Revenue		29,424
Working Loss		91,069
Subsidies		85,671
Overall Loss to Companies		5,398

In this first subsidy period, 5,804 passengers were carried, so that the figure of £120,493 for expenditure represented £20 15s. 3d. per passenger at a time when the single fare on the only route operated was £6 6s. 0d. The two companies' combined operating ratio* was about 400 per cent and, as can be seen, even with subsidies paid, a slight overall loss remained.

* Operating ratio is the percentage relation of total revenue to total expenditure, i.e.

$$\frac{\text{Expenditure}}{\text{Revenue}} \times 100$$

No similar figures covering all companies are available for the remainder of the period, 1 April 1922 to 31 March 1924. Figures for one representative airline, covering these two years, do however exist.[4] They cover the operations of the Daimler Airway and may best be summarised in a diagram (Fig. 1) which brings

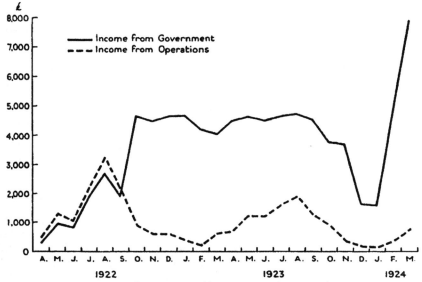

Fig. 1. *Daimler Airway Monthly Revenue, April 1922–March 1924*

out two points very clearly. First, that subsidy was closely tied to flying income under the "permanent" scheme, but hardly at all under the "revised" scheme. Second, the latter form of subsidy was on a very much more generous scale than the former, and the diagram shows graphically the extent of the airline's dependence on subsidies. The total figures for the one airline in the two years 1922–24 are as follows:

TABLE II

"Permanent" and "Revised" Subsidy Schemes: The Daimler Airway, April 1922 – March 1924

	£	£
Total Expenditure		131,242
Operating Revenue	21,317	
Subsidy and Grants	92,622	
Total Income		113,939
Total Loss		17,303

A breakdown of some of the more important items making up the Total

Expenditure figure is given in Table III. For comparison, the similar figures for B.E.A. (1957–58) are also included in the table. In a strict sense, the figures are not directly comparable, because the definitions of the items differ. They are, however, sufficiently similar to be worth using for this purpose.

TABLE III.

Breakdown of some items in the Total Expenditure of the Daimler Airway, 1922–24, with comparative figures for B.E.A., 1957–58

	DAIMLER AIRWAY		B.E.A.	
Items	£	per cent of total	£	per cent of total
Fuel and Oil	18,173	13.8	3,241,345	11.9
Aircraft and Engine Depreciation	8,407	6.4	2,180,441	8.0
Advertising	18,064	13.7	587,933	2.2
Insurance	14,772	11.2	349,520	1.3
Wages and Salaries	26,243	20.0	10,437,155	38.3
Total Expenditure	131,242		27,285,918	

The two notable figures here are the large percentages of Daimler expenditure devoted to advertising and insurance. Considerable advertising was probably necessary at the time and in the prevailing state of public opinion which regarded flying as an adventure. George Holt Thomas, founder of Air Transport & Travel, certainly regarded advertising as important.[6] Insurance premiums were inevitably high for such novel and untried vehicles of transport, but 11.2 per cent nevertheless seems a remarkably high figure. There is, unfortunately, no similar figure for another firm with which to compare it.

Subsidy and grants from government in the case of the Daimler Airway thus represented over 80 per cent of total income. This was certainly a greater proportion than for Handley Page Transport or Instone, both of which received substantially less than Daimler in total subsidies for their routes under the "revised" scheme. For this period, 1 October 1922 to 31 March 1924, Daimler received £69,807, Handley Page Transport £26,927, and Instone £39,775.[7] Nevertheless, the Daimler figures do illustrate the dependence of the airlines on state financial support. Without subsidies and grants, Daimler's operating ratio would have been about 620 per cent. In fact, of course, no company would have stayed in business on such terms, and it is clear that British scheduled air transport could not have existed without government financial assistance.

It is worth noting at this point, however, that one company, in a different form of air transport, did manage to survive over a long period without direct subsidy. The De Havilland Aeroplane Hire Service, a subsidiary of the De Havilland Aircraft Company, Ltd., used its parent firm's airfield at Stag Lane, Edgware, for air-charter operations. A fleet of converted D.H. 9c's (carrying two passengers in a cabin and one outside) and of D.H. 16s (four in a cabin) was maintained for charter at inclusive charges of 2s. and 2s. 6d. per mile, respectively. Apart from frequent flights within the U.K. and to the nearer parts of Europe, a considerable number of long tours were undertaken in eastern and southern Europe and in North Africa, for which Alan Cobham was frequently the pilot. The firm also undertook special newspaper work, air photography, and flying tuition. The hiring arrangement gave the service a number of advantages over the scheduled airlines. The inclusive charge meant that payment was always made for a full aircraft.[8] In addition the firm's activities must have helped to spread the overhead costs of the parent company's ground installations at Stag Lane. This is the only example, however, of a British company which can reasonably be regarded as being in the field of air transport and operating without state subsidies between March 1921 and March 1924.

It was, of course, widely realised that air transport was proving unprofitable. In 1923, for example, it was bitterly remarked that "the only people who make profits out of aviation are the petrol people".[9] The extent of the operators' losses, however, does not seem to have been generally understood. That this was so, even in official circles, in 1921 is shown by the "temporary" scheme which had been designed to yield a profit at the London–Paris fare of £6 6s. As Table I shows, revenue from this fare fell short of covering overhead costs. Again, in 1922, it was estimated that with an 80 per cent load factor,* the airline would break even on the London–Paris route.[10] As will be shown below, very poor load factors contributed to the airlines' troubles, but it is doubtful whether even 100 per cent load factors could have eliminated operating losses equal to six times revenue. When the Daimler Airway opened, Frank Searle, its managing director, was confident of showing a profit and hoped to dispense with subsidies within a year.[11] It has already been shown how far wide of the mark was this expectation.

As would be expected, no single factor was responsible for the airlines' large losses, but a number of reasons combined to produce them. In the first place, perhaps most obviously, the scale of the undertakings was too small. This becomes clear if they are compared in this respect with a modern airline which has, in the last few years, achieved profitability. In contrast to the £148,750 which was the price paid in 1924 for all the assets of the four vendor companies by Imperial Airways, the book value of B.E.A.'s aircraft, engines, and spares alone, quite apart from auxiliary equipment and fixed installations and buildings, is over £18.5 millions. The total revenue of all British air transport companies for the year 1921–22 was £29,424. This is to be set against the total revenue of B.E.A. for 1957–58 of over £28 millions.[12] It is only in recent years that much effort has been made to determine optimum scales for airlines.[13] To apply similar analyses to airlines before 1924, even if the material were fully available, would probably reveal that no such optimum existed, except in the

---

* Load factor is the percentage relation of payload to capacity offered.

sense of a point of minimum loss. The airlines of 1919-24 were too small to cover the fixed charges due to management, administrative staff, buildings and other ground facilities, and, as will be shown, too large relative to existing levels of traffic.

As a result of this conclusion, the fact that the aircraft operated by these airlines were inefficient as transport vehicles may seem to be of minor importance. It is, however, worth considering, because it was a problem which had to be solved before air transport could be profitable; and some progress towards its solution was made in this period. The converted military aircraft used in 1919 were most unsatisfactory. Holt Thomas wrote of the D.H. 4s and D.H. 8s used by Aircraft Transport & Travel that they lost money on every flight "even when we were able to fill them with as much as they would carry".[14] Sir Samuel Instone said much the same about the various early aircraft operated by his company.[15] This state of affairs was improved upon, but aircraft productivity remained low. Although it is not easy to measure the efficiency and output of aircraft for comparative purposes, Table IV summarises the trend in this period.

Although great significance should not be attached to the actual figures of operating costs, they do clearly indicate the general increase in efficiency as measured by cost per seat-mile. Both single and twin-engined aircraft showed marked improvement

TABLE IV
Characteristics of British Civil Transport Aircraft, 1919-1924

First Airline Service (month/year)	Aircraft	Engine	No.	Take-off power h.p.	Maximum take-off weight lb.	Cruising speed m.p.h.	Normal no. of pass. seats	Approx. total operating costs
8.1919	DH 4A	Rolls Royce *Eagle* VIII	1	360	3,700	110	2	36
8.1919	DH 16	Napier *Lion*	1	465	4,750	105	4	23
4.1920	DH 18	Napier *Lion*	1	465	7,000	95	6	15
4.1922	DH 34	Napier *Lion*	1	465	7,200	95	6	18
9.1919	HP o/400	Rolls Royce *Eagle* VIII	2	720	12,800	70	6	24
10.1921	HP W8	Napier *Lion*	2	930	12,500	90	12	13
5.1922	HP W8b	Rolls Royce *Eagle* IX	2	720	12,500	85	12	12
8.1923	Supermarine Sea Eagle	Rolls Royce *Eagle* IX	1	360	6,500	75	4	24

* The table is taken, with the author's permission, from Peter W. Brooks's unpublished paper, "The First Transport Aeroplanes". The approximate operating costs were calculated by "relating formula costs for the various types to such contemporary data as is available". Several of the aircraft listed were designed to carry more seats than are indicated, but the author regards the figures shown as nearer the actual averages for each aircraft.

† Pence per seat-mile in 1919 money values.

from the converted wartime designs (D.H. 4A, D.H. 16, and H.P. o/400), the costs of both being about halved in this period. Flying-boats (represented here by the Supermarine *Sea Eagle*) have always been generally less efficient than comparable land-planes—carrying less and being slower and more expensive to operate. Despite the improvements indicated here, aircraft still remained very expensive to operate in 1924. It has even been asserted that there was "a marked retardation in aircraft design after the war".[16] Modern total seat-mile costs average less than half the lowest figure shown in Table IV, and in 1919 values would be very much less again.

On such a small scale and with equipment so expensive to operate, one might be justified, without pursuing the matter further, in concluding that the airlines' commercial position was hopeless. There are, however, several other points worth noting, and a consideration of the nature and volume of air traffic in the period will introduce these.

Passengers were not, originally, expected to take more than a subsidiary part in the business of airlines. Two weeks after it began operations, Aircraft Transport & Travel was described as maintaining "mainly an express parcels and goods service".[17] In these early stages, mail was frequently regarded as the traffic most likely to provide a staple payload for aircraft. It is not intended here to say much about the development of airmail services, because it is a subject deserving study of its own. Apart from the pre-1914 experiments, the first British civil airmail was carried in November 1919 by Aircraft Transport & Travel, and surcharged airmails thereafter continued to be carried on a small scale throughout the period.[18] As late as October 1920, the Director General of Civil Aviation was of the opinion that mail was "the basis on which commercial aviation must at present develop".[19] With closer co-operation from the Post Office this might have become the case, as it did in the United States. Instead, although surcharged airmail contracts were received from the Post Office, the main bulk of British airlines' traffic always consisted of passengers. Table V gives a summary of 1919–24 passenger traffic.

TABLE V
U.K.—Continent Air Passenger Traffic: 1919–1924

Year Ending	British		Total including Foreign		Per cent of British to Total	
	Flights	Pass.	Flights	Pass.	Flights	Pass.
31 Mar. 1920 (7 months)	754	1,155	896	1,255	84	92
31 Mar. 1921	2,641	5,754	3,610	6,720	73	86
31 Mar. 1922	1,156	5,692	3,494	11,042	33	51
31 Mar. 1923	2,965	10,066	5,137	13,172	58	76
31 Mar. 1924	2,714	11,648	4,665	14,777	58	79

British aircraft carried a greater percentage of the total traffic than their modern counterpart. The nearest comparable figure for B.E.A. shows that in 1957–58 it carried 42 per cent of the total U.K.-Continent traffic.[20]

Perhaps more instructive than annual totals of passengers is the variation in the monthly totals shown in Fig. 2.[21] The problem of marked seasonal variation illustrated here has always characterised air transport, and that it remains critical even now is shown by the comparative figures for B.E.A. in 1957–58. In the 1919–24 period, however, the proportionate fluctuation was very much greater, with an August–December ratio of about 30:1 compared with B.E.A.'s less than 4:1. Winter traffic in fact fell to almost negligible levels in this early period. Standing charges, of course, remained constant, and even aircraft operating costs could not be greatly reduced when a schedule—even a much reduced winter schedule—had to be maintained. The bulk of the airlines' large operating losses were incurred in the "off-season" periods. It was even claimed that Aircraft Transport & Travel covered its costs in the late summer of 1920, and, although this is doubtful, it was naturally true that airlines' financial returns were better during the summer holiday

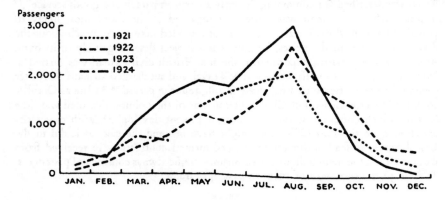

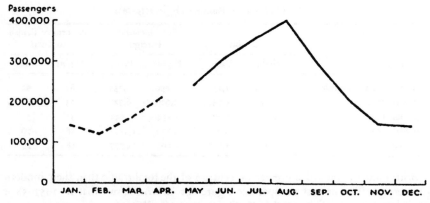

Fig. 2. Passenger Traffic Monthly Totals: British Airlines, May 1921–April 1924 (above); British European Airways, May 1957–April 1958 (below).

period. A reluctance to fly in bad weather and more frequent delays and interruptions of schedules in winter contributed to the annual traffic and revenue fluctuation. The main single factor, however, was the dominance of tourists among
passengers. The relatively high proportion of "business men" on Daimler's German
and Manchester routes in their early days was noted as being unusual.[22] It was also
remarked how many of the early airlines' passengers were American visitors. This
proportion was put as high as 85 per cent for Handley Page Transport before
June 1922,[23] and such visitors were much more numerous in summer than in winter.

It was realised that freight would not have such a marked seasonal incidence, and
a development of this traffic was frequently, as it still is, recommended as the solution
to the problem of seasonal fluctuations in passenger loads. The early goods services,
however, were even less lucrative for the airlines than passengers. They were
conceived rather as express parcels services and involved collection and delivery
facilities which were expensive to maintain. So poorly did this sort of business pay
that the Instone Airline withdrew from it altogether during the summer of 1922.
The Daimler Airway never undertook a service of this kind with collection and
delivery, although it would accept freight by particular arrangement and at special
rates. When, in October 1922, Instone began to concentrate on their London–
Brussels–Cologne route, they also began to develop a true freight service, consign-
ment being from aerodrome to aerodrome and the delivery period three days.
During 1923 Instone built up the largest British air freight service and successfully
obtained substantial contracts for carrying such cargo as motor-cycles. By July 1923
the company found it worth while to convert their Vickers "Vimy" into an all-cargo
aircraft. It is perhaps significant that this development took place on the only
British route not subject to foreign competition. Although Handley Page Transport
did carry substantial quantities of freight on the Paris route, it was the foreign
airlines—Air Union and K.L.M.—which carried the bulk of this type of traffic.
Thus, with the exception of the Instone Airline in its last year, no British airline
developed freight-carrying to significant proportions in this period. To some
extent, although the absolute figures have changed greatly, this small proportion
of freight to total traffic has remained true to the present day. In 1957–58, out of
B.E.A.'s total of 102m. load ton-miles sold (worth £23.9m.) only 9.9m. (worth
£1.75m.) were freight ton-miles.[24]

The best single indicator of whether an airline's carrying capacity is well, or
badly, matched to the traffic offering is its load factor. Although experience differs
quite widely, most modern short and medium-haul airlines operate with break-even
load factors around 60 per cent. For example, in 1957–58 B.E.A.'s break-even load
factor was 61.3 per cent and the actual load factor achieved was 63.7 per cent. For
an airline to return annual percentages of 80 or over would normally be taken to
indicate that traffic is sometimes being turned away—that is, that capacity is
inadequate.

There is not much exact information about load factors in the 1919–24 period, but the overwhelming impression is that, overall, they were very low, indicating that even the small capacity offered was in excess of demand. It has already been suggested that the overall load factor for Aircraft Transport & Travel was 30 to 40 per cent against a break-even figure estimated then at 70 per cent and probably very much higher—perhaps over 100 per cent. Early in 1922, it was estimated that on the London–Paris route, with the existing £6 6s. od. single fare, an 80 per cent load factor was necessary to break even.[25] In practice, the average load factor achieved was well below this and probably actually declined during 1922 under the "permanent" scheme of subsidy. For the three months April–June the average passenger load factor on British aircraft was 33 per cent, and during the two best months, July and August, it was only 48 per cent.[26] For the first ten months of its existence after April 1922 the Daimler Airway had an average monthly load factor of 29.8 per cent and in no month exceeded 40.5 per cent.[27] The nearest thing at present available to figures of annual load factor comparable over the whole period 1919–24 is given in Table VI. This shows numbers of passengers carried per flight and is based on Table V. These figures are not, of course, simple substitutes for load factor because the capacity of the aircraft in use changed. The increase of the second over the first figure, for example, is probably wholly accounted for by the introduction of the D.H. 18; it may even disguise a fall in load factor. On the other hand, almost certainly the increase in 1921–22, and without doubt the fall in 1922–23, reflect changes of load factor in the same direction. Some indication of the level of load factor (as a percentage) may be gained when it is remembered that, apart from the two and four-seat aircraft of 1919–20, nearly all British aircraft on scheduled

TABLE VI

Average Passenger-Loads: all British Airlines: 1919–1924

Year	Number of Passengers per Flight (British aircraft only)
25 Aug. 1919 – 31 Mar. 1920 (7 months)	1.53
1 Apr. 1920 – 31 Mar. 1921	2.18
1 Apr. 1921 – 31 Mar. 1922	4.93
1 Apr. 1922 – 31 Mar. 1923	3.39
1 Apr. 1923 – 31 Mar. 1924	4.29

routes had design capacities over 8 and sometimes 10 or 12. Thus, despite the small scale of operations, it is evident that, overall, the airlines offered capacity well in excess of demand at the time. It is therefore necessary to attempt an explanation of why demand was relatively so low. Quite apart from the sheer novelty of the new mode of transport, three specific factors weighed heavily against any very rapid increase in passenger traffic. These were reliability, safety, and fares; and attention will be given to each in turn.

Some indication of the difficulties facing early airlines in trying to maintain advertised schedules can be gained from the experience of Aircraft Transport & Travel. This firm began well in its first nine weeks, up to the middle of October 1919, by carrying out 97 per cent of its scheduled flights. With winter, however, this level of reliability slumped badly. In the next period of nearly four months—October 1919–February 1920—the percentage was only just over 72. This set the pattern for the future: reasonable reliability in summer, falling away markedly in winter. The 1922–24 trend appears in Table VII,[28] which shows the seasonal nature of efficiency, but also indicates a general improvement of winter efficiency over that achieved in the winter of 1919–20. Considering the many difficulties, these figures represent a creditable performance, although modern standards of regularity and punctuality are considerably higher. B.E.A. claims 97.4 per cent "regularity" and 80.1 per cent "punctuality (arrival)" for the year 1957–58.[29]

TABLE VII

Operational Reliability: all British airlines, 1922–1924

	Flights Completed to Terminal			
Period	Within Subsidy time*	Same day	Not same day	% completed in Subsidy time
Oct. 1922 – Mar. 1923	672	30	106	83
Apr. 1923 – Sept. 1923	1725	71	93	91
Oct. 1923 – Mar. 1924	902	78	116	82

* "Subsidy time" was the maximum period of time allowed under subsidy agreements for the complete journey on any route. The period varied for each approved route, but was in excess of the scheduled time.

Safety has always been a major weakness of air transport companies. They have never fully succeeded in persuading the public that flying is a comparatively safe method of travelling, and there was certainly a widespread opinion to the contrary during the period being considered. In fact, however, although forced landings were not at all unusual in this early period, fatal accidents to aircraft passengers on scheduled flights were surprisingly few, as Table VIII shows.

TABLE VIII

Accidents to British Transport Aircraft on Scheduled Flights, 1919–1924

Period	Passengers killed	Passengers injured	Crew killed	Crew injured	Total
Aug. 1919 – Mar. 1920	1	2	2	1	6
Apr. 1920 – Mar. 1921	2	2	2	—	6
Apr. 1921 – Mar. 1922	—	—	—	—	—
Apr. 1922 – Mar. 1923	—	1	2	1	4
Apr. 1923 – Mar. 1924	3	—	2	3	8

Overall, six passengers and eight crew members lost in four and a half years may not appear to be a bad record compared with the total of 55 passengers killed in B.E.A. aircraft during 1958.[30] Relative to the total number of passengers carried, however, it is a poor figure by modern standards. Over the full period August 1919–March 1924, one passenger was killed for every 5,719 carried on British scheduled flights. B.E.A.'s figure for 1957–58 was one for every 145,557 carried. A comparison on the basis of passenger-miles flown would be more realistic and more revealing of the modern improvement, but accurate figures of this kind for the 1919–24 period do not at present exist. The only conclusion to be drawn from the figures available is that, although the totals involved were small, air transport was in this period still a relatively unsafe mode of travel, although not as unsafe as was often believed.

Fares for travel by air on scheduled routes have nearly always exceeded surface charges. Aircraft Transport & Travel began by charging 20 guineas for the single journey to Paris, although this was reduced to 10 guineas before the end of 1920. Handley Page Transport continued to charge its original 15 guineas until the temporary suspension of services early in 1921. With the granting of subsidies the single fare became 6 guineas (£12 return) and remained at this figure throughout the rest of the period.

This compared with the first-class *return* fare by surface-transport of about £5 15s. in 1922. The difference between the fares of the two forms of transport was much greater then than now. The single ordinary fare between London and Paris by B.E.A. or Air France is now £9 1s. (return £16 6s.) and the first-class surface fare (Dover–Calais route) is £6 12s. 6d. (£13 5s. return). Night tourist air fares are, of course, lower and below first-class surface fares.

On other routes than London–Paris before 1924, air fares were generally similar or lower in proportion to the distance covered. Daimler's original single fare between London and Berlin was £6 10s., which represented only about half the London–Paris cost per mile. Surface fares were, however, considerably less. The London–Manchester single fare of £2 5s. was comparable with the first-class railway fare, but the journey was not markedly different in time after allowing for travel to and from the aerodromes.

These three factors—varying regularity, a doubtful safety record, and high fares—together explain why demand for air transport was generally poor. Herein lay the economic dilemma of the new industry. While traffic was lacking, airlines could not use the capacity they possessed to its full advantage and, until this was possible, it was clearly useless to provide greater capacity. Yet an increase in the scale of operations was probably a prerequisite of success in air transport, and certainly became increasingly so as aircraft, ground installations and services, and operating techniques became increasingly complex. Civil air transport was not a commercial success in this period. It was only a limited technical success, failing above all to develop a reasonably efficient transport aircraft. But it served its pioneering purpose in revealing the problems and in suggesting some of the solutions. Imperial Airways, formed in April 1924 from all four existing British airlines, was, among other things, a solution to the problem of size, being the first attempt to give resources to an air transport company which would enable it to develop on a considerable scale.

NOTES

1. The best short accounts are in *Report of the Civil Aerial Transport Ctee.*, Cmd. 1811. Cf. also E. Birkhead, "The Daimler Airway", *Journ. Transport Hist.*, III (1957–8), 195–200.

2. W. Armstrong, *Pioneer Pilot* (1952), 78.

3. Cmd. 1811, 6. The period began on 21 March for Instone.

4. Monthly Accounts of the Daimler Airway. The originals are kept by Daimler Hire, Ltd.: a copy, by kind permission of the owners, is in the Library of the University of Leicester.

5. The source for the B.E.A. figures is *B.E.A. Annual Report, 1957–8*, 6.

6. *Nineteenth Century*, LXXXVIII (1920), 341.   7. *Aeroplane*, XXVI (1924), 198.

8. *Proc. Third Air Conference, 1923*, Cmd. 1848. Report of the Director of Civil Aviation.

9. *Aeroplane*, XXIV (1924), 198.   10. *Ibid.*, XXII (1922), 83.

11. *Flight*, XVI (1922), 207–8.   12. *B.E.A. Annual Report, 1957–8*, 6.

13. See S. Wheatcroft, *Economics of European Air Transport* (1956), chap. III.

14. *Nineteenth Century*, loc. cit., 334.   15. *Proc. Air Conference, 1920* (Cmd. 1157), 21.

16. M. J. B. Davy, *Aeronautics: Heavier-than-Air Aircraft*, Part. I, Hist. Survey, 49.

17. *Flight*, XI (1919), 1233.

18. *Air Mails Ctee.: Interim Report, 1924* (Cmd. 2038), 3.

19. *Proc. Air Conference, 1920* (Cmd. 1157), 14.

20. There are, of course, more competitors involved now. B.E.A.'s share of the traffic over all its own normal scheduled routes was 58 per cent: *B.E.A. Annual Report, 1957–8*, 18.

21. *Flight*, XVI (1924), 371; *B.E.A. Annual Report, 1957–8*, 58.

22. *Flight*, XV (1923), 201.   23. *Aeroplane*, XXII (1922), 388.

24. *B.E.A. Annual Report, 1957–8*, 58.   25. *Aeroplane*, XXIII (1922), 83.

26. *Flight*, XIV (1922), 456.   27. *Modern Transport*, 31 Mar. 1923, 9.

28. *Annual Report of Director of Civil Aviation, 1923–4* (Cmd. 2210). 31.

29. *B.E.A. Annual Report, 1957–8*, 7.   30. *Flight*, LXXV (1959), 112.

N.B.   This paper was not passed for the press by the author, owing to his premature death: see p. 186.

4 Imperial Airways, 1924–40

A. J. QUIN-HARKIN

THE story of Imperial Airways is sixteen years of pioneering and development—sixteen years of glorious achievement. From its birth as a public company in 1924 to its absorption within the state-owned British Overseas Airways Corporation, this virile airline, begotten of the first generation of a new form of transport, had by the outbreak of war in September 1939 surveyed, opened, and put into regular operation air services between the United Kingdom and the Dominions and Colonies of the British Commonwealth. From a beginning with a heterogeneous fleet of thirteen single and twin-engined serviceable aircraft, and operating only services to the nearby capitals of Western Europe, with the tourist traffic to Paris featuring as its most popular and lucrative service, at the outbreak of war fifteen years later its four-engined fleet of over thirty flying boats and twenty landplanes were then carrying passengers, mail, and cargo to South Africa, India, Burma, Malaya, and the territories between, and also to Australia and New Zealand, in association with Queensland and Northern Territories Air Service (QANTAS) and Tasman Empire Airways (TEA). It had, further, inaugurated a service between the USA and Bermuda, joined Bangkok to Hong Kong, and Khartoum with Kano, and had moreover operated in the summers and early autumns of 1937, 1938, and 1939 a series of experimental transatlantic flights.[1]

Imperial Airways acquired on formation the landplanes of Handley Page Transport, Instone Air Lines, and Daimler Airway, and two flying boats of Scott Paine's British Marine Air Navigation. It was a ramshackle collection which included twin-engined Handley Page W.8's and a Vickers Vimy, the *City of London*—the pride of Instone Air

---

[1] The author, having been personally concerned with Imperial Airways throughout the company's life, has relied largely on his personal notes and recollections for this article. In addition, the published annual reports and accounts have been used, as well as a few official publications: the text indicates where these materials have been used.

Lines—single-engined D.H. 34's and Supermarine Sea Eagles, also a Vickers Vulcan, and even a grounded Handley Page converted o/400 bomber. Their tractive units were water-cooled Rolls "Eagle" VIII's (and IX's) and Napier "Lions" developing respectively 355, 365, and 450 h.p. The new concern shortly acquired a Handley Page W.8f, its first three-engined landplane. This disposed of two Siddeley "Pumas" of 240 h.p. outboard and an "Eagle" IX in the nose (incidentally also in the pilot's view). Besides appearing on the routes at 75 m.p.h., this multi-engined monster was featured at the head of the company's share certificates as evidence, no doubt, of the marvels to follow.

Beginning with a staff of about 260 (including sixteen pilots), mostly based at Croydon at the old Plough Lane site, the personnel grew to 3,500 by 1939, employed in Europe, the Middle and Far East, Central, South and West Africa, and in the U.S.A. and Bermuda. During this period its accounts staff alone had increased from about ten at one site to 400 in four continents! With an initial staff recruited from the four taken-over companies, Imperial Airways acquired many who had served civil aviation since its birth in 1919. These "Old Contemptibles", who later became the corner and keystones of the new and later structures, carried many strange burdens and performed many strange duties. It was a period when an ounce of experience was worth more than a ton of knowledge; when engines were hand-started and forearms broken; when pilots were also their own navigators and radio telephonists; when traffic staff were salesmen, loaders, and foreign exchange brokers; when passengers were few—and optimists! Many of the staffs still serve in honourable and responsible positions in the British Corporations; others have carried their knowledge, skill, and enthusiasm to those corners of the British Dominions and territories whence they first served Imperial Airways as pioneers; and others we shall never see again.

In the United Kingdom, civil aviation began on 25 August 1919 by a flight from Hounslow to Paris flown by Capt. W. Lawford, late of the R.A.F.; the operators were Aircraft Transport & Travel Ltd. On the same day a flight carrying a party of journalists was also operated by Handley Page Ltd, piloted by Lieut Sholto Douglas, now Lord Douglas of Kirtleside, Chairman of British European Airways Corporation. The birth of civil aviation stemmed from a Civil Aerial Transport Committee, convened by the Government in 1917 under the chairmanship of the first Lord Northcliffe. The first commercial operator—Aircraft Transport & Travel Ltd—was formed before the end of the First World War by Mr G. Holt Thomas, then head of the Aircraft Manufacturing Co. (now the De Havilland Aircraft Co.). From this beginning, also, other ventures sprang, sponsored by Handley Page Ltd, the aircraft constructors; Instone, the shipping company; and Daimler Hire, the luxury London car hire service, then an associate of the B.S.A. Company of Coventry.

It had been laid down by the Government in 1920 that air transport "must fly by itself": that meant there must be no subsidy. Overcome by inevitable events and irresistible economic forces, there arrived a black period in 1921 when, for three weeks, no British air service could be operated in the face of heavily subsidized foreign competition and the resultant cut fares. Awoken to the urgency and seriousness of the problem, the Government of the day, inspired by Mr Winston Churchill, Secretary of State for Air, made swift temporary arrangements to restart the propellers of British Civil Aviation, on a subsidy per flight basis, a state of affairs which lasted until April 1922 when three companies—Handley Page Transport, Instone Air Lines, and Daimler Airway (who employed the writer)—were all subsidized to compete (and cut each other's commercial throats) on the single London-Paris route, which was then also served by two equally competitive French Companies—Cie. Messageries Aériennes and the Grands Express Aériens.

The Government, quickly shaken by the mounting financial losses of these keen competitors, parcelled out, by September 1922, the European routes and allotted subsidies appropriate to the reciprocals of their estimated commercial potentialities—i.e. their probable losses! Handley Page Ltd, the doyen operators with their twelve-seater "Queen Mary's" of the air, retained the lucrative London-Paris route, with seasonal extensions to Basle and Zürich, then subsidized by these towns and assisted by a mail grant from Berne. Instone Air Lines were allotted the Brussels-Cologne and Prague services, and Daimler Airway received the new London-Amsterdam-Hamburg-Berlin and London-Manchester services. Meanwhile, the "Sea Eagles" of Scott Paine's British Marine Air Navigation Co. were cutting down the sea crossing between Southampton and Guernsey and Jersey from many frequently unpleasant hours at sea to eighty minutes of flight. But in a review specifically devoted to the development of Imperial Airways, scant justice can necessarily be done to the struggles and triumphs of those who preceded. Each venture would itself merit an article; each would contribute its series of anecdotes.

The Imperial Conference of 1921 had sounded a call for air communication within the British Empire. Formed in 1923 under the chairmanship of the late Sir Herbert Hambling, the Civil Air Transport Subsidies Committee, known shortly as the "Hambling" Committee, gave it direction. This Committee recommended that the existing four subsidized companies should be welded into a single organization strong enough organically to accept the call of the Imperial Conference. It also emphasized the commercial aspect of the "chosen instrument" and therefore recommended subsidies, on a diminishing scale.

The Statute of Westminster was still to come; "Empire" and "Imperial" were still dignified, fashionable, and descriptive words. It was inevitable that the title and quality "Imperial" should be included in its name, though up to four months before its registration the euphonious, descriptive, and prophetic title "Imperial Airways" had yet to replace the clumsier original designation "Imperial Air Transport Co., Ltd", which featured in the agreement signed on 3 December 1923, between the Air Council and the promoters

"providing for the formation of a

HEAVIER-THAN-AIR AIR TRANSPORT COMPANY

to be called

IMPERIAL AIR TRANSPORT COMPANY LTD".

The preface to the agreement, signed by the President of the Air Council, Sir Samuel Hoare (now Lord Templewood), specified that the company was "to operate a heavier-than-air transport service in Europe (including the Mediterranean and Black Seas)". It also asserted that:

> "The Agreement carries out the recommendations made by the Civil Air Transport Subsidies Committee in their Report dated 15th February 1923."

(It will be noted that the Treasury Solicitor's department could not stomach such linguistic innovations as "airplane" or "aeroplane" for the vessel by which this new transport medium was to be operated under this go-ahead agreement.) The draft agreement provided, *inter alia*, that:

(a) The company should have a capital of £1,000,000;

(b) On or before 1 April 1924 it should operate an efficient air service between London and Paris, London and Brussels, London and Amsterdam, and Southampton and the Channel Islands, or such other places approved, etc.;

(c) During the first four years, it should complete a minimum of 800,000 miles annually, with an average over the whole period of 1,000,000 miles per annum;

(d) Annual subsidies to a total of £1,000,000 should be paid in ten years, beginning with £137,000 in the first year and terminating with £32,000 in the tenth;

(e) All aircraft and engines should be of British design and manufacture;

(f) All aircraft should be equipped with apparatus necessary for safe and proper navigation;

(g) The President should have the right to nominate two of the directors (as Government directors).

The new company was incorporated on 31 March 1924 under the title of "Imperial Airways, Ltd." It acquired the vendor companies for a consideration of £148,750, payable one-third in cash and two-thirds in fully-paid shares. Its prospectus was issued in June for 500,000 shares of £1 each at par, payable 2s. 6d. per share on application and 7s. 6d. on allotment, "the balance of 10s. per share payable in calls not exceeding 5s. ... but there is no present intention to make such calls." Whether the fact that the public were appealed to on Derby Day (a soaking one) or whether investors were unconvinced of its future, the underwriters were left to take up about 75 per cent of the issue.

The first directors were:

Chairman: The Rt. Hon. Sir Eric Geddes, G.C.B., G.B.E., then chairman of the Dunlop Rubber Co., earlier the first Minister of Transport;

Managing Director: Frank Searle, C.B.E., D.S.O., former managing director of Daimler Hire, also earlier associated with A.T. & T.;

Sir J. George Beharrell, D.S.O., managing director of the Dunlop Rubber Co., earlier associated with Sir E. Geddes in the North Eastern Railway;

Sir Samuel Instone, chairman of Instone Air Lines;

Lt. Col. J. Barrett-Lennard, C.B.E., director of Handley Page Transport;

H. Scott Paine, chairman of British Marine Air Navigation;

Sir Herbert Hambling, Bart., deputy chairman, Barclays Bank (Government director);

Major J. Hills, J.P., late Financial Secretary to H.M. Treasury (Government director).

The new company was fortunate to possess a board of such distinction, experience, and commercial acumen. The general manager was George Woods Humphery, formerly of Handley Page Transport, more recently manager of Daimler Airway.

The prospectus, issued with the concurrence of the Government, recited, *inter alia*, that all persons employed on British territory were to be British; no government subsidy was to be granted for ten years in respect of other heavier-than-air air transport; the balance of profit, after payment of a 10 per cent dividend, was to be divided, one-third to Government in repayment of subsidy, one-third to reserve for development, and one-third for additional dividends. It was proposed to maintain the existing services of the vendor companies and "to develop the same further by the establishment of new routes and, by the extension of the company's activities further afield, *ultimately linking up all parts of the British Empire*." The prospectus mentioned 33,000 passengers carried by British aircraft in the four and a quarter years between August 1919 and December 1923 (compared with 1,700,000 carried in 1953 by B.E.A. alone!). It promised: "In the future, as in the past, 'Speed with Safety' will be the company's paramount consideration"; further, "By the application of modern scientific methods, great improvements will be introduced in the company's services, tending to ever-increasing comfort and safety in Air Travel." Finally, it was asserted in large type: "The net divisible profit for the first year from all sources, including the Government subsidy, is estimated at £53,000", after providing for obsolescence of the aeroplanes at 33⅓ per cent and 25 per cent to 33⅓ per cent on the engines.

If, as will be seen, the financial results of the early years did not quite accord with these confident assertions, yet at least the technical and commercial development of the company progressed unswervingly and without pause to the fulfilment of the under-taking to extend the company's activities with the purpose of "ultimately linking up all parts of the British Empire".

The new company acquired from the vendors the following fleet of thirteen air-craft in a serviceable condition:

Single-engined aircraft

    7 de Havilland 34's, 8-seater landplanes each fitted with one 450 h.p. Napier "Lion";
    2 Supermarine "Sea Eagle" flying boats, each fitted with one 365 h.p. Rolls "Eagle" IX.

Twin-engined aircraft

    3 Handley Page W.8b 12-seater landplanes, each fitted with two 355 h.p. Rolls "Eagle" VIII;
    1 Vickers "Vimy" 12-seater landplane, fitted with two 355 h.p. Rolls "Eagle" VIII.

(It also inherited some unserviceable units which were later scrapped.) The fleet acquired was both inadequate and unsuitable to undertake the operations envisaged by the Board, so that their first concern was the replacement of single-engined aircraft by the projection of new, larger, and faster multi-engined machines. In the interim, the company obtained a three-engined Handley Page W.8f on loan from the Air Ministry and ordered from Handley Page four W.10's and additionally a single three-engined W.9. The W.8f, as already stated, was installed with a Rolls "Eagle" IX in the nose and two Siddeley "Pumas" outboard. The W.10's were modified versions of the W.8b, in which the Rolls "Eagles" were replaced by the more powerful Napier "Lion" engines, from which they gained a slight increase in speed and an increase in passenger seats from twelve to fourteen. The W.9, a 14-seater, was virtually a flying test bed for the Jaguar air cooled engine and later also for Jupiters. The single-engined D.H.34's were withdrawn from service progressively as their engines were required for installation in the W.10's.

The W.10's, the first accretion to its fleet, were flown in formation from Crickle-wood to Croydon. Shareholders were invited to inspect their new acquisitions, including the W.9, and witness a naming ceremony performed by Lady Maud Hoare (now Lady Templewood). As the first aircraft was named, a flight of pigeons was re-leased from the cockpit.

In its first year, the new company was afflicted by various technical vicissitudes dur-ing its process of welding together the heterogenous flight equipment acquired from the vendor companies and standardizing its maintenance and overhaul procedure. At the nadir of its technical efficiency, of its fleet of thirteen on one day only two single-engined aircraft were operational. The editor of *The Aeroplane*, the late C. G. Grey, wrote: "The fleet of Imperial Airways has now been reduced to This and That, and at any moment This may become That!"

In 1925 an agreement was signed with the Air Ministry for the inauguration of a service between Cairo and Karachi as the first link of the England-India route. For this operation, a fleet of six 3-engined landplanes, to Imperial Airways' specification, was ordered from de Havilland's. These, the D.H.66 or "Hercules" type, were to be powered by three 450 h.p. air-cooled Bristol "Jupiter" VI engines. To gain experience, a "Jupiter" VI was installed in a Bristol "Bloodhound", and a sealed test under flight conditions was undertaken. Weather permitting, the "Bloodhound" was flown anywhere in England the pilot wished, with one objective—to pile up 100 engine hours (but not the aircraft) as quickly as possible. In the interim, an order had been placed with Armstrong Whitworth for three 3-engined biplanes—the "Argosy" type—for operation on the European routes. Installed with three "Jaguar" IV's each developing 396 h.p., they cruised at 95 m.p.h. carrying twenty passengers and a crew of three, including a steward. The first of the series came into service in 1926. A further four Argosies were later ordered, but these were installed with "Jaguar" VI engines of 425 h.p. As in the case of the "Jupiter" VI, the "Jaguars" had been given a work-out on European routes in the 3-engined Handley Page W.9, the "Hampstead", later sold to a gold-mining concern in New Guinea for the transport of heavy mining machinery over impassable mountain ranges.

The de Havilland "Hercules" opened the Cairo-Basra section of the Cairo-Karachi route in December 1926, all five of the fleet being flown out from Croydon in about 300-mile stages, then quite a feat of flying—particularly the long oversea flight from Malta to Tripoli. One, which left Croydon on 27 December 1926, carried the Secretary of State for Air—Sir Samuel Hoare—and Lady Maud Hoare. The trans-desert flight from Cairo to Baghdad had been previously operated by the R.A.F. whose water-cooled twin-engined aircraft were unsuitable to the temperature, altitude, and other conditions of the route. Flying close to the arid, featureless, and burning desert, and lacking modern radio and navigational aids, these followed a double ploughed furrow with numbered circles at twenty-mile intervals from Amman to Rutbah and beyond. Besides furnishing direction, these furrows and circles assisted in tracing force-landed aircraft. In data lent by the Air Ministry to Imperial Airways for planning their trans-desert service, the suggestion was made that an allowance at the rate of 50 per cent should be made for unsalvable aircraft! Happily, the "Hercules", built to Imperial Airways' specification, with air-cooled engines, proved ideal for the conditions encountered, and, during their first year they operated to a 100 per cent regularity. Moreover, being of wooden construction, as a consequence of the dry climate in which they operated they were found, at their first re-weighing, to have lost 500 lbs of all-up weight, thus gaining a corresponding increase in payload!

In this section, more space has been given to these earliest types than to later ones, because each represented an outstanding advance in design and construction in the heroic period of civil aviation. Moreover, the "Argosies" and D.H. "Hercules" were the first British aircraft built for civil aviation which, under the conditions of the day, could operate at a gross profit. Earlier types, even when full, could still not cover their basic operating costs of fuel, oil, pilotage, maintenance, and overhaul. As will be seen later, from then onwards the new fleet followed the development of Imperial Airways' routes as these were successfully extended to India, to North and South Africa, to Malaya and Australasia, and finally, experimentally, across the Atlantic. The principal aircraft put into operation by Imperial Airways between 1924 and 1939 may be listed:

> "Argosy" (Armstrong Whitworth)
> D.H. 66 (de Havilland)
> "Calcutta" (Shorts) flying boat
> "Kent" (Shorts) flying boat
> H.P. 42 (Handley Page)
> "Atalanta" (Armstrong Whitworth)
> "Scylla" (Shorts)
> D.H. 86 (de Havilland)
> S.23 "C" or "Empire" Class (Shorts) flying boat
> A.W. 27 "Ensign" Class (Armstrong Whitworth)
> S. 30 (Shorts) flying boat
> D.H. 91 "Frobisher" (de Havilland).

The Handley Page 42, or "Heracles" and "Hannibal" class, have a unique claim to mention. These four-engined thirty-eight-seater aircraft, of which the "Heracles" class were employed in Europe and the slightly slower "Hannibal" on the Empire routes, by their safety, regularity, comfort, and silence unquestionably opened a new vista in civil aviation. They were the first four-engined aircraft employed in civil air transport and undoubtedly the greatest contribution to popularizing flight as a normal means of transport. From their introduction in Europe in 1932 until the outbreak of the war in September 1939, this fleet of giants (of which one was accidentally destroyed by fire in its hangar at Karachi) flew over 7,000,000 miles without causing death or injury to passenger or aircrew. In the first six months of their full operation on the Paris service in Europe, Imperial Airways carried as many passengers as in the whole of the preceding year, whilst their deployment to the Middle East, where they flew between Cairo and Karachi, and Cairo and Kisumu, enabled frequencies to be doubled and the capacity to be increased over sixfold.

The following three other aircraft also deserve mention here. The "Atalanta", besides being Britain's first commercial large-scale monoplane, was constructed with a high allocation of space for mail, and specially designed for operation from the high altitude aerodromes between Cairo and the Cape. The D.H. 86, designed specially for the Singapore-Darwin section of the Australian route, had a fuel reserve to cross the Timor Sea against a 40 m.p.h. headwind. The joint Imperial Airways—QANTAS tender was submitted on specified characteristics before flight testing, and the proto-type was built and flown in less than twelve months from drawing board to accept-ance. The "Scylla" class of two landplanes had mainplanes, fin, rudder, etc., inter-changeable with the "Kent" flying boat. Whilst they were much criticized because of their appearance and flight characteristics, it should be recorded that the placing of the order with Shorts, by deliberate decision of Imperial Airways, saved the imminent dispersal of their office drawing staff at a time when, through lack of military orders, their shops were empty. Later, this great firm was to design the "C" class boat and its military counterpart, the Sunderland, which contributed so much in the Second World War to the success of the anti-submarine campaign.

Whilst no specific mention has been made of the various classes of Short flying boats from the "Calcutta" and the "Kent" to the "C" Class (S. 23's), yet their development was an essential feature in the planned programme of Imperial Airways' development, and it was vital to the undertaking of the Empire Mail Scheme—the carriage of all let-ter mail by air unsurcharged. When in 1934 the Government decided to implement the proposals submitted for this project, such was the faith of the board in this British design that, with the consent of the Air Ministry, Imperial Airways took the unprecedented step of ordering twenty-eight S.23 flying boats from "off the drawing board", at an estimated cost in aircraft alone of almost £2,000,000. To back up this fleet of flying boats, orders were concurrently placed with Armstrong Whitworth for fourteen "Ensigns", of which the European version seated forty passengers and the Empire design twenty-seven, with seats convertible into sleeping berths for twenty.

The original capital of Imperial Airways was sought by the prospectus issued in June 1924, already quoted, which had indicated an estimated profit of £53,000 in the first year. In face of the expectations aroused, the actual results of the first two years—losses of £15,217 and £20,415 respectively—administered a severe shock to the share-holders, one of whom, in fact, moved the winding-up of the company at the presenta-tion of the second year's accounts. Whilst the financial results in the first three years did not fulfil expectations, those of the succeeding years, however, more than made amends and demonstrated that the advance of commercial civil aviation was irresistible.

The published annual working results are given on p. 206 in tabular form, with the carry forward, dividend paid, and the number and horse-power of fleet in operation or under construction.

The last published balance sheet at 31 March 1938 also disclosed the following special reserves:

Share premium account	£424,426
Reserve for contingencies and dividend fund	£235,000
Carry forward (after payment of declared dividend)	£5,447
	£664,873

There was also a reserve for obsolescence of £558,743, against a fleet in use and under construction of a value of £2,013,611. The issued share capital was then £1,648,669.

IMPERIAL AIRWAYS RESULTS AND FLEET NUMBERS, 1924-38

Year	Result £		Carry Forward £		Dividend	Fleet in Use or Under Construction No.	H.P.
1924-5	Loss	15,217	Dr.	15,217	—	Not published	
-6	,,	20,415	Dr.	35,632	—	Not published	
-7	Profit	11,461	Dr.	24,171	—	20	18,102
-8	,,	72,567	Cr.	4,049[5]	5%	22	22,187
-9	,,	78,861	Cr.	6,689[6]	7½%	31	41,324
-30	,,	60,139	Cr.	20,957	5%	34	48,117
-1	,,	27,140	Cr.	31,556	3%	41	58,770
-2	,,	10,186	Cr.	25,200	3%	40	58,060
-3	,,	52,894	Cr.	27,192	5%	40	60,080
-4	,,	78,572	Cr.	49,245	6%	42	58,935
-5	,,	133,769[1]	Cr.	64,503	6% & 1% Bonus	42	55,620
-6	,,	140,705[2]	Cr.	65,118	6% & 2% Bonus	76	171,030
-7	,,	164,735[3]	Cr.	64,713	7% & 2% Bonus	79	185,065
-8	,,	97,267[4]	Cr.	5,447	7%	77	191,485

The progress of these years is recorded in the annual reports on which the following paragraphs are based. In 1924-5 (April to March, as in all following years) owing to labour troubles at the outset, all services were suspended for one month and only skeleton services were flown during the next month. It became evident that the basis upon which the Government subsidy was paid to the company did not further the intentions and aims which the Government had in granting the subsidy, and therefore a modification of the agreement was negotiated.

(All aircraft mileage qualified for subsidy, whether flown by the more costly twin-engined aircraft of twelve seats or a cheaper-operated single-engined 3-seater aircraft. The modification agreed was that a "subsidy mile" should be a mile of 425 h.p. and that the company's subsidy obligations would be satisfied by a *minimum* of 425,000,000 h.p. miles. An inducement was therefore created to operate larger-capacity units.)

Heads of agreement were arranged whereby the company would receive an additional subsidy of £93,600 p.a. in consideration of establishing an Eastern service between Egypt and India.

In 1926-7 the accounts covered the first full year of operations with the multi-engined aeroplanes. From the beginning of 1925 to autumn 1927, 52,000 passengers

[1] Plus £31,593 not attributable to 1934-5.   [3] Plus £12,229 not attributable to 1935-6.
[2] Plus £7,487 ,,   ,,   ,, 1936-7.   [4] Plus £1,205 ,,   ,,   ,, 1937-8.
[5] After providing for dividend and writing off £20,664 preliminary expenses.
[6]   ,,   ,,   ,,   ,, £20,664 balance of preliminary expenses.
[7] After the following transfers to reserve for contingencies: 1934-5, £30,000; 1935-6, £40,000; 1936-7, £95,000; 1937-8, £10,000, and £60,000 dividend reserve.

were carried and 2,500,000 miles flown without a single accident causing injury to passengers. The Cairo–Basra service, over a desert route of 1,100 miles, was operated since 27 December 1926 with 100 per cent regularity and reliability.

In 1927–8, the third consecutive year closed without a single accident causing injury to passengers. In 1928–9, the first aeroplane left Croydon on 30 March 1929 to inaugurate the weekly air service between England and India. Mail and passenger traffic grew steadily in accordance with forecast. 25,000 deferred shares of £1 each were issued to the Air Ministry, credited as fully paid, as "Consideration for Waiver of any Claims by the Air Ministry for repayment of Subsidy under the Agreement of 9 March 1929". (Whilst carrying remote dividend rights, these shares possessed very valuable rights in the event of liquidation.)

In 1929–30, the Board reported that, generally, the restriction of travel had been felt by all branches of transport. The preparation of the ground organization for the Cape to Cairo route was commenced. In December 1929 the England to India service was extended from Karachi to Delhi. The general manager, Mr G. E. Woods Humphery, was elected to a seat on the Board and was appointed managing director.

In 1930–1, on the European services the steady rate of progress did not continue. On the England to India service, however, the total traffic showed a satisfactory increase. Generally, air fares and freights were reduced in sympathy with the fall of values throughout the world. During the year, the final call of 5s. per share was made on 649,055 ordinary shares, previously 15s. paid, and 25,000 ordinary shares of £1 each, credited as fully paid, were issued as the "Cost of Acquisitions of Interests of Cobham-Blackburn Air Lines Ltd and of Survey and Initial Expenses in connection with the African route."

In 1931–2, when travel generally declined throughout the world, traffic by Imperial Airways improved, but the financial results were adversely affected by the late delivery of certain new aircraft. The directors submitted a consolidated statement of assets and liabilities so that the proprietors and the Government should be informed as to the position of the company as a whole. The Board recommended the dividend, with reduced carry forward (£25,200 compared with £31,556), in view of the improved traffic.

In 1932–3, passengers carried on regular European service were 42,892, compared with 24,192 in 1931–2. The Empire service was extended to Calcutta and Rangoon. The further extension to Singapore was to be begun before Christmas. The results of the first complete year of the Cape to Cairo service were encouraging.

In 1933–4, the Government of Australia accepted the tender submitted by the associated company, Qantas Empire Airways, Ltd (QEA) for the extension of the main route from Singapore to Brisbane. Fifty per cent of the capital of QEA was owned by Imperial Airways and 50 per cent by QANTAS. The service between London and Australia, 11,600 route miles, would be the longest air service in the world. Over the

Atlantic arrangements were made to start a weekly service between New York and Bermuda.

In 1934–5, the Board reported progressive improvement, illustrating the success of the policy which had consistently had as its objective the establishment on a commercial basis of a new system of communications of vital importance to the British Empire. £50,000 was set aside as the nucleus of a fund for a staff provident scheme. The Under-Secretary of State for Air and the Postmaster-General announced the Government's plan that all first-class letter mails should be carried by air to the Dominions and Colonies on the existing routes, and the Board said: "This far-reaching scheme is one of the most important events in the history of postal, as well as aviation, development and is of immense importance to the British Empire." This plan demands a more extended mention.

In the spring of 1933, the company had presented a memorandum to the Government on the future of civil aviation within the Empire. This led to the proposal that the company should carry all "first class" letter mail from the United Kingdom to Empire destinations by air without surcharge. The Postmaster-General and the Secretary of State for Air being finally won over, the company began four years' hard planning, staffing, and training, to provide for the progressive introduction of the scheme from 1937. The last published accounts included a sum of over £190,000 for expenditure under this heading held in suspense. An order for twenty-eight Short flying boats and fourteen Armstrong "Ensigns", and an accompanying increase in capital, flowed from this great project.

Such a complex scheme could only be introduced by stages. Beginning, therefore, on 29 June 1937, with the carriage of all first-class mails without surcharge to South Africa, the scheme was extended in February 1938 to India, Burma, and Malaya, and the final stage, to Australia, was inaugurated on 28 July 1938. The following appeared in a souvenir booklet issued for the occasion:

"28 July 1938
"As from today, 28 July 1938, all letters and postcards in the British Isles for delivery to 'Empire' destinations on the England-Australia (Imperial) air route will go by air in the airliners of Imperial Airways and of its associates, Indian Trans Continental Airways and QEA. The postage for letters is now three-halfpence a half-ounce and a penny for postcards. *The air mail fee has been abolished.*"

To resume, in 1935–6, new services were operated outside Europe: from Khartoum to Kano (Nigeria) in February 1936, and from Penang to Hong Kong in March 1936. In 1937, on the night of 5–6 July, the first commercial survey flights across the North Atlantic were flown, by Imperial Airways' flying boat *Caledonia* in fifteen hours from east to west and simultaneously by the Pan-American "Clipper" in the opposite direction.

The following extracts from the log of *Caledonia* (A. S. Wilcockson, Commander) speak for themselves of the cool courage and endeavour which preceded the commonplace of today. They are typical of the undramatic performance of dramatic events.

"Monday, 5 July 1937

"Weather was slowly deteriorating at Foynes (Eire), clouds had come down on the surrounding hills and it was raining steadily. . . . I slipped moorings at 18.42 G.M.T. . . . The take-off was good, and I put the aircraft direct on course for Loop Head and Botwood (Newfoundland). . . At 22.30 darkness was practically complete. At approximately 23.05 we made wireless contact with the S.S. *Alaunia*, who was in position 52° 47' N. 20° 55' W.

"Tuesday, 6 July 1937

"At 02.20 it was raining, 10–10 covered and pitch black. . . At 03.26 the clouds broke and we were able to take a star sight on Jupiter and Arcturus. At 05.06 we were flying in fog or cloud at 2,000 ft. At 08.05 the fog started to clear and we were flying in ideal conditions. Our E.T.A. (estimated time of arrival) for Botwood was 10.00 G.M.T. . . At 09.40 to 09.55 I received a succession of Q.D.M.'s (magnetic bearings) and went to Botwood on them, arriving there at 10.02, or two minutes behind my E.T.A. We landed at 10.08 and moored at 10.13."

Captain Wilcockson's log continues, after flying from Botwood to Montreal on 8 July and Montreal to New York on 9 July:

"Everything had run to schedule . . . the trip from Ireland had been from all aspects 100 per cent successful."

In 1936–7 the death was reported of the Rt. Hon. Sir Eric Geddes, G.C.B., G.B.E., who had been chairman of the company since its inception in 1924. Sir J. George Beharrell, D.S.O., also a director since 1924, was elected chairman.

The 1937–8 report recorded that in June 1937 a prospectus was published in respect of an issue of 1,000,000 ordinary shares of £1 each at 30s. per share, payable as to 2s. per share on application, 8s. on allotment, 10s. on 1 September and 10s. on 1 December. The objects of the issue were described as primarily to "provide a first instalment towards the cost of the fleet and equipment now being delivered for working the new contract with the Government."

The traffic results (Empire) for the year showed an increase in the traffic ton miles operated of over 60 per cent, due to the progressive introduction of the Empire Mail programme.

Meanwhile, however, events of another kind were taking place. After a trenchant debate on British civil aviation in the House of Commons on 17 November 1937, a special committee was appointed under the chairmanship of Lord Cadman.

Various questions had been raised previously in the Commons concerning staff conditions in Imperial Airways, its technical efficiency and development, and concerning the subsidies needed for the Empire Air Mail Scheme and other developments. Disquiet had been caused and criticism levied by the declaration of a dividend of 7 per cent plus 2 per cent bonus in October 1937. In a long and vigorous debate, various accusations were levelled not only at Imperial Airways but also at the Air Ministry in its administration of British Civil Aviation.

Besides Lord Cadman, the chairman, the committee was composed of Mr J. W. Bowen, J.P., Mr T. Harrison Hughes, and Sir Frederick J. Marquis, J.P. (later to become Lord Woolton); the secretary was Mr W. W. Burkett, O.B.E., M.C., of the Air Ministry.

In a statement to the House of Commons on 24 November 1937, the Under-Secretary of State for Air quoted from a letter to Lord Cadman from Lord Swinton, the Secretary of State, in which he wrote:

"I do not think it necessary to give the committee formal terms of reference, as the scope of the inquiry was clearly stated ... in the course of the debate ... I should wish the committee to exercise the fullest freedom in examining any matters raised in the debate, whether affecting the Air Ministry or Imperial Airways. . ."

The preamble of the committee's report to the Secretary of State stated:

"In sum, our reference required us to investigate:
(a) Charges of inefficiency in the Air Ministry and Imperial Airways Ltd;
(b) The present state of British civil aviation, particularly in Europe;
(c) The system employed by Imperial Airways for dealing with its staff (in supplement to the discussions between the Secretary of State and Government directors of Imperial Airways); and
(d) Other questions not specifically raised during the debate."

The committee held thirty meetings between December 1937 and February 1938 and received oral and written evidence from over eighty persons, who included representatives from eighteen bodies or associations. The report, of approximately thirty pages, was published by the Stationery Office (Cmd. 5685). It was supported by an appendix of fifty or so pages in small print, including statistical data. It was also preceded by twelve pages of observations by the Government in rejoinder, rebuttal, or confirmation of the views of the committee. The extracts which follow are limited to specific references to Imperial Airways and the accusations made against them. Only about eight pages in all (of the thirty-page report) related to Imperial Airways specifically; these found much to praise.

In matters affecting the relations of Imperial Airways with the Air Ministry and the Ministry's dealings with staff and internal management, the committee recorded:

"We have given very close consideration to these matters and are profoundly dissatisfied in regard to them."

After narrating the recommendations of the Hambling committee with respect to the relations between the company and the Ministry, and giving the commitee's views, the report said:

"Although the carriage of air passengers in safety and comfort, and the conveyance of mails and freight, have been achieved by Imperial Airways with considerable efficiency, we cannot avoid the conclusion that the management of Imperial Airways has been defective in other respects. In particular, not only has it failed to co-operate fully with the Air Ministry, but it has been intolerant of suggestion and unyielding in negotiation. Internally, its attitude in staff matters has left much to be desired.

"It appears to us that the managing director of the company—presumably with the acquiescence of the Board—has taken a commercial view of his responsibilities that was too narrow, and has failed to give the Government departments, with which he has been concerned, the co-operation we should have expected from a company heavily subsidized and having such important international and Imperial contacts. There should, in our opinion, be an immediate improvement in these respects, and this may well involve some change in directing personnel."

The immediately succeeding paragraphs dealt with and stressed the desirability of a full-time chairman, of whom it was written:

"Close personal intervention on his part is immediately necessary to restore the mutual confidence and goodwill which have been seriously prejudiced but are essential in relations of the management to Government departments, the company's staff, and outside organizations."

Concerning a criticism raised in the House of Commons debate with respect to the 9 per cent dividend the report stated:

"There is little doubt that capital was attracted to the enterprise by the prospect of substantial dividends. During the early years . . . no dividends were paid, and over a period of thirteen years (1924–37) shareholders received, on an average, 4½ per cent on their capital";

and, with respect to subsidies:

"The subsidies paid to Imperial Airways have always been on a contractual basis for specific services and normally on a descending scale. . . A lower amount (on a ton mileage basis) was paid to Imperial Airways for work done than to any other companies [in Europe]."

The report added that, expressed as a percentage of the company's total revenue since 1934, subsidies had been reduced for all services from 45·4 per cent to 23·8 per cent. "As will be seen . . . none of the four large foreign companies can approach these figures." Concerning an allegation that the dividend was paid from increased subsidies, the committee declared:

"It is incorrect to state that the dividend of 9 per cent in respect of the year ended 31 March 1937 was paid out of an increased subsidy. There was, in fact, a reduction in subsidy for that year. During the last three years, dividends have increased while the subsidies have decreased, a result indicative of improved trading."

There had also been criticism concerning the proportion of traffic carried by Imperial Airways in Europe, on which the committee commented:

"We see no reason for dissatisfaction with the proportion of the traffic carried by Imperial Airways."

Besides these matters, the Report covered various technical matters affecting equipment and operating personnel.

The Government, in their observations on the report, made the following comment relating to Imperial Airways:

"The Government share the view taken by the committee that the conveyance of air passengers in safety and comfort, and of mail and freight, has been achieved by Imperial Airways with considerable efficiency, and they agree that the company's record with regard to safety of its services . . . is an exceptionally good one. The committee's findings on the allegations of defects in equipment are all favourable to Imperial Airways."

The Government also expressed its concurrence with the committee's recommendations concerning a full-time chairman and other matters of management.

The consequences of the November 1937 debate and of the resulting Cadman Report altered the whole course of development of British civil aviation. Even today, whether its ultimate effect was good or harmful remains conjectural and debatable. So far as Imperial Airways was concerned, it caused the resignation of the managing director, Mr G. E. Woods Humphery, and the appointment of the then Director-General of the B.B.C., Sir John Reith, to be full-time chairman of Imperial Airways; and it produced the conception of an Airways Corporation to amalgamate Imperial Airways and British Airways, by a means of a public issue of stock bearing a guaranteed rate of interest.

After the appointment of Sir John Reith, in the period of fifteen months from June 1938 till the outbreak of war in September 1939, the Board was strengthened, the internal management organization was altered from a direct to a functional responsibility, and various administrative measures were taken to meet the parliamentary criticisms affecting relations with Government departments and in respect of personnel matters. As the concept of the new Airways Corporation emerged, management policy was directed towards prestige and away from the "dividend motive". A leader in the *Financial News* of 5 November 1938, on the report for the year ended 31 March 1938, reveals the City's quick appreciation of this feature:

"It was implicit in the recommendations of the Cadman Committee that commercial aviation was to pay far more attention than hitherto to 'carrying the flag', and national prestige and profitability do not go hand in hand in commercial aviation."

Civil Aviation had produced in several countries, in the formative years, exceptional managers whose advancement and experience paralleled the development of commercial aviation from parochial beginnings to global networks. Their consequential familiarity with all aspects of international operations, coupled with their developing experience in an industry in which they were creating the precedents, was unique and invaluable. In the United Kingdom, there could, however, be no comparable replacement for a Chief Executive whose experience in Civil Aviation had begun with it in 1919, whose faculties had been developed between then and 1924 through Handley Page Transport and Daimler Airway, and whose management of Imperial Airways had comprehended the heroic era from the initial three European services in 1924, operated by a fleet of 7,000 h.p., to the Empire Mail and Atlantic services of 1938, with their fleets of seventy-seven landplanes and flying boats of almost 200,000 total horse power. It has remained the conviction of many of the former staff of Imperial Airways that British civil aviation generally, rather than Imperial Airways only, was the greater loser by the resignation of their managing director as an unavoidable consequence of the Cadman Report.

But during the period after the inception of the new order in July 1938, all considerations were overshadowed by grave world events which gave the air of unreality to future planning. The Munich crisis and the near escape from war were almost concurrent with the changes in management. It provided an urgent reminder of the ministerial decision needed concerning the role to be played by civil aviation in the event of war. Consultations with the Air Ministry which followed Munich led to a plan for combining the services and resources of Imperial Airways and British Airways in war-time. At the same time, with the legal amalgamation in a single corporation in view, joint discussions at management level began, and joint panels were initiated to facilitate the impending amalgamation and to avoid in the meantime the creation of wider divergences in procedure.

The new head office of Imperial Airways in Buckingham Palace Road, under construction for about two years, was occupied in June 1939, only to be evacuated two months later. The War Book, started after Munich and completed by August 1939, was based on the Air Ministry's decision to co-ordinate all the resources of civil aviation in time of war under the name of "National Air Communications Service" (N.A.C.). The role of Imperial Airways (and British Airways) was to lie principally in maintaining overseas communications with their combined fleets, all operations to be at the cost of His Majesty's Government. Like all such plans, it made broad arrangements for operational and staff movements to meet a variety of potential situations, leaving the detailed execution to the executives concerned as the situation developed. It further provided for an immediate suspension of the Empire Mail Scheme—a suspension which, in the event, became an absolute abandonment.

In harmony with general Government dispersal arrangements affecting large organizations from London, the Air Ministry had decided that Imperial Airways (and British Airways) should evacuate London and Croydon within forty-eight hours of the outbreak of war and establish a provisional base at Bristol, to which the Director-General of Civil Aviation and his department were also to move. By June 1939, heads of departments had decided on the essential staff to be retained, and these had been notified. By August 1939 all broad details had been agreed and provisional billeting arrangements made with local authorities.

Events moved quickly in the last month of peace and notices to staff concerning their part in the emergency became more frequent. Thus, on 9 August, one headed "National Emergency'" was issued to all in England, giving them details concerning Evacuation and Pay (for those to be released or retained or with Reserve commitments). Meanwhile, the normal European and Empire services were, of course, being operated and the normal administration problems dealt with, but all with an increased sense of unreality.

On 31 August, the code-word was received which set in motion the emergency plans throughout the company. On 1 September, the date of the invasion of Poland, the advance party arrived at Clifton, Bristol; the main party followed on 2 September and other arrivals on 3 September. As the lights of England and Europe went out for six long years, an entry in the War Diary recorded prosaically:

"3 September 1939
"All staff had been instructed to report at 11.00 At 11.15 broadcast announcement of declaration of war. Thereafter, sundry administration announcements made. Staff told to report on Monday."

By the accident of war, the planned amalgamation of Imperial Airways and British Airways had been precipitated and their staffs integrated. It was, therefore, decided to give effect forthwith to the functional appointments and duties as planned for the unborn Corporation. A notice issued on 1 September by the Director-General-Designate, the Hon. W. L. Runciman, stated:

"The move of Imperial Airways and British Airways to Bristol (Whitchurch) necessitates the working of the two companies as a single unit and this anticipates the formation of the Corporation."

It continued to define various *ad hoc* duties and appointments.

A history of Imperial Airways' war operations must thus fortuitously merge into that of British Overseas Airways Corporation to form a single vivid narrative of courage, enterprise, endeavour, and tragedy, of which much is described in the official narrative entitled: *Merchant Airmen* (The Air Ministry Account of Civil Aviation 1939–44: H.M.S.O., 1946).

The natural events of birth and death still require their legal recognition. Thus, also, the impending obsequies of Imperial Airways were preceded by Parliamentary formality and concluded with company law procedure.

Their start was on 11 November 1938, when the Secretary of State announced in Parliament the proposed introduction of a bill to set up a new Public Corporation to acquire the existing undertakings of Imperial Airways Ltd and British Airways Ltd. The chairman of Imperial Airways a few days later by a statement at the annual general meeting acquainted the shareholders of the proposal and negotiations.

By May 1939, the negotiations with the Treasury for the take-over price had reached finality. At an extraordinary meeting of shareholders on 22 May 1939, to ratify the directors' acceptance of the Government's offer, shareholders were also told that they would be permitted to take up an amount of corporation stock corresponding to the amount purchasable by their redemption money. (In the event, and as a consequence of the outbreak of war, none of the Airways Stock was actually issued to the public; it was all held by the Commissioners for the Reduction of the National Debt.) Except for a further purely formal meeting in July 1939, required by parliamentary procedure to approve the Bill, the meeting of 11 May 1939 was the legal swan song of the proprietors of Imperial Airways Ltd.; and in the event no accounts were published for the twenty-four months from 1 April 1938 to 31 March 1940, the last day of its existence.

The British Overseas Airways Act received Royal Assent on 4 August 1939, and the corporation was established by the Secretary of State for Air on 24 November 1939. Under this Act it acquired the "undertaking" of Imperial Airways Ltd upon the "appointed day", 1 April 1940. Thus came to an end, in this coldly embracing term, sixteen years of pioneering—sixteen years of glorious achievement, which, in retrospect, have already become sixteen years of Aviation History.

5 British Airways Ltd, 1935–40

ROBIN HIGHAM

A SERIES of mergers among the non-subsidized airlines in Great Britain ended in November 1935 with the creation of British Airways, Ltd. Within the space of a few months the new company obtained both air mail and development contracts and proceeded to explore two vital areas not exploited by the older monopoly, Imperial Airways. Services were started to Berlin and to Scandinavia, on which night flying became routine, and surveys and plans were pushed ahead for a line to South America. These promising developments, and the reasons for their frustration, are the theme of this article.[1]

I

In 1928 Oliver Simmonds formed Simmonds Aircraft, Ltd, with W. D. L. Roberts (later of British Airways) and Col. L. A. Strange. The organization manufactured Spartan aircraft in the former government rolling mills at Southampton. During 1929–30 a reorganization took place in the process of raising additional finances, and Simmonds resigned as managing director. Spartan Aircraft, Ltd, in which the then Whitehall Trust Company (now Whitehall Securities) had acquired an interest, took over the Simmonds company assets, but it farmed out the manufacture of Spartan aircraft to Saunders-Roe, the flying-boat makers. Owing to severe competition, the manufacture of Spartan planes was discontinued in 1935. In the meantime, Spartan Air Lines, Ltd, was created in 1933 to operate to the Isle of Wight, and a sister company, United Airways, Ltd, to operate connecting lines as far north as the Isle of Man.

At about the same time an independent busman, Edward Hillman, organized Hillman Airways and carried the war against the railways into the third dimension. Hillman soon became unpopular with Imperial Airways, now allied with his opponents in Railway Air Services, because of his ability to fly faster and cheaper on the cross-Channel routes than the monopoly. Hillman died a few days after his organization was made a public company late in 1934. However, the London banking house of d'Erlangers had now stepped in, and his concern continued to grow. Meanwhile the Spartan group had been strengthened by the addition of United Airways, and in the autumn of 1935 the two groups were merged financially, but not operationally. In November Highland Airways and Northern and Scottish Airways were brought in, and the whole was designated British Airways. In April 1936 the new company bought out Crilly Airways' foreign undertakings and gained priorities for routes to southwest Europe. In mid-1936 the last corporate addition to British Airways was completed by a merger with British Continental Airways. Before Crilly and B.C.A. were acquired, however, there remained the matter of obtaining government financial support without which few airlines in Europe could operate without loss or hope to acquire regular schedules in competition with the nationalized lines of other foreign states.

Immediately after World War I the British Government had attempted to make civil air transport "fly by itself". The result had been temporary elimination of all British airlines by the French. From 1921 to 1924 the pioneer British airlines were, with great reluctance, granted financial and other aid. In 1923 the government created a single monopoly, Imperial Airways, which came into being on 1 April 1924. In 1928 this "chosen instrument" was granted exclusive privileges in regard to all British subsidies which might be paid for any overseas air services.[2] Thus in the following years Parliamentary questioners were unable to obtain the slightest assurance of financial aid for new projects.[3] However, after the rise of Hitler came re-armament and a reappraisal of British national policy, and the Fisher Interdepartmental Committee on International Air Communications was set up in 1935.

In the interim, the promoters of British Airways had been negotiating with the Post Office since May 1935 for an air mail contract. These talks were brought to a successful conclusion only shortly before the award of a subsidy early in 1936. At that time the company surveyed the route London–Amsterdam–Hamburg–Copenhagen–Malmö (Stockholm's new aerodrome not yet being open). The government had now determined that for reasons of prestige as well as strategy Britain should have expanded air services in Europe. Pressure was, therefore, put upon Imperial Airways to relinquish some of the areas in which it was inactive, and on 18 February the monopoly agreed to give up its rights to the territory north of the line London–Berlin. On the day before the official announcement British Airways' first service took off; and on the day after the company was awarded both a mail contract and a subsidy. But, though now officially recognized as a co-monopoly, British Airways was by no means fully airborne.

In their war against the busmen the railways had enlisted the aid of their former enemy, Imperial Airways. Railway Air Services was created in 1933 with railway money and Imperial Airways personnel. In the ensuing war between the railways and their airline and the busmen and theirs, the notorious "booking ban" developed. This was a form of boycott. Travel agents were told that if they sold tickets for airlines not approved by the railways, they would lose their franchises. It has been estimated that this action cost British Airways and its allies 80 per cent of their potential business. The ban was not finally withdrawn until after the Air Ministry threatened to obtain an Order in Council against it in 1938.

On giving up unoccupied territory to British Airways, Imperial Airways had agreed to co-operate with the new, non-competitive monopoly. But to do so placed the older company in an embarrassing position. In 1926 Imperial Airways had given up a number of the pioneer British routes in Europe, remaining merely the English agent for the state-owned foreign companies operating them. British Airways was now to operate in direct competition with Deutsch-Luft-Hansa (D.L.H.), for whom Imperial Airways was agent. The result was that the *Imperial Airways Gazette* refused to carry British Airways' advertising (unless paid for), and the company generally avoided booking their passengers on British Airways planes. Not unnaturally such actions raised a storm of protest in Parliament against the older company for its unpatriotic, if commercially reasonable, stand.

In order to operate these schedules the company purchased DH 86 aircraft.[4] When these were found to be unsuitable for winter operations, permission was obtained from the Air Ministry to purchase Junkers Ju 52s in December 1936. Two weeks later, the government sanctioned another departure by authorizing the purchase of Lockheed Electras (Lockheed 10s) and later Lockheed 14s. The subsidy arrangements required the company to operate 200-m.p.h. aircraft by 1937 in order to compete effectively with foreign operators, who were for the most part using Lockheed or Douglas models. Unfortunately, no British aircraft which would fill the bill was available. The de Havilland Frobisher/Albatross, which was on order for Imperial Airways, though designed as a trans-Atlantic mail-plane, and the Bristol Blenheim, commandeered for the R.A.F. as a light bomber, were not obtainable.

Amongst the reasons for the creation of British Airways was the fact that Britain had no regular night air services in Europe. Imperial Airways did run a banking flight, but this was an exclusive business. In 1935 they began plans for a joint night-mail service to Berlin with D.L.H., but their biplane crashed before it was inaugurated. Once British Airways was established operationally, night services became routine. In June 1936 a co-operative service with the Swedes began, with mail loads exchanged at Hanover. A year later a direct service to Berlin came into being. On 9 August 1937 the first direct night air mail to Berlin carrying all British first-class mail for central and eastern Europe left London. From then on this service was operated co-operatively with D.L.H., whereas in the old days it had been a German monopoly to fly the night mails out of England to northern Europe.

British Airways suffered for almost the whole of its life from the lack of a permanent base. It began life at Heston, but moved to Gatwick because the latter was more convenient for north German services, had railway communications with London, and was provided with Lorenz (Standard Beam Approach) equipment. But as Gatwick became water-logged, a temporary move had to be made to Croydon. This was not satisfactory, for the field was crowded, less well equipped for night operations, and less accessible than Gatwick. In the meantime, the Air Ministry had been working on Heston. So, in the end, British Airways was moved back again to its original field in May 1938.

During the summer of 1936 British Airways continued to expand both its fleet and its holdings. Four more DH 86s were acquired; so was British Continental Airways. B.C.A. was a private enterprise of Sir Percy MacKinnon, the chairman of Lloyds, and his son Graham, and it had the distinction of being a member of the International Air Traffic Association at a time when the only other British member was Imperial Airways. However, this had not saved it from the booking ban. Originally it operated from Croydon to Le Zoute and Brussels. About six months after operations began (June 1935), the company pioneered a British route to Malmö. After its efforts in this direction had been frustrated by the subsidy granted to British Airways, which had not flown the Scandinavian service, B.C.A. was less well off. Failing to obtain any government assistance, it was forced to accept a public hint given by the Secretary of State for Air on 13 May 1936 and merge with British Airways.[5] For about a year, two B.C.A. men had seats on the board of the enlarged company, but before the end of 1937 they had resigned.

After a series of accidents to their own DH 86s and to an ex-Crilly Fokker operating the night mail to the Continent, British Airways introduced German Junkers Ju 52 aircraft on this service. Meanwhile the other Fokkers were run to Paris in competition with Imperial Airways, as the Spanish government refused a permit for the planned Portuguese operations. As soon as the Electras became available in April 1937 they were placed on both the Scandinavian and Paris services. On the latter they cut the time to 90 minutes, against the two hours or more of the stalwart biplanes of the older concern. In July services were doubled to four daily. Thus the company was well established in Europe.

II

By mid-1937 the Air Ministry was beginning to envisage a wider role for the co-subsidized company. Imperial Airways was deeply involved in the inauguration of the Empire Air Mail Scheme, by which all imperial first-class mail went by air at surface rates, and with the development of the trans-Atlantic routes. The older company's neglect of the important South American and northern European areas soon brought British Airways development and subsidy contracts. Now that the company was recognized as the second "chosen instrument", it gained the inestimable advantage when tendering for the new services of being able to speak from experience. It became, in other words, a known factor, not merely an aggregation of names, capital, and ideas on a scrap of paper. This worked in its favour in 1936-7.

In December 1935 Crilly Airways had proposed running a service to Lisbon, and Mr Baldwin, then Prime Minister, had given Leo Crilly a letter of introduction to the leading Portuguese minister. The upshot was a rapid scissoring of red-tape and the immediate granting of a Portuguese mail contract. Ancient Anglo–Portuguese amity no doubt helped. But perhaps equally important was the sense of urgency which was beginning to move the British government of the day, suddenly turned air-minded in 1934. Crilly purchased four of K.L.M.'s old Fokker F.XIIs, and these were immediately certified by the Air Ministry. An experimental London-Paris-Bordeaux-Biarritz-Madrid-Lisbon survey flight completed the arrangements. But the Franco government withheld permission, indefinitely.

Despite the fact that the South American service ultimately depended upon this London-Lisbon link, British thinking appears to have remained wedded to commercial concepts. While it must be admitted that direct flight was at first beyond the endurance of the aircraft available unless Empire flying boats, Ensigns, or Frobishers, were co-opted, wartime services by Lockheed 14s showed that a Cornwall-Lisbon hop was practicable. This would, of course, have meant neglecting some profitable traffic; but that was scarcely as important as the strategic, prestige, and commercial value of a service to South America.

Interest in a South American service went back to the Handley Page world-wide proposals of 1919. But nothing had come of them, owing largely to adverse financial conditions in the immediate post-war years. The French, however, with their adequate state support, began in 1924 a service to Dakar. This was extended three years later to Buenos Aires, using fast steamers across the South Atlantic. By 1933, however, both French and German companies operated air services all the way and carried British mails at a cost approaching £100,000 a year by 1937. This figure was a large enough proportion of a possible subsidy to demand serious reconsideration of British air postal policy.

In March 1936 Sir Warren Fisher's Committee began to study the factors involved in subsidizing a British line to Latin America. The prospects of increased sums being available under the Air Navigation Bill then in Parliament gave this work practical application. At the same time the South African government began to press for an alternative route from London to Cape Town, in view of Mussolini's bellicose interest in the Mediterranean theatre. The Fisher Committee rejected all the original proposals, and revised tenders were not examined until late summer 1936. One of the immediate difficulties was the requirement that British aircraft with British engines be used. Apart from the Empire flying boats and the Armstrong-Whitworth Ensigns, both fully reserved for Imperial Airways, no British designs were available. Eventually this condition was modified. The Fisher Committee and the government then finally agreed to British Airways as the "chosen instrument" in March 1937, nearly eighteen months after proposals were first called for. By July the details were settled and the contract for survey work signed.

The White Paper containing the heads of agreement provided for the reimbursement to the company of development expenses incurred in establishing the Lisbon-Bathurst route,[6] Crilly having already studied the run to Portugal. The exploratory group returned in February 1938 and submitted their report. The result was an agreement for a subsidy and postal payments of £116,000 a year, with services beginning on 2 January 1939 between London and Lisbon. Lockheed 14s were at

once ordered and hopes were expressed that a through service to South America
would be operating by 1940. (Originally the Fisher committee had called for these
services to start in May 1937.) In September 1938 the first 14 flew up to Heston from
assembly at Southampton, and in early October arrangements were completed with
a test flight to Lisbon and back via Bordeaux. Everything looked fine, except for
Franco. He blocked the January starting date, but hinted that recognition of his
régime would clear away all obstacles. Though this was accorded in March 1939,
the ban remained until almost the end of World War II.

Meanwhile another British Airways team had been surveying the situation in
South America. It reported late in 1938, and steps were taken to bring the next leg
of the route into operation. At the end of December one of the 14s flew out to
Bathurst and back, and British Airways indicated that when two more aircraft were
in hand a West African service would be inaugurated.

By this time, however, a number of other complications had arisen. On 11 November 1938 the Secretary of State for Air had announced the intention of the government to form a public air transport company; some development work was held up
because of the necessary concentration of management on the coming amalgamation
with Imperial Airways in B.O.A.C. A second cause of delaying was the loss of
Empire flying boats by Imperial Airways. *Cavalier* succumbed to ice and rough seas
between New York and Bermuda in January 1939. It was intended to replace her
with *Champion*, which was to fly a South Atlantic ocean survey en route. But owing
to further accidents with other boats on the African and Australian routes, *Champion*
was not available before war killed the whole scheme. Even before war came the
government was beginning to think that there might be no British South American
service until 1943. And lastly, but not to be overlooked, Franco still blocked a
democratic airline running to Portugal.

III

In the latter part of 1937 British Airways was operating efficient services in Europe
with high-speed aircraft. Apart from one Electra which overshot while making a
single-engined landing at Croydon and got entangled with a hangar, accidents were
negligible. But that autumn ushered in an eventful eighteen months, ending with
nationalization and war.

Robert Perkins, M.P., on behalf of the British Air Line Pilots Association (B.A.L.
P.A.), threw down the gauntlet to Imperial Airways and the government in November. The result of the ensuing struggle, which included the report of the Cadman
Committee, brought profound changes to the younger as well as to the more
venerable monopoly. Partly because of the animosity against Imperial Airways
which had been growing since the early thirties, Lord Monsell, the retiring First
Lord of the Admiralty, joined British Airways as its government director even

before the Cadman Committee reported. By its willing acceptance of Lord Monsell British Airways moved with the times. Parliament, happily *laissez-faire* in air matters until 1934, had by 1936 come to feel that the public should have some control in any company which was largely dependent on government subsidies.

When the Cadman Committee reported in May 1938,[7] British Airways found itself directly affected. While its management was not under fire, nevertheless the committee suggested that it needed a full-time chairman instead of a man who spent most of his day in the financial world. As a result the Hon. Clive Pearson devoted himself solely to British Airways for the remaining period before the British Overseas Airways Corporation came into being. The committee's report also suggested that British Airways should run to Oslo, the London–Paris service should be pooled with Imperial Airways in a joint company, and subsidies for all operations should be increased considerably.

The bulk of the Cadman Committee's criticisms related to the affairs of Imperial Airways and the Air Ministry. To deal with these, the government transferred Sir John (now Lord) Reith from the British Broadcasting Corporation to the chairmanship of Imperial Airways. With him he carried the concept that a heavily-subsidized national monopoly should be run for the benefit of the country and not of the stockholders. He accepted his new post in July 1938 only on the understanding that he would ease the shareholders out with fair compensation. Reith set to work at once, and Sir Kingsley Wood, then Secretary of State for Air, was able to announce on 11 November 1938 the proposed formation of a publicly-owned, national air transport company.[8]

In the meantime, an event of international importance had served to emphasize the backwardness of British airliners. During the Munich crisis Neville Chamberlain was conveyed to and from Germany in British Airways' American aircraft. All his journeys were made in Electras, except the last, which was in a brand-new Lockheed 14. In addition to grumblings about appeasement, there were a number of chagrined comments about a British prime minister having to travel in American aircraft to appease an Austrian corporal in Germany. Obviously the time had come to put Britain back in the forefront of world aviation, where she had been in 1918. Whatever else Munich did, it helped to accelerate plans already afoot for vastly improved British air services.

Since B.O.A.C. (though it was not yet even known as the "BOA Constrictor") was expected to begin operations in October 1939, contractual agreements between the Air Ministry and British Airways were limited to a period ending during the autumn. As Franco was still blocking services to the south-west, it was decided to follow the Cadman Committee's suggestions and inaugurate prestige services to the capitals of Europe. By April 1939 British Airways had acquired eight Lockheed 14s for the service to Lisbon and beyond, though one had been lost on a demonstration flight. As this service could not be operated until Franco relented, new arrangements were made. With the seven 14s and the Electras, services were opened to Berlin, Warsaw, and Budapest; an Oslo schedule was also considered. It was agreed that subsidies should be paid at the rate of £19,500 a year for a twice-daily Electra service to Brussels, £53,500 for a daily Berlin-Warsaw run with 14s, and £53,000 for one to Budapest, also with 14s. The last-named route had been operated by Imperial Airways up to 1938, but its DH 86s had suffered from icing and had had to be withdrawn in the winter.

In addition to the services mentioned, British Airways aircraft were also employed as substitutes on Imperial Airways schedules until the latter company received its full equipment. Armstrong-Whitworth Ensigns, ordered in 1934 for 1936 delivery, were at length going into satisfactory service in limited numbers when war came late in 1939. Useful de Havilland Frobishers, designed as trans-Atlantic mailplanes but converted to medium-range passenger planes, had under-carriage troubles at muddy grass-covered Croydon. These aircraft were Britain's best answer to the Douglas DC3 and the Lockheeds used by European competitors, and they performed excellently otherwise. But when they had to be withdrawn occasionally from the Zürich and Paris services, British Airways was called upon to find substitutes. It was on one of these assignments that the second 14 was lost near Luxeuil on 11 August 1939. Fortunately there were no casualties. But four days later an Electra fell into the sea off the Danish coast; only the pilot was saved.

In June the shareholders of British Airways agreed to sell out to the government. A secret valuation of the company had been made and the shareholders were paid 15s. 9d. a share, or a total for the company of £262,000. In addition the principal shareholders were reimbursed the £311,000 they had advanced. Critics of the transaction felt that British Airways owners had gotten the short end of the deal, as Americans would say, in comparison with Imperial Airways shareholders, who were paid 32s. 6d. per share. There was certainly some plausibility in the argument that, after all, Imperial Airways' worth had been very largely created by government funds.

The British Overseas Airways Bill had a very rapid passage through Parliament in mid-summer and received the Royal Assent on 4 August. It was intended that both private companies should cease operations on 31 March 1940, at the end of the fiscal year. Equipment and personnel were to be taken over by B.O.A.C. on 1 April. But war came in September 1939. All aircraft and personnel came at once under government control. Evacuation to the Bristol area took place immediately. All personnel who had not joined the armed forces were handed buckets of paint and brushes and told to camouflage their machines. Thereafter services were severely restricted; in British Airways' European bailiwick they became virtually extinct, only the London-Paris run being maintained. The name *British Airways* did not, however, die at once. For some time after B.O.A.C. came into being its aircraft and passengers' baggage continued to bear the words "British Airways" with an Imperial Airways Speedbird emblem added beneath.

IV

Statistically, British Airways made a commendable showing. The number of passengers carried rose from 15,500 in 1936 to 22,500 in 1938, and it appeared to be heading for another record in 1939. Route mileage rose from about 1,200 in 1936 to 3,800 by mid-1939. Subsidies began at £2,960 for the fiscal year 1935–6 and were £110,653 in 1938–9 and still growing. If 1939–40 had been a full year the company would have been taking in some £126,000 for European services, plus whatever was agreed for the opening of the London-Lisbon-Bathurst line. But as it takes time to get any brand-new commercial organization on its feet, it is not surprising to notice that the first year of operations entailed a loss of £159,618, the second one of £177,975, and the third a deficit of £80,721. The actual loss for the year (excluding accumulated deficits) was only £24,128.[9] Given one or two more years, British Airways should have been in a position to pay substantial dividends.

The company was well managed, efficient, adequately equipped with competitive aircraft, and with sufficient financial resources to enable it to do what Imperial Airways did not do in Europe. It must, however, be admitted that British Airways, because of government commitments to Imperial Airways, was forced to remain out of the field until both technology and national affairs made its admission desirable. On behalf of Imperial Airways, it should be noted that that company was originally established to carry out a programme which was ill-defined at first and which, when it was clarified in 1928, laid the emphasis on Imperial rather than European services. It wanted to abandon European services altogether, but the Air Ministry refused to allow that. Nevertheless, Imperial Airways did not until 1937 possess the capital which the Hambling Committee of 1923[10] had felt was the minimum desirable, nor did it maintain as modern a fleet as subsidy contracts envisaged. British Airways, however, enjoyed adequate capital and government backing; at the same time it was willing and able to purchase American and German airliners because no suitable British aircraft were available owing to rearmament and prior orders from Imperial Airways. (If the war had not occurred, British Airways would have been able to buy British by 1942, for the Air Ministry was developing aircraft, such as the Fairey FC-1, which would have been comparable to American designs by that date.) In addition to its commercial assets, British Airways also possessed the inestimable boon of entering the field when civil aviation had come of age. Thus it had far less pioneering to do than any of the older companies had had.

The establishment of a non-competitive, comparative-cost monopoly company with limited fields of endeavour would appear to have been a wise move in 1924.

It was tried successfully in 1936, but abandoned in the 1939 legislation, only to be reborn in 1946 in British European Airways. In the highly nationalized field of European air transport before the war, British Airways was a necessity both for strategy and prestige. The country was lucky to have men willing to take the risks to establish such an airline.

BRITISH AIRWAYS STATISTICS, 1936–9

Government subsidies and other payments (with the exception of postal payments):

	Financial Year	1935–6	£2,960
		1936–7	£11,565
		1937–8	£61,888
		1938–9	£110,653

Source: 348 *H.C.Deb.5s.*, 54, 5 June 1939.

	Year ended 30 Sept.		
	1936	1937	1938
Passengers carried			
Regular services	38,897		
Other services	19,445		
Excluding subsidiaries	15,508	17,130	22,562
Baggage (pounds)	343,747	480,699	732,480
Mail (pounds)	186,185	605,708	1,525,888
Freight (pounds)	889,545	1,177,002	1,401,915
Loss incurred	£159,618	£177,975	£80,721*

*but only £24,128 for the year.

Source: Annual Reports of British Airways.

NOTES

1. This paper is based on chapters included in my doctoral dissertation for Harvard University, "Britain and Imperial Air Ways, 1918–1939", 1957. The complete work is shortly to be published in London under the title *Imperial Air Routes*. For British Airways the principal sources used included *The Aeroplane*, Command Papers, Hansard, the annual reports of British Airways, and correspondence with the Hon. Clive Pearson, former chairman of the company.

2. See Cmd. 3143 (1929).

3. A typical reply is that of Sir Philip Sassoon, Under-Secretary of State for Air, on 2 May 1935 in which he repeated the usual statement about obligations to Imperial Airways. (See 301 *H.C.Deb.5s.*, 552–3.) His reply on 12 Feb. 1936, however, clearly indicated a change of policy, if not of heart, on the part of the government. (See 308 *H.C.Deb.5s.*, 943–4.)

Notes

4. British Airways registered the following numbers of aircraft during its lifetime:

Spartan Cruisers	7	
DH 84s	2	
DH 86s	11	
DH 89s	11	
Fokker F VIII	2	
Fokker F XII	6	(B.O.A.C. inherited 1 on 1 Apr. 1940)
Junkers Ju52	3	„ „ 3 „ „ „ „
Lockheed 10	7	„ „ 3 „ „ „ „
Lockheed 14	9	„ „ 5 „ „ „ „

5. See 312 *H.C.Deb.5s.*, 392–3, 13 May 1936.

6. The agreements between the government and the airlines ceased to be published in their full legal form starting with Cmd. 3143. In their stead the Command Papers promulgated only the heads of agreement. For British Airways the following White Papers indicate the nature of the contracts: Cmd. 5203 (1936), Cmd. 5524 (1937), Cmd. 5898 (1938), and Cmd. 6005 (1939).

7. Cmd. 5685.

8. See 341 *H.C.Deb.5s.*, 453–5, 11 Nov. 1938. Also Lord Reith, *Into the Wind* (1948).

9. Statistics are included in the annual reports available at the Companies Registration Office, Somerset House, London. See also the Air Ministry, *Civil Aviation Statistical and Technical Review* for 1937 and 1938 and the *Report of the Progress of Civil Aviation, 1939–1945* issued only as a mimeograph. See also table on p.122.

10. Cmd. 1811.

6 The new road to the Isles: Highland Airways and Scottish Airways, 1933–39

A. J. ROBERTSON

Internal air transport enjoyed a patchy history in Britain in the period between the two world wars. Initial enthusiasm and growth in the immediate aftermath of the Great War was rapidly succeeded by insolvencies and decline. By 1924, when Imperial Airways took over from the main independent airlines, scheduled domestic flights had come to an end. Imperial Airways concerned itself exclusively with external flights, in its early days at any rate, and it was not until the early 1930s that new independent scheduled domestic air services re-appeared. From 1931 the independents tried to build up their business in the face of well established services offered by large-scale surface transport concerns. For many of these fledgling airlines the struggle was too much: in Sir Peter Masefield's phrase, they 'flitted like brief shadows across the scene'.[1] But some were able not only to survive but to expand (if not thereby to prosper), and to lay the foundations before the outbreak of war in 1939 of the modern network of internal air services that covers the United Kingdom.[2] This article is concerned with one of the most prominent of these pioneering internal airlines, which began its existence as Highland Airways Ltd in May 1933, being transmogrified in August 1938 into the northern division of Scottish Airways Ltd. The change of name did little, however, to alter the character of the original undertaking. In both its manifestations, the concern's tone was set by the man who ran it throughout the years from 1933 to 1939, Captain Ernest Edmund Fresson.[3] It is the aim of this article to examine the development of Fresson's airline up to the outbreak of war in September 1939, which put an end to normal civil flying in Britain, with particular emphasis on the natural and man-made problems it faced and on the means that were devised to overcome them.

I. Growth and development

Highland Airways Ltd was incorporated in April 1933, with a share capital of

£2,675 subscribed by no fewer than seventeen shareholders, all but two of whom were resident in the north-east of Scotland. The bulk of the capital, indeed, came from business and professional men in the towns of Inverness, Elgin and Wick. There was no candlestick maker among their number, but there certainly was a butcher and a baker, together with a doctor (who was chairman), a couple of solicitors, a brace of garage proprietors, an architect, a builder, and two ladies whose status was simply defined as 'married woman'. The company's head office was to be in Academy Street in Inverness, and its declared object was 'to inaugurate an air service between Inverness, Thurso and Orkney, and also West to Stornoway and East to Aberdeen'. Fresson, with the third largest allotment of shares, was appointed managing director.[4]

The airline appears to have been very much Fresson's personal creation. An ex-RFC flying instructor, he had been touring the north of Scotland since 1931 with a superannuated Avro 504 training biplane, giving 'joy rides' at fairs and resorts — cheap, brief flights from impromptu airfields for people to whom aircraft and flying were still great novelties. On several occasions, however, Fresson had been engaged on a charter basis for more serious purposes by local businessmen, to make business trips between towns such as Wick and Kirkwall (the county town of Orkney) which by surface transport could take several days and involved the rigours of a sea passage over the notorious waters of the Pentland Firth. Air travel could enable them to compress the exercise into a single day. Recognising the potential market for regular air transport services in the Highlands and Islands, albeit on a modest scale, Fresson went about cultivating his local contacts to raise the necessary capital while creating the facilities (by way of airfields and ground installations) necessary for regular air transport operations and obtaining an aircraft more suitable for the purpose than his Avro. By 8 May 1933 all was ready. After due civic ceremonial at the new Inverness municipal airport in which Highland Airways' new and sole aircraft — a General Aircraft Monospar ST4 twin-engined cabin monoplane with four passenger seats — was christened in whisky by the Provost's wife, the inaugural flight took off bound for Kirkwall via Wick. The Edinburgh daily newspaper *The Scotsman* reported the event very fully, recording the Lady Provost's description of the flight as 'a unique occasion in the history of transport in the Highlands' and describing the affair as 'epoch-making' — a touch of hyperbole that could be excused by the fact that the paper itself was a key sponsor of Fresson's venture.[5]

Highland Airways may have started life as a one-plane, almost one-man, outfit, but it did not remain like that for long. Within a few months of the inaugural flight an additional and much larger aircraft — a De Havilland DH 84 Dragon eight-seat biplane — had been added to the fleet and an additional pilot hired. Further additions both to the fleet and to the staff followed regularly, so that by 1938, in its new guise as Scottish Airways' northern division, Fresson's airline operated the Monospar, two DH 84s and three new DH 89 Dragon Rapide biplanes giving employment to eight pilots as well as Fresson himself. By that time, however, he himself had been constrained by the weight of administration to give up regular flying on the company's scheduled services. Over the period from 1933 to 1938 the original daily scheduled flight from Inverness to Kirkwall via Wick (with a return service the same day) had been substantially augmented. New stages had been added to provide a daily service between Inverness and Aberdeen to the south and between Kirkwall and Shetland (Sumburgh) to the north; and an Orkney inter-island service was also in operation. The creation of services to Thurso and Stornoway, which had been among the declared objectives of Highland Airways' prospectus, had run into difficulties with regard to the availability of suitable landing fields for regular operations, though frequent charter flights were flown to both towns, indicating a significant level of demand for such services. By the end of 1938 the Inverness–Stornoway service was at least the subject of an agreement with the local authorities on the isle of Lewis: implementation in the summer of 1939 was intended.[6] According to figures given by Fresson himself, the average monthly number of passengers using his services rose from 175 in 1933 to 682 in 1938, while the average daily mail and freight loadings had risen over the same period from 60 lb weight to nearly 1,200 lb. If his figures are at all reliable, they show that the proportion of total UK domestic air passenger traffic carried by Fresson's aircraft remained fairly constant at between 5 and 6 per cent from 1933 to 1938. His freight loadings, on the other hand, accounted for perhaps two-fifths of the admittedly very small total amount of internal UK air freight in 1933, and about an eighth of the larger total for 1938.[7]

2. Finance and organisation

As the airline developed, it underwent several metamorphoses in terms of finance, organisation and control. In this Highland Airways simply reflected the rapidly changing scene in the field of British domestic airline development in the 1930s. Small companies came and went; liquidations, mergers and take-overs were commonplace; large concerns from outside the sphere of air transport took a hand in developments, sometimes in a positive way by injecting capital into the airlines, sometimes more negatively by trying to obstruct airline competition with established forms of surface transport.

From its earliest days Highland Airways was subject to all these influences, both positive and negative. On the occasion of the very first flight, in May 1933, Fresson had noted that this welcome by the civic authorities in Kirkwall had been decidedly cool. 'Provost Slater,' he recorded in his memoirs, 'cut me dead on arrival . . . I suspect the Provost was more interested in other means of transport. Whatever it was I got no support from him for some time to come.'[8]

Slater, he suspected, was in the pocket of the North of Scotland Orkney & Shetland Steam Navigation Company, of Aberdeen, which had until then enjoyed a monopoly of passenger and freight traffic between the mainland and the Northern Isles. On the mainland itself, Highland Airways had to contend with the hostility of the railway companies, particularly the London Midland & Scottish and the London & North Eastern, both of which had lines in the area in which Highland Airways operated and both of which saw in air passenger transport a threat to their own operations. Fresson found that travel agents were being warned off booking pasengers on to his services by the threat of the cancellation of their more substantial railway booking business.[9] However, it will be seen that in the longer term Fresson was able to turn this early hostility to his airline to advantage, and to develop strong positive links with the established surface transport concerns in the Highlands and Islands, both rail and sea.

The rapid build-up in the scale of Highland Airways' operations, manifested by the expansion both of the fleet and the payroll, soon outstripped the modest financial resources with which the airline had first been established. The original capital of £2,675 had been entirely absorbed in the purchase of the Monospar and the establishment of ground facilities at Inverness, Wick and Kirkwall in the spring of 1933. The purchase of the first DH 84 in August that year necessitated a further capital expenditure of £2,500 and further expenditures on crew, etc., by a company which was far from profitable. The money was found by increasing the share capital to £8,000 and by accepting a large-scale investment in the new shares from none other than the North of Scotland Orkney & Shetland Steam Navigation Company. George Law, proprietor of *The Scotsman*, also took a parcel of shares.[10] The matter was evidently not uncontentious, since the chairman of Highland Airways, an Elgin doctor named Thomas Alexander, resigned after what Fresson described as 'a hectic Board meeting of disagreement', but it gave the airline the wherewithal to finance its continued expansion and turned a potentially dangerous enemy into a powerful and well connected ally. Not the least beneficial effect of the involvement of the steamship company in Highland Airways was that the attitude of the civic authorities of Kirkwall towards the airline mellowed considerably. Fresson put the shipping line's action down to its realisation that air transport had come to stay, and that participation was the only way to minimise the effects of the inroads that it was making into seaborne passenger traffic in the region.[11] While it may be true that the steamship men had decided to join what they could not beat, there is no doubt that in the short term at least the benefits of the transaction nearly all flowed in the direction of Highland Airways.

In 1935 the development of domestic air transport in Britain took a new turn. Until that date the activities of the internal airlines had been completley unconnected and unco-ordinated. Perhaps because of the hostility of the railways, the various companies began in that year to draw closer together. One of the first moves in the process was the take-over in May 1935 of Highland Airways by United Airways, which in turn was controlled by Whitehall Securities Ltd, a component of the rich and powerful Pearson group, based on London and with extensive interests in civil engineering, oil, and shipping. The advantages to Fresson, Highland Airways and its shareholders were obvious. In the first place, Highland Airways retained its identity, its distinctive green-and-white livery and its operational independence in the north of Scotland. Fresson himself remained in effective managerial control, but with access to greatly enhanced resources of capital, and with the possibility of extending his services south of Inverness to link up at Glasgow with United Airways services southwards to London, with full through booking facilities. Most of the original Highland Airways personal shareholders were bought out by United Airways at a price which gave them a handsome capital gain to compensate for the lack of operating profits since 1933.[12] The tie-up with United Airways in turn made Highland Airways a party to the next great merger promoted by the Pearson interests within the internal airline sector, which resulted in October 1935 in the emergence of British Airways Ltd. Once again, however, Highland Airways retained its identity and Fresson remained in control of its affairs.[13]

The increased financial strength and greater co-ordination of effort created among the airlines by these events considerably strengthened their hand in dealing with the railways. Fresson took up the matter of travel agency bookings directly with the LMS in March 1937, and secured some concessions.[14] But already matters were moving beyond his individual efforts to secure an accommodation with a single railway company. The railways had begun to operate their own air services in competition with the independent airlines from April 1933, with the intention of driving their fledgling competitors from the field. But gradually they shifted their ground and came to seek a *modus vivendi* between their own air services and the new larger airline grouping sponsored by the Pearson interests. A market, small but growing fast, clearly existed for internal air services; and the two competing groups had built up substantial investments by 1937 to serve that market. It made more sense to protect those investments by reaching agreement than for one group to pursue the destruction of the other at perhaps substantial cost to itself. The upshot was a series of agreements which, in effect, merged the airline undertakings of the railway companies with those of the Pearson group. As far as Highland Airways was concerned, the crucial development was a Minute of Agreement date 6–15 April 1938 between the LMS, British Airways Ltd, Scottish Airways Ltd, Northern Airways Ltd, Highland Airways Ltd, Western Isles Airways Ltd and David MacBrayne Ltd to promote 'the formation of new air service companies for Scotland'.[15] In essence, the assets of Scotland's two existing operational airlines (Northern Airways and Highland Airways, both British Airways subsidiaries) were to be taken over by the newly formed Scottish Airways Ltd, which would operate their services and those of the as yet non-operational MacBrayne subsidiary, Western Isles Airways. The new company would have an issued share capital of £100,000, the main shareholders being British Airways, the LMS and David MacBrayne's. Fresson remained in control of all the routes formerly flown by Highland Airways, but he was no longer a completely free agent. Rather he was a divisional manager answerable to a powerful board of directors and to head-office managers in London. He made no secret of the fact that he did not find his new subservience congenial. Meanwhile the company he had founded in 1933, having ceased to operate in August 1938, was gradually run down to its liquidation in the summer of 1940.[16]

3. Operating conditions and problems

Introducing air transport into an area which had never experienced such a service before, at a time when aviation in general was still rather a novelty, posed several problems for the founders of Highland Airways. Not the least was that not even the most basic provision for air transport existed in the localities they intended to serve. Fortunately, the standards applied by the Air Ministry in 1933 to airfields for civil use were not very exacting. Any reasonably flat grass field whose surface and boundaries were free from obvious obstructions in the form of buildings and power lines, and which gave a run of a couple of hundred yards into the prevailing wind, would do, more or less. Highland Airways was fortunate that Inverness Burgh Council was sufficiently sympathetic not only to provide such a field but to equip it with facilities for the use of airline passengers and ground staff. The use of this municipal airport was available to Highland Airways on payment of fees according to use. Elsewhere the airline was not so lucky: Kirkwall obstructed its attempt to secure the use of a suitable airfield at Hatston, obliging Fresson to take the lease of a field at Wideford Farm, which was more remote from the town and more often affected by fog and low cloud. This turn of events nearly put an untimely end to both Fresson and his airline. In other places Highland Airways had no difficulty in reaching agreement about the availability of airfields by arrangement with local farmers. Given the financial constraints under which the airline operated, the facilities constructed at these fields were usually minimal.[17] In the outer isles particularly, the landing surface itself was usually the sole facility, and it often had to be cleared of sheep or cattle before use as an airfield.

To begin with, navigational aids such as radio beacons and direction-finders were non-existent on Highland Airways routes. Fresson and his pilots flew their services until 1936 by visual navigation when weather permitted or by dead-reckoning and aviator's instinct when it did not (as was frequently the case in the far north of Scotland). One of the benefits of the increasing interest of the State in civil aviation that was manifested by the Maybury and Cadman inquiries of 1936–38 was the installation by the Air Ministry of radio direction-finders at Sumburgh and Kirkwall in 1936 and at Inverness the following year.[18] Fresson was happy to acknowledge their utility, but there was another side to the government's interest in civil aviation with which he was less enamoured. The Maybury committee had recommended the regulation by licence of internal air routes, the control of local airports by local authorities, and an upgrading of airport standards and amenities enforced by the Air Ministry. Perhaps because they reflected feeling within civil aviation at large, Fresson's characteristically plain-spoken objections to these ideas were reported at length in the technical press.[19] He objected especially vociferously to being forced by the new Air Transport Licensing Authority to share routes that he had pioneered and facilities that he had been instrumental in creating with upstart competitors such as Eric Gandar Dower's Allied Airways, especially when the ATLA imposed a settlement that marginally favoured his competitor.[20]

Once the technical facilities to carry on airline operations had been established, people had to be induced to use them in sufficient numbers to sustain regular services and to offer some prospect of making them pay. Fresson had chosen to operate in one of the poorest parts of Britain among people who are often very set in their ways and suspicious of innovations and Englishmen. He had to work hard to generate what he called 'airmindedness' in the area, to impress the people with the benefits that air transport could bring in their everyday lives and to promote confidence in the quality and reliability of the service he was offering. In this he was assisted by the obvious advantages offered by air transport over surface transport for journeys between the main centres of the region. Several specific examples are quoted in his memoirs, and he did not need to embroider the truth to make his point. The journey from Inverness to Stornoway — about one hundred miles as the crow flies — took all day and much of the night by surface transport as against fifty minutes by air. Kirkwall to Stornoway took two days by land and sea, just about an hour by air. Even the short stage from Wick to Kirkwall, less than forty miles on the map, showed air travel to advantage, with a twenty-minute flight contrasting with a four-hour sea passage. The benefits of air travel, in terms of time saved, greater convenience and reduced hotel costs, were perhaps especially appreciated by the more mobile business and professional men. Accountants travelling to audits and commercial travellers were among the most faithful users of Highland Airways' scheduled and charter services.

The advantages of transport by air for small-bulk/high-value freight — especially time-sensitive items such as letters and newspapers — were also apparent both from the point of view of the consumer in the Highlands and Islands and from that of Highland Airways. Such routine amenities enjoyed by less remote communities as newspapers that were available on the day of publication or letters that arrived on the day of or the morning after posting were by no means commonplace in Kirkwall or Lerwick, far less on Stronsay or Foula (where even the necessities of life were not always readily available). By speeding the mails and the papers Fresson could demonstrate in ways that touched the lives of almost everybody in the region the benefits that air transport could offer over its competitors. And contracts for the delivery of the mails and the newspapers would also provide Highland Airways with a secure core of basic revenue, especially important in the early days, when passenger traffic might be uncertain.

With this kind of consideration in mind, Fresson approached the Post Office in 1933 with a view to securing an air-mail contract on his proposed Inverness–Wick–Kirkwall route. One of his local backers in the establishment of Highland Airways was an acquaintance of George Law, proprietor of *The Scotsman*, and he arranged a meeting to try to interest Law in granting a contract to deliver the paper to Kirkwall.[21] The approach to the Post Office was not immediately successful, the Postmaster General feeling that Highland Airways should demonstrate its ability to maintain a reliable service for one year before he could consider granting such a novelty as a contract for the carriage by air of His Majesty's inland mails. Law, on the other hand, could see the commercial advantage of having his paper on sale in Kirkwall several hours ahead of its mainland rivals and agreed to a contract, exclusive to *The Scotsman*, which assured Highland Airways of a revenue of some £750 in its first year of operation. Law agreed in May 1935 to open up the carriage of newspapers by air between Inverness and Kirkwall to his rivals, who had been pressing Fresson to let them in, and from then on *The Glasgow Herald*, *The Aberdeen Press and Journal* and other mainland newspapers added significantly to the daily revenues of Highland and Scottish Airways.[22] In the summer of 1934 the Post Office itself followed suit. Expressing satisfaction with the way Highland Airways had functioned in its first year, it awarded the airline Britain's first ever contract for the carriage by air of inland mail at normal postal rates.[23]

Highland Airways was also awarded a contract in November 1934 by Orkney County Council for the provision of an air ambulance service between the outer islands of the county and the Balfour Hospital in Kirkwall and even, where special treatment was required, with hospitals on the mainland. Fresson had already made several such flights by private arrangement with the Chief Surgeon in Kirkwall, undoubtedly from the highest of motives. But he must also have been aware of the value to Highland Airways of such services in terms of promoting public awareness of the airline's value to the community, and hence support for its services. The award of a formal contract had the added advantage of generating further regular revenue.[24]

It is clear, indeed, that Captain Fresson was a very able publicist for Highland Airways, and was fully cognisant of the value of publicity in consolidating the position of his undertaking among the people of the north. He cultivated the press assiduously, exploiting his connection with *The Scotsman*, developing links with the local newspapers of the Highland towns,[25] making sure the press was informed of any notable flight, and even taking journalists along on special flights.[26] Thus he kept his own name and that of Highland Airways regularly before his potential customers. He also kept them before his peers in the world of civil aviation: *Flight*, the official organ of the Royal Aero Club and in effect the trade paper of the civil airlines, carried regular notices of Fresson's activities. Nor did his publicity work end when Highland Airways was superseded by Scottish Airways, and *Flight*, for example, praised the Scottish Airways route guide published in August 1939, noting that 'Other airline people might usefully try as hard as Scottish Airways to interest the prospective traveller.'[27]

It was, in truth, fairly easy to obtain publicity for the activities of Highland Airways. Aviation was still newsworthy, and the achievements of Fresson and his pilots were in their own way as thrilling, diverting and worthy of notice as those of the great public figures of aviation at the time, such as Sir Alan Cobham or Amy Johnson. Air travel in the south might be getting more civilised, routine and unexciting. But in the regions where Fresson operated it remained much more obviously a contest between the flyer and the environment, a test of the skill and courage of the pilot (to say nothing of the nerves of his passengers). Climate, terrain and the necessarily primitive character of some of the airfields were the main factors making for this. Fresson's aircraft flew over some of the most daunting and forbidding country in Europe. Snow, fog, blinding rain and gales were so common that to ground aircraft because of them would have meant interruptions so frequent and prolonged to schedules that they would hardly have qualified for the name. Airfields were often so small, or their approaches so restricted by cliffs or hills, as to bring pilots into intimate acquaintance with the technical limits of their aircraft's landing and take-off performance. Fresson seems to have revelled in this kind of flying, and to have gathered round him a body of pilots of similar temperament. Between them they had no difficulty in keeping the press supplied with tales of aeronautical intrepidity. Some events were clearly organised as much for their publicity value to Highland Airways as anything else. Such an occasion occurred, for example, in February 1938 when the Shetland island of Foula, having been isolated by storms for five weeks and simultaneously stricken by a 'flu epidemic, was 'relieved' by an improvised supply drop by parachute from a Highland Airways Dragon Rapide. The following month it was Stornoway's turn. With the mail boat stormbound in Mallaig, Fresson flew the mails in from Inverness through conditions he described as the worst he had experienced in his forty-one years of flying. Nothing pleased him more, however, than being able to show that his aircraft could get through when more earthbound forms of transport failed.[28]

This was very much the spirit that motivated all the pilots of Highland and Scottish Airways alike. Their motto, as Fresson somewhat melodramatically put it, was 'This plane must get through'.[29] They prided themselves on keeping up the schedule as advertised, no matter what the weather or the ground conditions. This was done not out of mere bravado or foolhardiness but out of a consciousness of the need to maintain confidence among the people who used their services — whether big concerns like the Post Office or small crofting communities — that they could be relied on. To maintain regular and reliable services in that part of the world inevitably meant flying in adverse conditions. Equally, however, passengers and freight consigners had to be assured of the safety of the service, and indeed Highland Airways and the Scottish Airways northern division under Fresson's management enjoyed a safety record that was second to none before 1939. Only one serious accident occurred, when in July 1933 Fresson himself crashed the Monospar (then Highland Airways' sole aircraft) attempting to land in fog at Wideford Farm, near Kirkwall. No deaths or significant injuries resulted, though the aircraft was out of service for six weeks and schedules were only maintained thanks to the loan of an aircraft from John Sword's Midland & Scottish Air Ferries Ltd.[30] This successful record appears to have been based first of all on a sober recognition of the hazards that were bound to attend commercial flying in the Highlands and Islands, and secondly on the adoption of pilot training and equipment which were as well adapted as possible to ensuring that the hazards might be safely overcome. Fresson described in some detail in his memoirs the training of Highland Airways pilots to fly as a matter of course out of makeshift airfields at night (a common experience on the air ambulance service), in fog and low cloud, and in winds of up to 70 m.p.h.[31] These were all conditions that might be commonly encountered in their operational flights, so, as Fresson put it, 'all our flying staff had to learn the drill before being let loose' in them. Equipment too was selected with a close eye on the conditions. For services on which high winds were regularly experienced the Monospar monoplane was preferred to the larger De Havilland biplanes, for the simple reason that it was less likely to be blown on to its back. And before Fresson adopted the DH 89 Dragon Rapide for service, over routes where very short take-off and landing capabilities were at a premium, he required the manufacturers to develop a variant fitted with wing flaps to reduce its take-off and landing runs.[32]

Thanks to the care with which training and equipment were matched to operating conditions, the aircraft under Fresson's management maintained, between the foundation of Highland Airways in 1933 and the outbreak of war in 1939, not only an excellent safety record but an enviable reputation for the regularity and reliability of their services. Scheduled flight regularity seems never to have fallen below 94 per cent, and commonly ran at rates as high as 99 and even 100 per cent, attracting favourable comment in the authoritative columns of *Flight*.[33] And as the safety, regularity and sheer social utility of their services came to be recognised, passenger and freight loadings on Fresson's aircraft rose. They came to be patronised by all classes and conditions of passenger: business and professional men, politicians and high officials of state, admirals *en route* to the Scapa Flow naval base, tourists, crofters with their produce on the way to market, and 'fisher lassies' following the herring from one northern port to another.[34] All could benefit from the dramatic cuts in journey times that air travel made possible.

4. The final year

For all its success in attracting passengers, Highland Airways never succeeded in running at a profit. The best that Fresson could claim was that, when merged with Northern Airways to create Scottish Airways in 1938, Highland Airways was on the brink of profitability. Since Northern Airways was at the time returning substantial losses, he wanted the accounts of the two divisions of the merged company to be kept separate. This attempt to retain a measure of financial autonomy was not acceptable to the London overlords of Scottish Airways, whose continued unprofitability Fresson was apt to ascribe wholly to the southern division of which he was not in charge. The old Highland Airways had been very much Fresson's own show, and his memoirs make it clear that he found his new position of subordination in the Scottish Airways scheme of things irksome. 'It was clear,' he observed, 'that they had a very different outlook on operational methods from my own. Moreover, I did not wish to lose my identity and authority to possible bureaucracy, restrictions and planning unsuitable to our part of Britain. And indeed there were difficulties in the early days of the merger arising out of Fresson's unwillingness to fall in with the wishes of remote higher management in London who, in his view, knew nothing of conditions in the north of Scotland. His new superiors however, seem to have been willing to give Fresson his head in the running of the northern division, and to keep their intervention to a minimum once the new set-up had overcome its teething troubles. The traditions and the ethos that had been established in Highlands Airways continued, by and large, to operate in Scottish Airways until, on 4 September 1939, 'the Air Ministry ordered the cessation of our air services and withdrew the radio facilities along our routes'.[35]

Notes

1 P. G. Masefield, 'Some economic factors in air transport operation', *Journal of the Institute of Transport*, XXIV (March 1951), p. 83.

2 The Maybury Committee report (*Parl. Papers*, 1936–7, XVII, Cmd 5351) had noted that, for all their growth, British internal airlines were chronic financial loss-makers: see also Masefield, *loc. cit.*, pp. 84–7.

3 Anyone who concerns himself with the history of Highland Airways/Scottish Airways is inevitably in-

debted to Fresson, whose posthumously published memoirs, *Air Road to the Isles: the Memoirs of Captain E. E. Fresson, OBE* (1967) are an invaluable if not a detached source. For a brief account of Fresson's general career see the entry under his name in A. Slaven *et al.* (eds.), *Dictionary of Scottish Business Biography* (Aberdeen, forthcoming), II.

4 Scottish Record Office, Board of Trade Company Files BT 2/17238: Highland Airways Ltd; items 4–6 (Statement of Capital, etc., 30 March 1933) and

item 8 (Return of Share Allotments, 1 May 1933).

5 The ceremony and flight were fully reported in *The Scotsman*, 9 May 1933.

6 This account of the fleet and the development of services is based on Fresson, *op. cit.*, ch. 9; *Jane's All the World's Aircraft, 1938* (1939), Sect. A — Civil Aviation; *Flight*, XXXIV (July–December 1938), p. 282.

7 Fresson, *op. cit.*, pp. 174–5. Highland/Scottish Airways' market shares are calculated from Fresson's figures and the official UK aggregates reproduced in D. H. Aldcroft, *Studies in British Transport History* (Newton Abbot, 1974), p. 212. The crudity of the calculation is evident, but it is roughly suggestive of the signifcance of Fresson's operation in the general context of UK domestic air transport at the time.

8 Fresson, *op. cit.*, p. 84.

9 On the attitude of the railway companies generally to air transport see D. H. Aldcroft, 'The railways and air transport', *Scottish Journal of Political Economy*, XII (1965). For Highland Airways' specific problems, Fresson, *op. cit.*, pp. 146–7.

10 S.R.O. BT 2/17238, item 13: Highland Airways Ltd, Notice of Increase of Nominal Capital; items 15–17, Allotments made on Ordinary Shares, 6 October–10 December 1933. The steamship company's stake is given as £2,000, George Law's as £500.

11 Fresson, *op. cit.*, p. 103.

12 *Ibid.*, pp. 129–30. The Highland Airways records (S.R.O. BT 2/17238, items 20–8; Particulars of Directors, Notice of Increase of Capital, Special Resolutions, Returns of Share Allotments, 10 May 1935–11 December 1936) give details of the transactions. Paid-up capital was doubled to £16,000 in August 1935, with United holding the bulk of the new shares. The Return of Allotments of 11 December 1936 shows the nominees of British Airways holding over 10,500 £1 ordinary shares, the North of Scotland S.N. Co. and its proprietors holding most of the balance. Only five of the original shareholders of 1933 retained a stake in Highland Airways by that date, including Fresson himself. Fresson recorded (*op. cit.*, p. 95) that those who sold out to United Airways did so at a premium of 50 per cent.

13 Masefield, *loc. cit.*, p. 83.

14 Fresson, *op. cit.*, pp. 145–7.

15 S.R.O. Company Microfiche SC19 907: Scottish Airways Ltd; Minute of Agreement, 6–15 April 1938; Minutes of Extraordinary General Meeting, 16 May 1938.

16 S.R.O. BT 2/17238, item 38: Highland Airways Ltd; Return of Trial Winding-up and General Meeting, 25 May 1940; Final Return, 1 July 1940.

17 S.R.O. Microfiche SC19 907: Scottish Airways Ltd; Minute of Agreement, 6–15 April 1938, contains a list of Highland Airway assets, including airfields and their facilities, together with the terms of leases, etc., by which access was obtained.

18 *Report of the Committee of Inquiry into Civil Aviation* (Cadman committee), P.P. 1937–8, (VIII, Cmd. 5685), p. 76.

19 *Flight*, XXXI (January–June 1937), p. 379. Fresson was not opposed to government intervention as such: indeed, his objection to the Maybury recommendation on local authority provision of civil airports was that many local authorities lacked the means to finance this and that national government ought to be responsible. In general, he though the Maybury report's recommendations would add disastrously to the operating costs of an airline like his, and that it 'entirely overlooked those airlines which so valuably serve remote parts of the county'.

20 The dispute with Allied Airways concerned traffic between the mainland and the Northern Isles. The ATLA granted licences to both airlines to operate such services, but the airlines were unable to agree on how the traffic should be shared. Fresson, as the larger operator and the pioneer of the routes, wanted the lion's share. The problem took over six months to resolve and then only by the imposition of a settlement by the ATLA: *Flight*, XXXIV (July–December 1938), p. 216; XXXV (January–June 1939), p. 204.

21 The negotiations with the Post Office and with George Law are described in Fresson, *op. cit.*, ch. 4.

22 Fresson, *op. cit.*, p. 174.

23 *The Scotsman*, 30 May 1934.

24 On the early development of the air ambulance service, see Fresson, *op. cit.*, pp. 102, 116.

25 For example, he arranged that *The Orcadian*, Kirkwall's local paper, would act as local booking agent for Highland Airways: *ibid.*, p. 87.

26 His memoirs describe one such flight to Fair Isle on coronation day, 1937, accompanied by 'Sandy McLaren, the local representative of Star Photos, Perth, who kept the daily newspapers well supplied with photos of Highland Airways' developments': *ibid.*, p. 153.

27 *Flight*, XXXVI (July–December 1939), p. 139. Events early in September, of course, rendered the publication unfortunately obsolete.

28 For the Foula incident, *Flight*, XXXIII (January–June 1938), p. 127; Fresson, *op. cit.*, pp. 167–8. For the Stornoway mail flight, Fresson, *op. cit.*, p. 169.

29 Fresson, *op. cit.*, p. 180.

30 *Ibid.*, pp. 87–92. Fresson had never regarded the Wideford site as especially suitable for an airfield. He would much have preferred Hatston, but was prevented from using it by the local council. Hatston was later developed as an airfield for the Fleet Air Arm (Fresson claimed it was on his advice) and is now the Kirkwall civil airport.

31 The problems and the training adopted to overcome them are graphically described in Fresson, *op. cit.*, pp. 116, 121–5.

32 *Ibid.*, pp. 119, 121.

33 *Flight*, XXIX (January–June 1936), pp. 95, 448; XXXIV (July–December 1938), p. 604.

34 Fresson, *op. cit.*, pp. 116, 172.

35 *Ibid.*, pp. 151, 161, 184.

Acknowledgements

I owe a considerable debt in connection with this paper to Professor Tony Slaven and Mrs Sheila Hamilton of the University of Glasgow. They first drew my attention to the subject in connection with the *Dictionary of Scottish Business Biography* (2 vols., Aberdeen University Press, forthcoming) which they were preparing, and supplied me with much valuable documentation.

7 The Bermuda Conference and Anglo-American aviation relations at the end of the Second World War

DAVID MACKENZIE

'Several times when Englishmen have asked me what I think the United States wants in the post-war air', the American Civil Air Attaché in London wrote in 1944, 'I reply, "to fly airplanes." That is what they are afraid of.'[1] The American official could afford to be smug; indeed, there were few areas in the international arena in which American superiority was more pronounced than in civil aviation. Before the war Pan American Airways (Pan Am), the American flagship carrier, operated services across Central and South America, to Europe via the Azores and Portugal, and held a monopoly on the Pacific route to the Far East. While wartime developments either destroyed or forced most European international carriers drastically to cut their services, Pan Am continued to expand thanks, in part, to War Department contracts to construct bases in Latin America and the West Indies and to establish an air route to Africa via South America. By 1939 Pan Am's route system totalled more than 60,000 miles; two years later it surpassed 98,000 miles — approximately 2.5 times the route mileage of BOAC, and more miles than all European services combined.[2]

In Washington the debate continued between those who wished to designate a single airline as a 'chosen instrument' (like most European nations) and those who preferred to allow private companies to compete internationally, but in other areas there was growing unanimity. It was clear that for economic and strategic reasons (as well as for national prestige) international civil aviation would be an important factor in the post-war world, and the Americans were determined to play their part. 'Whoever controls the main strategic postwar air bases, together with the technical facilities to keep them manned, will unquestionably be the world's strongest power', proclaimed one author in *Fortune*. 'We have no commercial bases except in the Pacific and the Caribbean; our problem, therefore, is not to restore the *status quo ante* but to break out ... Shall we withdraw? Or shall we insist upon our right as a great power to fly anywhere? And whose air is it, anyway?'[3]

For the British government American aviation superiority posed a very serious challenge. In the 1930s Imperial Airways — the predecessor of BOAC — operated routes across Africa, to India and Australia, and, in 1935, formed a joint operating company with Ireland, Canada and Newfoundland to operate a transatlantic service. In addition to the Empire services, Imperial Airways operated routes to several European capitals, and in 1935–36 an Anglo-American agreement was negotiated for services to the United States. The early transatlantic routes consisted of a series of intermediate refuelling stops, depending on the specific route, at Bermuda, the Azores, Iceland, Ireland or Newfoundland. These refuelling stops decreased in importance over the years with improvements in aircraft performance and the introduction of jet-engine aircraft in the 1950s.

The lack of suitable long-range aircraft limited the operation of the transatlantic service to a few scheduled flights late in the summer of 1939. After the outbreak of war, all available aircraft were requisitioned for the war effort, European services were reduced and then dropped altogether, and transatlantic flights were limited to military services. In aircraft design, meanwhile, the technological advantage had swung in the United States' favour in the 1930s, and during the war American industry far surpassed British in the production of long-range transport aircraft. Moreover, Britain's one significant advantage — its widespread Empire — was increasingly seen in American eyes as the major obstacle to the expansion of international aviation.

Given the great disparity between American and British strength in civil aviation, it is not surprising that American calls for wide-open competition in the air after the war were met with considerable trepidation in British circles. The British government was determined to receive its fair share of international air traffic, and it feared that if the Americans were allowed to compete without regulation it would be next to impossible for Britain ever to catch up. Furthermore, there was no desire on the British side to return to the era of cut-throat competition of the 1930s, when most European states heavily subsidised their national airlines, more for prestige than economic reasons.[4] Thus, the two allies approached the end of the war with differing viewpoints: the Americans advocated the negotiation of unrestricted bilateral agreements which would open the airways of the world to all who could compete; the British, on the other hand, called for a multilateral solution — a regulated international system with controls on routes and frequencies and safeguards to protect the weaker nations.

Informal bilateral negotiations — between Britain, the United States and other nations — were held beginning in 1943, and hopes ran high that a truly multilateral aviation agreement could be reached. These efforts culminated with the international aviation conference held in Chicago in November 1944. The Chicago Conference is remembered as the single most important aviation conference of the era, and this is a fair assessment. Fifty-two nations participated and over a period of six weeks dozens of technical and geographical problems in aviation were solved, laying the groundwork for the smooth transition to peacetime civil aviation once the war was over. International agreements were negotiated and, perhaps most important, the conference spawned the birth of the Provisional International Civil Aviation Organization (PICAO), which, in 1947, became the International Civil Aviation Organization (ICAO), which continues to function today.

The very real successes of Chicago, however, have tended to obscure the fact that on the fundamental commercial issues of international civil aviation — routes, rights and rates — these nations could not reach a satisfactory agreement. The settlement of those economic questions left over from Chicago had to wait for the smaller and less celebrated Anglo-American conference at Bermuda early in 1946. Given that in 1945 the United States controlled an estimated 72 per cent of the world's air commerce and Britain 12 per cent,[5] — thanks in part to the growth of BOAC's total route mileage to almost 70,000 miles by the end of the year — it is no surprise that an agreement between the two leading aviation states would have a profound effect on international air transport. What is perhaps more surprising, is that the final outcome was not the multilateral solution that many had hoped for in the early post-war period, but, rather a bilateral agreement negotiated in private at Bermuda.

The Bermuda Conference, even though it has been overshadowed by Chicago, deserves a closer look for several reasons. First, the agreement negotiated at Bermuda broke the Anglo-American impasse over commercial privileges in international air transport and set the standard for most bilateral civil aviation agreements since the end of the war. Secondly, for a brief time international civil aviation issues were linked with, and threatened to disturb, crucial Anglo-American financial negotiations. Finally, the Bermuda agreement underlined the great disparity between the United States and Britain in international air power at the end of the war. Bermuda did not produce this disparity, but an understanding of the forces and events leading to its negotiation helps to shed some light on the politics of Anglo-American aviation relations.

Discussion of international civil aviation in the mid-1940s usually included the 'five freedoms' of the air. The first two freedoms were essentially transit rights: the right of innocent passage over foreign territory and the right to land for non-traffic purposes. Freedoms three and four were at heart commercial privileges: the right to land passengers and cargo in a foreign territory, and the right to pick up passengers, etc. in a foreign country for return to the country of origin of the aircraft. Most of the toughest debating focused on the fifth freedom, which gave the right to convey traffic between two countries neither of which were the country where the aircraft originated. The root of the trouble over the fifth freedom was perhaps best described by one observer who wrote in 1947 that 'everybody's fifth freedom is someone else's third and fourth freedoms'.[6] To grant fifth-freedom rights was, in effect, giving a foreign operator the right to compete with direct international services. The problem, of course, was how to negotiate this right without endangering domestic airlines.

The Chicago Conference broke down over the fifth freedom. British proposals called for the establishment of an international aviation authority with regulatory powers to divide routes and frequencies and a rigid formula to set rates. If the number or frequencies of flights flown over a given period of time and the rates charged by the various airlines were placed under the control of an international body, then the British government was willing to tie the first four freedoms to a multilateral convention and, moreover, was willing to negotiate the limited use of fifth-freedom privileges with foreign operators. In contrast, the American delegation advocated the unrestricted granting of the fifth-freedom and the creation of a less powerful international organisation restricted to technical matters and with no control over rates, routes or frequencies.[7]

The failure of the Chicago Conference meant that the burden of finding an acceptable multilateral solution to the commercial problems of international civil aviation fell to PICAO and, later, ICAO. In the meantime, the United States, Britain and other states returned to negotiating bilateral agreements for the operation of international air services. On fundamental issues the United States and Britain remained far apart, and, with the end of the war and the resumption of international civil air transport, friction between the two was certain. The change from military to civilian control over aviation began in Europe and North America as national airlines were revived and a number of military air services were transformed into commercial ones.

In Britain the transition to peacetime aviation was gradual and necessitated, at least in the initial stages, limitations on the rights afforded foreign operators in British airspace and at British airports. The American negotiation of air agreements with North Atlantic states — like Ireland — only confirmed British fears that the United States was intent on bypassing Britain on its European services. Moreover, American pressure to negotiate a bilateral agreement which included fifth-freedom rights but no regulation of capacity and frequencies was regarded as an attempt by the United States to use its superiority in aircraft to monopolise the North Atlantic air service.[8]

The Americans argued that the British were blocking the spread of American aviation by refusing to negotiate for the commercial use of American-leased bases, and by using their influence in foreign and imperial capitals to thwart American negotiating efforts. In Egypt, for example, the American government exchanged the American-built Payne Field for landing rights at Cairo, but it encountered stiff resistance to the negotiation of similar agreements from other Middle Eastern states; resistance, it was believed, inspired by the British government. The State Department accused the British of obstruction; London protested, of course. 'It has been part of our policy', one memo in the Prime Minister's Office explained, 'to secure the maximum support in Europe and the Middle East for the principles to which we adhere. Many countries have voluntarily sought our advice and we have tendered it to others. Naturally, in advising these countries we advocate the British and not the American wide open door policy. This is a natural corollary of the failure to agree at Chicago and American resentment is clearly illogical'.[9]

Anglo-American air transport difficulties did not disappear following the election of the Labour government in July 1945, but they were overshadowed by more pressing economic issues. The abrupt termination of Lend-Lease only a few weeks after the end of the war in the Pacific precipitated a major financial crisis in Britain. Faced with staggering domestic economic problems caused by the war, the Labour government introduced an austerity programme at home and turned to North America for huge loans. Estimates put the amount of foreign aid needed in the neighbourhood of $3·75 billion. Late in the summer a team of British officials, led by Lord Keynes, was dispatched to Washington to undertake the financial talks.

Shortly before, on 24 August, informal talks were held between Lord Winster, the British Minister of Civil Aviation, and William Clayton, the U.S. Assistant Secretary of State, and Stokely Morgan, head of the State Department's Aviation Division. The conversation covered well-worn ground concerning fifth-freedom privileges, with little progress being made. There were suggestions from Clayton and Morgan that their government might seek 'to take advantage of the financial talks to negotiate, under pressure, an Agreement favourable to them'. Lord Winster was invited to visit Washington to settle the outstanding aviation problems, but he, along with Ernest Bevin, the Foreign Secretary, 'agreed with Lord Keynes' recommendation that negotiations on this topic should, in time and space, be kept as far apart as possible from the financial talks'. [10]

Another complicating factor was introduced early in the autumn, when Pan Am declared its intention to lower unilaterally its fare on its New York–London service to $275 — $100 lower than the rate set earlier that year by the International Air Transport Association (IATA), an operator's organisation formed in 1945. Pan Am operated two services per week to London (under the terms of the 1935–36 agreement) and was free to set its own rate, but this action prompted some discussion in British circles about the possibility of denouncing the agreement.[11]

The British government responded with a proposal to negotiate a limited bilateral agreement which would divide Anglo-American traffic on a roughly 50:50 basis, with both sides limited to a capacity of 500 seats per week. Pan Am's two services would be included as part of the 500 seats, while rates would be set by IATA and approved by the two governments. No fifth-freedom rights were included, but it was hoped that such an agreement would be suitable, at least in the interim, for the North Atlantic service. Still opposing any limitations on capacity and frequencies, Washington rejected the British proposals and continued to seek a more comprehensive arrangement.[12]

The threats from Pan Am served only to deteriorate further Anglo-American aviation relations. In mid-November Prime Minister Attlee was in Washington to discuss the control of atomic energy with President Truman, and at one stage during his visit he discussed civil aviation matters with Truman and James Byrnes, the Secretary of State. The Americans pressed Attlee to agree to participate in an Anglo-American aviation conference in the near future and again linked civil aviation to the loan negotiations which were then reaching a critical stage. 'Mr Byrnes stressed the point that the Aviation Lobby was very strong', Attlee recorded. 'He was afraid that when finance matters came up the Aviation Lobby would induce a number of Senators [and] Representatives to vote against the proposals with a view to bringing pressure to bear on the Civil Aviation problem.'[13]

Lord Halifax, the British Ambassador in Washington, received comparable signals. He reported to the Foreign Office that he had met Dean Acheson, the Undersecretary of State, and the American had told him 'that the civil aviation question constitutes one of our greatest dangers in the forthcoming congressional discussions on the loan. Mr Acheson asked whether it would not be possible to get one or two fair minded people on both sides to come over to Bermuda or to the Azores and explore the ground.' Others on Halifax's staff had 'been similarly warned by other friendly officials . . .'.[14]

Linking the settlement of aviation problems with the far more crucial loan negotiations forced the hand of the British government. Lord Winster was dismayed with the American tactics, and he wrote Hugh Dalton, the Chancellor of the Exchequer, that Halifax's telegram seemed 'to suggest once again that a Congress lobbied by Pan American Airways might try to force complete freedom of action in the air as opposed to the regulated competition which we know to be right'. [15] But he saw no alternative other than to agree to the discussions. Winster's views were shared by most of the Cabinet, and it was agreed to participate in the proposed aviation talks, to be held in Bermuda early in the new year.[16]

The Bermuda Conference opened on the morning of 15 January 1946. The British delegation was chaired by Sir Henry Self, who had been director of the British Purchasing Commission during the war. Accompanying Self were a number of officials, including Sir William Hildred, the Director General of Civil Aviation. The American team was led by George Baker, the Director of the Office of Transport and Communications Policy in the State Department, and included his Deputy Director, Garrison Norton, Stokely Morgan and Welch Pogue, the head of the Civil Aeronautics Board. At an early meeting, Baker outlined his government's view that there were two principle issues to be examined.

The first dealt with the negotiation of a bilateral aviation agreement dealing with rates, frequencies, capacity and the fifth freedom. The second concerned the commercial use of American-built bases in British territory. To deal with these questions, two committees were established: a Rates and Traffic Committee, to discuss the civil air agreement; and a Leased Bases Committee.[17]

The committees hammered out over the next ten days a tentative bilateral agreement. The American delegation was willing to concede the issue of rate-setting, but on frequency control and the fifth freedom it was unwilling to budge. 'We have stated no go on any frequency control theoretical or actual', Baker reported to Washington on 23 January. 'I believe UK Delegation here including Self would follow Hildred if London weakens. Will appreciate hearing loan situation in Washington.'[18]

Four days later Baker informed Washington that a 'meeting of minds' had been reached with the British delegation. 'Agreements involve British giving way completely from Chicago position on control of frequencies and capacity and our giving way completely on rate control. On Fifth Freedom, the British have also given way.' The Americans also conceded the right of consultation if the British believed they were being treated unfairly, but such consultation would happen only after the fact and would not detract from the real benefits of the agreement. 'Since our delegation, including all the CAB [Civil Aeronautics Board] members, all believe rate control desirable, anyway', Baker concluded, 'we believe this arrangement constitutes a real victory.'[19]

The American government signalled its approval to sign the agreements, but the British government still had to agree. The loan agreement, meanwhile, had been finalised in December and was inching its way through Congress. Public opinion was not fully behind the deal and the aviation companies were lobbying hard to slow up its progress. Moreover, there were strong interests in Congress opposed to the loan. As one Congressman exclaimed, a loan to the British government would serve only to 'promote too damned much Socialism at home and too much damned Imperialism abroad'. [20]

The still uncertain future of the loan agreement gave the Americans some leverage on the aviation issue. On 31 January Byrnes telegraphed Ambassador Winant in London that 'the signature of this [Bermuda] Agreement as soon as possible would not only be desirable as a fair and reasonable settlement of the long standing civil aviation controversy, but would contribute materially toward a favourable reception in Congress to the loan agreement.' For these reasons, Winant was instructed to talk with Bevin and Attlee and press the American case.[21]

At almost the same time in Washington, Lord Halifax was summoned to a meeting with Acheson and Clayton. The Americans explained that their government had approved the tentative agreement and 'expressed the very strong hope that His Majesty's Government would find it possible to authorize

Sir H. Self to accept the agreement also. They emphasized the powerful effect which a successful outcome to the Conference would have on Congress in connexion with consideration of loan agreements.' Halifax had received a copy of the agreement that evening and had 'no doubt' that certain aspects raised 'a number of difficult technical questions'. Nevertheless, he concluded, 'on broad grounds of policy, I have no hesitation in urging you to accept settlement of this inflammatory question, which is recommended by our negotiators at Bermuda. Moreover, I would also recommend that we should act as quickly as possible and strike so that full impact of success of negotiations should come while the iron is hot.'[22]

The American pressure began to have its desired effect. On 4 February the Bermuda negotiations came up for discussion in Cabinet, although the focus of the debate was not on aviation but, rather, on the loan agreement. Lord Winster explained his reasons for not liking the Bermuda agreement, but added that 'if the Cabinet felt that the signing of the agreement was of vital importance from the point of view of our general relations with the United States and the consideration of the loan agreement by Congress, he was willing that our Delegation should be authorized to sign.' Hugh Dalton reiterated that Britain was 'not likely to secure anything better' through continued negotiations. He, too, recommended acceptance of the agreement.[23] The other Ministers present were of a like mind. Bevin agreed that the agreement was 'not entirely satisfactory and would be difficult to defend in Parliament'. But, he continued, 'in view of the weakness of our position, due to the delays in the production of suitable British civil aircraft, there seemed to be no alternative but to accept this draft.' Prime Minister Attlee revealed that he had been urged by Ambassador Winant to accept the terms of the Bermuda agreement. He surmised, 'from the point of view of the loan debate in Congress, it was desirable that we should meet the desires of the American Government.'[24]

Attlee still had serious concerns over the text of the agreement and argued that 'it was essential that, before the Cabinet reached a final decision, they should understand clearly what was involved in the grant of Fifth Freedom rights . . .'. At this stage in the negotiations, fifth-freedom rights centred on what was known as 'change of gauge' or the right of a foreign airline to change aircraft at intermediate stops along a trunk route. 'If we agree to change of gauge', one Cabinet memo explained,

a United States operator running a service, say from New York to Paris, would be able to bring a load of passengers to this country in a trans-oceanic aircraft and thereafter carry on those who wished to proceed to Paris or elsewhere in one or more smaller aircraft. The fear expressed at the Cabinet was that this would enable the American operator to run an unlimited number of smaller aircraft from this country to Paris or elsewhere in competition with our air lines, and thus virtually establish an advanced base here.[25]

The British reservations on change of gauge, however, met with strong opposition. The Americans insisted on the right to change to smaller aircraft at intermediate points (in this case in Britain) if thought necessary, and were unwilling to request the permission of the British authorities to do so. There was room for compromise, however, and late in the evening of 9 February an understanding was reached. It was agreed that a change of gauge was to be permitted but on condition of 'there being adequate volume of through traffic'. In addition, the following clause was added:

> Where change of gauge is made at a point in the territory of the United Kingdom or in the territory of the United States, the smaller aircraft will operate only in connection with the larger aircraft arriving at the point of change, so as to provide a connecting service which will thus normally wait on the arrival of the larger aircraft . . . Where there are vacancies in the smaller aircraft such vacancies may be filled with passengers from United Kingdom or United States territory respectively. It is understood however that the capacity of the smaller aircraft shall be determined with primary reference to the traffic travelling in the larger aircraft normally requiring to be carried onward.[26]

The addition of the above clause seemed to offer sufficient protection to British interests by forcing the smaller aircraft to wait for the arrival of the larger aircraft before leaving, thereby preventing the operation of American airlines in Britain as semi-regular services. In any event, the Americans would go no further, and the texts of the agreements were telegraphed to London. The documents were studied first by the Civil Aviation Committee and then, on 11 February, by the Cabinet. That same day, across the ocean, the Bermuda Air Transport Agreement was signed.

There were no real surprises on the route selection. The British requested services from London and/or Prestwick to New York, Chicago, Washington and several other American cities; Bermuda to New York, Washington and Baltimore; from the West Indies to Miami; and from Singapore/Hong Kong to San Francisco. The Americans requested services from New York (and other major American cities) to London and on to points in Europe and Asia; through the West Indies for services to South America, and for the use of Hong Kong and Singapore. The agreement itself set out what became known as 'Bermuda Principles'. At Chicago the two countries agreed to exchange the first two freedoms (transit rights); the Bermuda agreement added freedoms three, four and five, or the commercial privileges. For example, a British service, London to the Far East via New York, San Francisco and Hawaii, could stop at all of these airports and drop off British traffic. Passengers bound for the Far East could be picked up at these stopovers (i.e. fifth-freedom traffic), but no passengers picked up in New York could be dropped off in San Francisco or Hawaii. The same rules applied to American services flying through Britain.

Fifth-freedom rights were central to the deal and could not be removed from it, but they were to be utilised under rather broad principles and only on designated routes and at agreed airports set out in an Annex attached to the bilateral agreement. Routes across any other states on the service could be changed without mutual consent. On the issue of rates, it was agreed to allow IATA to establish fares which would then be subject to government approval. On the crucial question of capacity and frequencies, the two states were free to set their own levels, again within general limitations. The key clause stipulated that the two states would

> retain as their primary objective the provision of capacity adequate to the traffic demands between the country of which such air carrier is a national and the country of ultimate destination of the traffic. The right to embark or disembark on such services international traffic destined for and coming from third countries at a point or points on the routes specified in the Annex to the Agreement shall be applied in accordance with the general principles of orderly development to which both Governments subscribe and shall be subject to the general principle that capacity should be related:
> (a) to traffic requirements between the country of origin and the countries of destination;
> (b) to the requirements of through airline operation, and
> (c) to the traffic requirements of the area through which the airline passes after taking account of local and regional services.[27]

If one of the countries believed that the other was not acting in the spirit of the agreement and a mutual understanding could not be reached between them, then the issue could be given to PICAO for an impartial judgement. Clearly, such a request would only be made after the disputed activity was in effect, and PICAO would have no power to enforce any of its decisions. The British government had won the right of consultation with the international authority, but, equally, the United States could ignore any PICAO decision it did not like.

The Bermuda agreement has usually been depicted as a compromise that settled the nagging Anglo-American problems in international civil aviation. 'The Bermuda bilateral agreement was not just a compromise, it was a landmark compromise', one American author has written. 'It ratified the new balance of commercial air power for the Western world. When the French quickly followed the British example and in March 1946 signed a Bermuda-like pact with the United States that opened the door to Paris and beyond, the pattern was set.' With the extension of entry rights into Britain, transatlantic permits were issued to Pan Am, TWA and American Overseas Airlines. By the summer of 1946 BOAC (using four Lockheed Constellations), Air France and KLM had inaugurated air services to New York. That same year saw an explosion in transatlantic aviation, with over 120,000 passengers flying the Atlantic, with more than half — 66,500 — in Pan Am aeroplanes.[28]

A closer examination of the agreement and the events surrounding its negotiation suggests that Bermuda was anything but a compromise. On the key points on the American agenda — fifth-freedom rights, no regulation of frequencies or capacity, change of gauge, limited powers for the international authority — the United States got its way. In contrast, the British won the right to have rates set by IATA (something the Americans were willing to accept in any event) and won the right to appeal to PICAO if the Americans acted unfairly over questions of capacity and frequencies. The latter was a questionable victory at best; as one American author later wrote: 'in theory there could be "ex post facto consultations", but since the facts always changed for next year, the understanding and practice were that capacity would be essentially unregulated.'[29] Moreover, the looming Anglo-American loan negotiations cast a long shadow over Bermuda, and forced the British government at all times to weigh its interests in aviation against the possible negative effects a collapse in the talks could have on the loan.

The Bermuda agreement did not spark the vast increase in transatlantic commercial aviation that occurred after the war; such an increase would likely have happened in any event, although along different lines. What it did do, however, was establish the tone and style of Atlantic aviation, by opening it up to more aggressive international competition than would have been the case under more traditional bilateral arrangements that divided routes and traffic along equal lines. In the immediate post-war period, such developments greatly favoured the Americans, who were better placed financially, industrially and strategically to compete successfully in international civil aviation.

The Bermuda agreement came into effect immediately, and over the next two years the United States negotiated more than twenty-five similar agreements with other states. The British were more reluctant converts, and soon ran into conflict with the United States over agreements BOAC negotiated with France and Argentina, both of which stipulated a strict division of capacity. American protests led to further discussions and in September 1946 the two countries issued a statement declaring that 'both parties believe that in negotiating any new bilateral agreements with other countries, they should follow the basic principles agreed at Bermuda . . .'.[30]

The importance of the Bermuda agreement and 'Bermuda principles' became more pronounced over subsequent years as efforts by PICAO and ICAO to negotiate a multilateral convention ended in failure. Not all air transport agreements signed over the following years were exactly the same as Bermuda, but the principles laid down in that agreement served as a model and became the standard style for American and most other bilateral civil aviation agreements.

Indeed, Bermuda, together with the agreements negotiated at Chicago and the power of IATA to establish rates, laid the foundations for the post-war system of international air transport.

The Bermuda agreement lived a long life. For thirty years 'Bermuda principles' remained at the heart of Anglo-American aviation relations. In 1976 the British government — faced with stiff competition from American wide-body aircraft, and with the rise of charter air services and the desire of non-scheduled carriers to operate more international routes — announced its intention to denounce the agreement. A new round of Anglo-American negotiations ensued and a second Bermuda agreement was signed in July 1977.[31]

In 1946, two months after the signing of the Bermuda agreement, Livingston Satterthwaite reported to Washington that there were still elements in British government circles that opposed Bermuda and were looking for ways to get around it. He had recently heard a speech by Ivor Bulmer-Thomas, Parliamentary Secretary in the Ministry of Civil Aviation, in which he described several recent aviation agreements negotiated by Britain, but made no reference to Bermuda. After the speech Satterthwaite approached Bulmer-Thomas and asked why he had omitted any reference to Bermuda. 'Thomas colored', Satterthwaite noted, and 'said it was so important he forgot it. He would not say it was a good aviation agreement, but thought it was good for Anglo-American relations.'[32]

Notes

1 Livingston Satterthwaite memo, 2 March 1944, National Archives, Washington (NAW hereafter), RG59 Records of the Office of European Affairs (Matthews-Hickerson file) Box 11.
2 See D. Ray, 'The Takoradi route: Roosevelt's prewar venture beyond the western hemisphere', *Journal of American History*, LXII (2) (September 1975), pp. 340–58; M. Bender and S. Altschul, *The Chosen Instrument* (New York, 1982), p. 365.
3 'The logic of the air', *Fortune*, XXVII, (4) (April, 1943), p. 73.
4 See, for example, O. Lissitzyn, 'The diplomacy of air transport', *Foreign Affairs*, XIX (1) (October 1940), pp. 156–70, and his *International Air Transport and National Policy* (New York, 1942).
5 N. Taneja, *U.S. International Aviation Policy* (Lexington, Mass., 1980), p. 12.
6 A. McKim, 'World order in air transport', *International Journal*, II (summer 1947), p. 228.
7 For more on Chicago, see Department of State, *Proceedings of the International Civil Aviation Conference, Chicago, Illinois: November 1–December 7, 1944*, 2 vols (Washington, 1948).
8 See 'Brief for Prime Minister on United States – United Kingdom Relations in Civil Aviation', n.d. (probably September–October 1945), Public Record Office, Kew (PRO hereafter) PREM 8/16.

9 *Ibid.*; Taneja, *U.S. International Aviation Policy*, p. 12.
10 'Brief for the Prime Minister', PREM 8/16. On the discussions, see Satterthwaite to State Department, 4 September 1945, NAW RG59 841.796/9–445; and Winster memo, CAC (45) 4, 12 September 1945, PRO, CAB 134, 57.
11 Chargé in the UK to Secretary of State, 20 October 1945, Department of State, *Foreign Relations of the United States* (FRUS hereafter) 1945, VI, pp. 224–5.
12 Halifax to Secretary of State, 13 November 1945, FRUS 1945, VI, pp. 228–9. For the American response, see Department of State to British Embassy, 19 November 1945, FRUS, p. 230.
13 Attlee note, 15 November 1945, PRO, PREM 8/16.
14 Halifax to Foreign Office, t.8551, 24 December 1945, PRO, FO371 50272, W16612/24/802.
15 Winster to Dalton, 1 January 1946, PRO, FO371 50272, W16612/24/802.
16 Foreign Office to Washington Embassy, t.44, 2 January 1946, PRO, FO371 50272, W16612/24/802. See also Dalton's diary for 7 December 1945, British Library of Economics and Political Science, Dalton Papers, XXXIII.
17 Briefly, a broad agreement on commercial

privileges at the bases was reached, but the talks hit a snag over the American desire to link the bases deal with the aviation agreement and, secondly, to include a clause which would call on the British government to use its influence to 'persuade' Newfoundland and Canada to agree to a settlement for the use of the American bases in Newfoundland. The British negotiators resisted both proposals. Ultimately, the Americans agreed to delete the clause regarding the use of British influence on Newfoundland and Canada, and in its place accepted Britain's 'oral undertaking to facilitate discussions with Canada and Newfoundland'. It was also agreed that the two agreements would remain separate, and that the bases Heads of Agreement 'should merely be initialled *ad referendum*'.

18 Baker to Clayton, t.8365, 23 January 1946, NAW RG59 841.798/1-2346.

19 Baker to Clayton, 27 January 1946, NAW RG59 841.796/1-2746.

20 Quoted in A. Bullock, *Ernest Bevin: Foreign Secretary, 1945-1951* (London, 1983) p. 202.

21 Byrnes to Winant, 31 January 1946, FRUS, 1946, I, pp. 1464-5.

22 Halifax to Foreign Office, t.663, 30 January 1946, PRO, PREM 8 /138.

23 Cabinet Conclusions, 4 February 1946, PRO, CAB 128.

24 *Ibid.*

25 Cabinet Memo, CP (46) 44, 6 February 1946, PRO, CAB 129.

26 *Bilateral Air Transport Agreement Between the Government of the United Kingdom and the Government of the United States of America Relating to Air Services Between Their Respective Territories*, Cmd. 6747.

27 *Ibid.*

28 C. Solberg, *Conquest of the Skies: History of Commercial Aviation in America* (Boston, 1979), pp. 291, 300; B. Gidwitz, *The Politics of International Air Transport* (Lexington, Mass., 1980), pp. 51-5. See also J. C. Cooper, 'The Bermuda plan: world pattern for air transport', *Foreign Affairs*, XXV (1) (October 1946), pp. 59-71.

29 A. Lowenfeld, 'A new takeoff for international air transport', *Foreign Affairs*, LIV (1) (October 1975), p. 38.

30 Acting Secretary of State to Certain Diplomatic Officers, 19 September 1946, FRUS, 1946, I, p. 1489.

31 Taneja, *U.S. International Aviation Policy*, pp. 21-2.

32 Satterthwaite to Secretary of State, t.28775, 13 March 1946, NAW RG59 841.796/3-1346.

8 'A multiplicity of instruments': the 1946 decision to create a separate British European airline and its effect on civil aircraft production[1]

PETER J. LYTH

British air transport was an obvious target for nationalisation by the Labour government after 1945.[2] Although it was an industry still in its infancy, with none of the problems associated with older transport systems such as the railways,[3] it was a natural candidate for public ownership. Part of the reason lay in the wartime demonstration of air power which had made people aware of the important role that civil aviation could play in the post-war world. If the commanding lead which the Americans had built up in the manufacture of transport aircraft was to be challenged, and this seemed vital for Britain's technological prowess as well as for reasons of defence and prestige, then close government supervision of both airlines and aircraft construction was necessary. It is also important to place nationalisation in the context of British civil aviation history. Within that 'long tradition of growth' in the government's responsibility for the economy,[4] the establishment of the air corporations in the 1946 Civil Aviation Act can be seen as the last step in a process which had begun with the decision to subsidise Imperial Airways in 1924, and continued with the formation of the British Overseas Airways Corporation (BOAC) as a nationalised undertaking by the Conservative government in 1939.[5]

There was nothing especially radical about the creation of BOAC and its junior partners, British European Airways (BEA) and British South American Airways (BSAA).[6] While drawing very largely on the civil aviation plans of the preceding Coalition government, the 1946 Act exhibited a curious lack of clarity about long-term objectives for either the air transport business or the aircraft manufacturing industry. Indeed, it appears to be a good example of what one commentator has seen as an absence of 'systematic coherence about Labour's public ownership programme from the point of view of the economy as a whole'.[7]

In the following article, this judgement is applied to the case of BEA and Labour's choice of a divided 'instrument' through which to guide the nation's civil aviation effort. It argues that the separation of short- and medium-haul operations (BEA) from long-haul services (BOAC) made the road to profitability unnecessarily hard for the airlines and, more importantly, prejudiced the aircraft procurement process in such a way as to make it difficult for British manufacturers to build a world-class airliner. It begins with a review of the origins of the 1946 legislation before focusing on the special operational circumstances faced by BEA and the confused strategy that was adopted in finding a suitable replacement for the successful Viscount aircraft in the latter half of the 1950s.

I

By 1937 it was apparent that something was seriously wrong with British civil aviation. From a commanding position after the First World War it had deteriorated to the level where a number of unprofitable operators were competing for a share of an internal market that was hardly big enough to support one of them,[8] while the main international flag-carrier, Imperial Airways, was so preoccupied with its Empire routes to Australia and South Africa that it had let the European market go by default.[9] Worse, civil aircraft construction had fallen far behind new developments in the United States and Europe, and was now eclipsed by the priority that the government was giving to combat types as part of the rearmament programme.[10]

A first step towards rectifying this situation had been taken in 1935 with the creation of British Airways, a second 'chosen instrument' to tackle the European services. But this did not silence the strong criticism of the industry that was building up within Parliament, and the government set up a committee of investigation under the chairmanship of Lord Cadman. Its report, published in 1938, censured both Imperial Airways and the Air Ministry, castigating the poor management of the former, and accusing the latter of a lack of 'virility in the initiation of policy and forward planning'.[11]

The war accelerated the process of reform initiated by Cadman. Imperial Airways and British Airways were merged to form BOAC,[12] and in 1944 the status of the industry was raised by the establishment of a fully fledged Ministry of Civil Aviation, with Lord Swinton as the first Minister.

It was also during 1944 that serious proposals were put forward for civil aviation in post-war Britain. The BOAC Chairman, Lord Knollys, favoured an airline monopoly for international operations with financial participation by private interests. This would obtain for the chosen carrier 'the advantages of the commercial experience and facilities of surface transport', while providing ' a means of giving a stake in the enterprise to those who may claim they are prejudiced by its activities [i.e. rail and shipping interests]'.[13] This extraordinary piece of logic was tantamount to saying that firms already operating in a market should be compensated for the entrance of a newcomer, and it was characterised by the Director-General of Civil Aviation, Sir William Hildred, as 'nothing but a twisted and complicated attempt to enable private interests to get a rake-off under the guise of a public corporation'.[14]

In October the four major railway companies, which had played an important role in pre-war domestic aviation,[15] joined the debate and submitted their own 'Railway Plan for Air Transport'. This document outlined a scheme which far exceeded their activities in the 1930s, proposing a Continental as well as a British service. They planned to form an airline with the participation of the shipping companies and confidently predicted that it would function without government subsidy. They rested their case on their record and the fact that 'British railways have long ceased to be carriers by rail alone. They have become transportation companies affording the public co-ordinated transport by rail, sea and air.'[16]

The BOAC and the railway companies' proposals show that there was a distinct pressure on the government to perpetuate the air transport policy of the pre-war years, not only in the participation of established interests in the ownership of the national airline but also the tendency to see monopoly rights as a gift in return for which the 'chosen carrier' would consent to exist in a cosy relationship with other transport systems. It was not an inspiring formula for the development of British civil aviation, particularly in regard to the signals it would send to the aircraft construction industry, where the pronounced lead which the Americans had established since the beginning of the war was already a cause for grave concern.[17] However, during the brief tenure of Lord Swinton as Minister of Civil Aviation (1944–45), the government was clearly moving towards approval of the proposals. For Swinton, the primary concern was that the new airline, whatever form it took, should consume the minimum of state subsidy. In this respect, he represented that school of thought which had been concerned to limit government support ever since the creation of Imperial Airways.[18]

It was the railways that had the clearest ideas on which air routes would be operated in Europe after the war, and it was their estimates of air transport demand which to a large extent formed the network proposed in the White Paper, 'British Air Transport', presented by Swinton to Parliament in March 1945.[19] This is not to deny the important administrative role performed by the War Cabinet Committee on Post-War Civil Aviation, which met under the chairmanship of Lord Beaverbrook in 1944–45, but it is apparent from the record of this committee's deliberations that its assumptions on the preferred structure for British air transport (as opposed to the question of ownership) corresponded very closely to those of BOAC and the railway companies.[20]

As many of the ideas in the White Paper were later incorporated into the 1946 Civil Aviation Act, it is worth considering its chief features. First, it accepted that there were air transport services 'which are essential in the public interest, but which offer little or no prospect of a direct financial return'. The incentive for operators to run these services was monopoly rights, and Swinton made this clear in a memorandum to the Cabinet in May 1945.[21] Secondly, it restated the government's determination that the new air corporations should fly British aircraft.[22] Thirdly, it stressed the government's wish that the corporations 'operate as far as possible without subsidy', indeed the participating companies would be chosen not merely for 'the positive contribution which they can make in skill and experience' but also because they were 'prepared to invest their own money without any government guarantee'.[23] Fourthly, it envisaged not one but three 'flag-carriers', with ownership spread amongst the railways, shipping interests and travel agencies. The three airlines would offer services, respectively, to the Empire, North America and the Far East (BOAC), the European Continent and destinations within Britain (BEA) and South America and the Caribbean (BSAA).

By way of explanation for the assignment of the most lucrative long-range operations to BOAC, the White Paper simply noted that, as the successor to Imperial Airways, it was 'clearly the appropriate instrument for the operation and further development of these routes'.[24] BOAC would also have a sizeable stake (32 per cent) in BEA; the remainder of the new corporation being owned by the railways (43 per cent), the Short Sea Shipping Lines (15 per cent), the travel agencies (5 per cent) and the independent airlines (5 per cent).[25] BEA's creation as a short- and medium-haul carrier, restricted to the European Continent, betrayed its origins in the railway companies' plan. As its largest shareholder, the railways looked upon the new airline as the modern equivalent of their British surface network with its links to the European mainland.

Although in its proposals for the air corporations' ownership the White Paper was superseded by Labour's nationalisation plans, in other respects it remained a very durable statement of British civil aviation policy in the post-war era. The three-carrier approach, the commitment to British aircraft and the obligation to service unprofitable domestic routes were all retained. Even Swinton's rejection of government subsidy found an echo in the Labour policy, for the new government was as anxious as the Conservatives had been to see the corporations pay their own way. Moreover, the actual decision to nationalise can be placed within the context of the industry's troubled history. 'If, as we assume, the Government desire this country to take a leading place in civil aviation', the Cadman Report had said in 1938, 'much reorganisation and additional expenditure of public money will be necessary.'[26] Nationalisation signified recognition by the Labour government that state expenditure would be inevitable and that where there was subsidy there would have to be supervision.

The same reasoning, however, cannot be seen in the other parts of 1946 legislation, where the provisions of the 1945 White Paper were adopted without change. There was no serious thought given to how the commitment to British aircraft would be reconciled with BEA's obligation to fly the hopelessly unprofitable domestic routes,[27] or the general intention to see the corporation making profits as soon as possible. Equally inexplicable was the retention of the three-pronged 'chosen instrument'.

At the time Sir Stafford Cripps warned against 'matters of great national importance' being placed in the hands of a single managerial group. Accordingly, Britain's civil aviation effort would be shared amongst a 'multiplicity of instruments', conducive to the testing of different techniques and arrangements for civil air transport, and avoiding the rigid uniformity of ideas that might come from a single monolithic structure such as Imperial Airways.[28] This was a laudable sentiment in itself, but it took no account of the experience of other European operators such as the Dutch airline KLM, which had successfully combined short- and long-range operations in the inter-war period and was about to do so again in 1945. An objective test of different arrangements for air transport was more likely to have been achieved with a choice of airlines operating on the same route rather than by the geographically separated monopolies which Labour favoured.

It is hard to avoid the conclusion that Labour's 'multiplicity of instruments' was really no more than a replica of plans drawn up by wartime special interests like the railway companies, synthesised through the medium of the 1945 White Paper and made politically acceptable by the replacement of private with public ownership. It paid lip-service to the need to test different styles of airline management, but gave little indication that the intrinsic problems of airline operation were understood or that an integrated approach to British civil aviation, including the development of a new generation of transport aircraft, was part of its objective.

II

When it started operations, in August 1946, BEA had on lease from the Ministry of Supply a stock of surplus Douglas DC-3s (Dakotas), some Junkers JU-52s (reparations from Germany) and a large number of de Havilland 89s. All the aircraft were obsolescent, and the shortage of spares for them was so acute that in the first six months of operations 8–24 per cent of the fleet was unserviceable.[29] On the ground, things were not much better. BEA's base at Northolt, a former RAF station, was poorly equipped for maintaining civil aircraft, and the corporation actually had a 'long battle with the Air Ministry in order to get the RAF out'.[30] Even the weather conspired against the new enterprise, for hardly had regular services been established before Britain was hit by one of the worst winters on record. Ice on the tarmac caused surface vehicles to collide with aircraft and in the absence of adequate radio, navigational and blind-approach aids, weather conditions played havoc with timetables. During February and March 1947 only seven out of every ten scheduled services to the Continent could be operated, giving BEA an unfortunate image of unreliability in the mind of the travelling public.[31]

Within ten years the situation had been transformed. By 1956 BEA had increased its Capacity Ton Mileage (CTM) more than sixfold, halved its unit costs (measured in pence per CTM), eliminated its government subsidy and begun at last to show a modest profit.[32] The main reason for this remarkable turnaround was modern equipment: the DC-3s and Vikings (an 'interim' type based on the Wellington bomber) had been largely replaced with Elizabethans and Vickers Viscounts, the latter a truly path-breaking aircraft. The corporation seemed in excellent shape to meet the challenge of the fast-expanding European air travel market, and Chairman Lord Douglas of Kirtleside could tell his Minister without exaggeration: 'BEA is now one of the major airlines of the world, and, if I may say so, one of the most successful.'[33]

At this stage the 1946 decision to set up BEA as a short-haul airline might have seemed vindicated, but the highly favourable conditions of the 1950s were not to last. In Europe, the famous German airline Lufthansa had now returned as a major contender, while at home new independent airlines like British United Airways gained momentum after the 1960 Civil Aviation (Licensing) Act.[34] The growth of the independents was significant for BEA, not only because they tended to concentrate on the high-traffic 'holiday' routes to the Continent but also because the charter operators among them were able to outpace the corporation in its attempts to achieve high load factors.[35]

There is some difference of opinion as to whether or not long-haul air operations such as BOAC's are inherently more profitable than short-haul services like BEA's. It can be argued, for example, that the long-haul operator's aircraft are more expensive to purchase and the landing charges they attract will be higher. But, with a greater proportion of time spent in the air, fixed costs are spread further. In scheduling, the long-haul airline has greater flexibility in planning arrival and departure times, and this allows better utilisation of aircraft. Demand for long-haul services may be lower than that for short-haul flights simply by virtue of the fact that fewer people can afford the higher fares, yet that demand will be less price elastic and probably less subject to seasonal fluctuations, particularly on routes where the Equator is crossed.

Because they involve more landings and take-offs per miles flown, short-haul operations have higher unit costs than do long-haul. The 'block speeds' achieved between the points of departure and arrival are lower, the aircraft and crew utilisation is lower, and maintenance and station costs are higher per passenger mile flown. In other words, aircraft and crew spend more time on the ground, and less time in the air earning revenue.[36]

How, then, could a short-haul operator like BEA survive? — chiefly by concentrating on routes with very high traffic density and overcoming the inherently lower productivity of the shorter stage lengths by the maximum possible utilisation of aircraft. One method of achieving this was the use of flexible fare structures to entice people to fly at off-peak periods, and in this BEA excelled. However, in other areas of operational efficiency the short-haul handicaps were less successfully overcome.

When BEA is compared with its foreign rivals for 1957, its aircraft utilisation was below not only that of intercontinental airlines like KLM and TWA, but also domestic US carriers like National, United and Western, which had stage lengths comparable to BEA's. By the same token, both crew and maintenance costs, when measured per CTM, were high, especially in view of the fact that American wage rates were anything up to three times greater than British rates. The main cause of BEA's low aircraft utilisation was the summer traffic peak which could be met only with a capacity level that far exceeded demand in the slow winter months. As the figures below make clear, the ratio of summer to winter traffic was equalled only by TWA, and that airline had the advantage of a mean stage length four times greater than BEA's. A further problem was the corporation's low productivity level (measured as CTM per hour) stemming from the use of smaller aircraft on shorter routes. The considerably greater maintenance and overhaul costs per CTM which BEA incurred derived in large part from its lower aircraft productivity[37] (see table 1).

That BEA flew in the face of the conventional wisdom on civil aviation in Europe is indicated by the conclusions of the Weigelt Committee, which deliberated over the rebirth of Lufthansa in 1952. It argued that air traffic within Europe was not remunerative for distances under 200 miles, except in the rare cases where traffic was exceptionally dense and special geographical factors made substantial time savings possible with the use of aircraft, e.g. stretches of water. Otherwise it was only profitable if run in conjunction with intercontinental connections, and for this reason most of the Continent's carriers combined both operations.[38] In 1957 BEA was the European carrier with the most flights per day, but also the shortest average sector distance. Established competitors such as Air France and KLM cross-subsidised their European network, treating it as a traffic 'feeder' for their intercontinental routes. For them, the marginal cost of operating an additional flight from London to Paris, or from London to Amsterdam, was covered if a few extra long-haul passengers were attracted to their services to Africa or the Far East, and for this reason they could fly these short-haul routes at low load factors. In fact, the airlines which got the major part of their traffic from long-haul flights were also the ones which operated their European services at the lowest load factors, e.g. KLM and SABENA, and, to a lesser extent, Lufthansa, SAS and Swissair.

By comparison, BEA had no opportunity to cross-subsidise its more costly routes with the revenue from long-haul services, since the whole gamut of intercontinental flights to the Commonwealth, the United States and the Far

Table 1. *Comparative operating statistics: BEA and five other airlines in 1957*[a]

		Dutch		American		
	BEA	KLM	National	TWA	United	Western
Summer/winter traffic ratio	3·0 : 1	1·7 : 1	1·9 : 1[b]	3·0 : 1	1·7 : 1	1·5 : 1
Annual aircraft utilisation (hrs)[c]	1,731	2,260	2,355	2,040	3,025	3,060
Mean stage length (miles)	327	789	458	1,300	450	264
Average aircraft size (cubic tons)	4·9	7·4	8·1	7·6	7·6	6·3
Average block speed (m.p.h.)	174	224	224	256	252	222
Average CTM per hour	860	1,660	1,820	1,950	1,930	1,390
Crew costs (£ per hour)	12·6	25·3	15·3	53·2	21·4	16·8
Per CTM (pence)	3·5	3·6	2·0	6·5	2·6	2·9
Maintenance and overhaul costs (£ per hour)	24·1	35·4	22·8	41·8	41·5	22·7
Per CTM (pence)	6·7	5·1	3·0	5·1	5·2	3·9

[a]The domestic carriers National and Western were of similar size, in terms of CTM capacity, to BEA in 1957, as was the international airline TWA. KLM was somewhat bigger, while United had over six times the capacity of BEA.
[b]1956 figures.
[c]Not weighted to aircraft capacity.
Source. 'Why are BEA Costs Higher than Airline Costs in the USA?', BEA Engineering, Project and Development, Technical Note P/250, Prepared by R. A. J. Kiddle, 11 September 1959, RAF Museum, Hendon, Box 242.

East had been given to BOAC under the 1946 Act.[39] With the tariff level essentially beyond its control in the hands of the International Air Traffic Association (IATA) and access to long-haul revenue closed, BEA sought to sustain its profitability through 'pool' agreements with other airlines, high load factors and a rising rate of operating efficiency.

Its commitment to 'pools', however reluctant, is witnessed by the fact that it had entered into such agreements with almost every other European airline by 1960.[40] Its determination to achieve high load factors was relentless and reaffirmed in a 1966 lecture by its new Chairman, A. H. Milward.[41] But it was swimming against the tide. As Lord Douglas lamented in 1961: 'We cannot pursue our policy [of high load factors] if other European airlines adopt what is essentially a "dumping" policy and maintain frequencies irrespective of load factors.'[42] Moreover, high load factors required aircraft custom-built to the traffic characteristics of BEA's particular routes. This restricted the opportunities to interchange aircraft between different stage lengths, leading to a loss of aircraft utility and a reduction in general operational flexibility.[43] It also meant that BEA's aircraft suppliers had a daunting task to sell their products to any other airline.

III

Support for the British aircraft industry was always an integral feature of BEA policy. All the major types it brought into service were British airframes with British engines, i.e. the Viking, Viscount and Vanguard built by Vickers-Armstrong, and the Elizabethan and Trident made by de Havilland.[44] This was not simply compliance with the 'buy British' provision of the 1946 Act, although the legislation certainly influenced managerial decision-making. Rather, there was a genuine conviction that the best aircraft could be obtained from domestic manufacturers, given the right degree of co-operation at the development stage between the two sides. Indeed, both Lord Douglas and Peter Masefield believed that one of their tasks at BEA was to encourage the British aircraft industry to produce good, economic transport aircraft, in particular exploiting the lead which it had built up in jet and turbine engines.[45]

At times this intense loyalty to the home industry — a trait not found in the boardrooms of any other European carrier, including BOAC — was rewarded with the production of a world-beating aircraft like the Viscount, but this was the exception rather than the rule. More often, BEA's insistence on aircraft with specifications tailored to the peculiar needs of its short-haul network meant that these aircraft found few foreign buyers. It was a phenomenon which had also been a problem for British manufacturers in the 1930s, when the unique requirements of Imperial Airways' extended routes to Australia and South Africa had given birth to a hybrid collection of flying boats and biplanes at a time when the rest of the world was turning to stressed-metal monoplanes.[46] Indeed, in view of this pre-war experience, it is perhaps surprising that the limiting effect that a specialised airline like BEA could have on the British aircraft industry was not appreciated in 1946.

To begin with BEA found itself in the position of developing two new aircraft, the Elizabethan and the Viscount, simultaneously in the late 1940s, and introducing them into its fleet within a year of each other in the early 1950s. Since airlines generally benefit from operating a minimum number of different aircraft types, this was an early sign that the procurement process was faulted. When BEA introduced these aircraft, it was desperate to reduce costs and normal commercial requirements would have suggested taking either one or the other, but not both. However, it was not its own master in this respect. Both aircraft had originated in the wartime Brabazon programme and relied entirely on government support to reach production. Besides its statutory obligation to assist the manufacturers by serving as a proving ground for their products, BEA was bound to try both new aircraft since there was no previous operational experience with either and no other way to test their relative merits other than to bring them into scheduled service.

The forty-seven-seat twin-engined Elizabethan was not a great success. Although modern and attractive with its high-wing configuration, it was over a year late in delivery and had numerous shortcomings which eventually gave rise to claims for compensation by BEA. In the year of its introduction (1952), the *Annual Report* described it as an 'immense burden' for the Engineering Department, and there was even a serious proposal from BEA's Chief Engineer to dispose of them all, despite the fact that they were brand new, and replace them with an equal number of Viscounts.[47] Although they eventually made a modest profit, they were actually less flexible than the venerable DC-3s and substantially more expensive to use on domestic routes. The corporation withdrew them from service in 1958 after only six years in operation.

By contrast, the forty-seven-seat Viscount was Britain's major commercial achievement among post-war airliners, and the aircraft which brought BEA profits and prestige.[48] Over 400 were sold, mainly to foreign airlines, and the government more than recouped its initial investment. The Viscount was a success because 'like the DC-3 before it, it was a carefully balanced mixture of available techniques, which were both the most advanced at the time yet fully enough developed to be used without incurring heavy development costs while the aircraft was in service'.[49] Its sole claim to distinction was its revolutionary power plant, the Rolls Royce Dart turbo-prop, which, having no reciprocating parts, was not only simpler to maintain than a piston-engined unit but also had the advantage of running on a cheaper fuel (kerosene).[50] The Viscount was instantly popular with passengers; it was novel, it was fast and it had far less vibration in the passenger cabin than conventional airliners.

Impressed with the Viscount's lower unit costs, and in the expectation of continuously rising demand for capacity, BEA had no hesitation in ordering a 'stretched' version, the fifty-seven-seat V-800 series, in 1954. With the painful memory of the Comet disasters still fresh in everyone's mind, the reliability and cost efficiency of the Viscount were reassuring, and suggested that the turbo-prop, not the pure jet engine, was the power plant of the future. 'Our experience', Peter Masefield told an American gathering in 1955, '. . . has convinced us that the turbine power-plant is here to stay and that for short, medium and long range operations, the propellor turbine engine has a great potential future in world aviation.'[51]

It was understandable, therefore, that as BEA looked for a Viscount replacement to meet the traffic needs of the 1960s, it thought in terms of a second-generation turbo-prop aircraft. In 1955 the government was facing a balance of payments crisis and applying severe credit restrictions, but Masefield won the case for investment in a Viscount replacement by pointing to its likely contribution to exports and 'the future prosperity of this country'. With £50 million worth of Viscounts already sold, it would be disastrous, he reasoned, to stop now just as Britain seemed to be on the track of a winner.[52] This was the genesis of the turbo-prop Vickers Vanguard.

The Vanguard's development has to be seen in the context of BEA's belief that, while competition from big jets like the Boeing 707 and Douglas DC-8 was certain on the longer sectors, turbo-props would have the cost advantage for some time to come on short-haul routes. With its constant concern with load factors, the corporation was wary of the over-capacity which the faster jets seemed to signify. 'The only valid reason for BEA having a requirement for a pure jet aircraft would be the commercial advantage of the higher speed, and that only on longer sectors; i.e. the sales value of being able to advertise the higher cruise speed . . .', concluded BEA's Chief Project and Development Engineer, R. C. Morgan, in 1956. That alone was not 'enough reason for BEA buying a jet aircraft'.[53]

However, aircraft technology was poised to take a major leap forward, similar in effect to the introduction of the stressed-metal monoplane in the 1930s. Jets were coming and BEA's European competitors were scrambling to place orders for them. The effect of their introduction could not be foreseen, but the following year the corporation estimated that it would lose around £4 million annually in potential revenue between 1960 and 1964 if it did not operate jet aircraft itself.[54] Its fears seemed confirmed in 1959, when Air France began the first scheduled Caravelle service into London, gaining a competitive advantage over BEA at a stroke. The corporation's share of London–Paris traffic, which had risen from 50 per cent in 1957 to 58 per cent in 1959 with the introduction of the Viscount V-800s, fell back to 52 per cent by 1961.[55] The airline which had pioneered the Viscount only five years before now faced a desperate race to catch up.

The Vanguard order was not cancelled, although at this stage that could have been done at relatively low cost; instead a jet programme was tacked onto it. Like the simultaneous introduction of the Elizabethan and the Viscount in the early 1950s, BEA was heading for another twin birth in the early 1960s. The Vanguard would be used on the heavy traffic routes under 500 miles, while the new jet would be a smaller, 'complementary' aircraft to match the thinner traffic on the longer routes to the Eastern Mediterranean. In 1957 the order went to de Havilland and the DH-121, later known as the Trident. The specification called for an airliner with seating for seventy to eighty passengers, three engines at the tail and a cruising speed of around 600 m.p.h.[56]

There was then a year's delay as the government sought to use its control over the aircraft's manufacture to bring about a rationalisation of the aerospace industry. In the meantime 'interim' jets were needed to shore up BEA's competitive position until the Trident was ready in 1963. It was a situation reminiscent of the late 1940s, when the 'interim' Viking served as the airline's chief workhorse until the Elizabethan and Viscount were ready. Since French Caravelles were ruled out for political reasons, the only option was a short-haul version of the de Havilland Comet, the 4B, which BEA's Morgan had dismissed only months before as 'clearly of no interest at all'.[57]

Thus it was that by 1958 BEA had on order Comet 4Bs, Tridents, Vanguards and the remaining Viscount V-800s. The spectre of over-capacity loomed large and the corporation's management worried that the Trident was too big. In 1959 the decision was taken to downgrade it to an even smaller aircraft with less capacity and range, so 'condemning it', in the words of one writer, 'to the [Rolls Royce] Spey engine of limited development potential' instead of the more powerful and promising Medway.[58] Lord Douglas assured the Minister of Civil Aviation that the smaller Trident was 'a highly efficient economic aircraft of the right size in passenger capacity for BEA, and therefore for many operators world-wide', dismissing the larger aircraft which Vickers had proposed, and in which the Canadian airline TCA had shown an interest, as carrying 'undue penalties which BEA could not be expected to bear'.[59]

Unfortunately, by the time the Trident One finally began full scheduled operations in 1964–65, it was already carrying 'penalties' for BEA. Intended for longer routes, the aircraft had to be pressed immediately into service on the very short, but prestigious, London–Paris flight to meet intense competition from the jets of rival airlines. For this high-density route it was much too small, with operating costs that were too high for the revenue rate.[60] The jet aircraft which BEA should perhaps have ordered, and which Vickers or de Havilland should have had the opportunity to build, had by this stage already rolled out of a hangar in Seattle. This was the 150-seat Boeing 727, which was ordered by Air France in 1965 and went on to become the largest-selling commercial jet airliner of its time. It was this new American aircraft and the smaller Boeing 737, rather than the Trident, that offered the greater capacity and reduced operating costs necessary to make the jet supreme on European networks. It was a challenge for which BEA had no answer and in 1966 it applied to the government for permission to buy both the Boeing types. Its lengthy affair with turbo-props over, it was also ready to break its long record of loyalty to the British aircraft industry. Twenty years after a Labour government had written the 'buy British' clause into BEA's founding statutes, another Labour administration found itself having to enforce the ruling and deny the corporation's request.[61]

IV

In 1957, at the time when BEA was still deliberating on the Trident's specifications, Lord Douglas told his Minister that the new short-haul jet represented 'a gap in the world aircraft procurement picture which the British aircraft industry could fill'. He predicted that if Britain could 'seize the initiative, this aeroplace will stand a very good chance of repeating the world-wide success of the Viscount'.[62] This was by no means far-fetched. Boeing was uncertain of the commercial wisdom of the 727 in the late 1950s, but was encouraged to pursue the project by the news that the British were building a three-engined aircraft of almost identical layout.[63] There was a real chance at this point for Britain to carve out a notable segment of the market for short-to-medium-haul jets. What went wrong in the next eight years was typical of BEA's procurement process and the generally sterile relationship which existed between Whitehall, the British aircraft manufacturers and the air corporations.

First, the decision to proceed with the Vanguard in 1956, when the trend to jets in civil aviation was becoming clear, must be seen in terms of BEA's fear of over-capacity and determination to maximise load factors. Big and fast, jets were initially perceived as a major liability for the corporation. The mistake was to underestimate the value of their novelty in generating new demand, a mistake all the more surprising since BEA had benefited from the originality of the turbo-prop Viscount only a few years before. Indeed, it was precisely because the airline industry was so regulated by national and international sanctions (IATA, 'pools' etc.) that BEA was prevented from competing on price and had to concentrate on service, a field in which the sheer modernity of one's capital equipment played a critical part.[64]

The Vanguard was both a disappointment in operation and a waste of Britain's aeronautical resources, since its development coincided with that of another four-engined turbo-prop airliner, the long-range Bristol Britannia ordered by BOAC.[65] As early as 1958 it was realised that the Vanguard's economics (cost per seat mile) would be no better than that of the smaller and lighter Viscount, and the specification had to be changed to accommodate 130 instead of the original 105 passengers.[66] By the time it entered service, at the end of 1960, it was plagued with problems, including protracted difficulties with its Rolls Royce Tyne engines.[67]

Secondly, the Vanguard order illustrates the danger of basing aircraft specifications too closely on future traffic estimates. The fallibility of such predictions was shown in 1949, when BEA was choosing between a thirty- or fifty-seat Elizabethan. Peter Masefield worried that load factors on a fifty-passenger aircraft would be too low, and wrote that 'nothing bigger than the Elizabethan is foreseen as a major requirement on any BEA routes up to 1960'.[68] In fact, the next five years saw a staggering growth in air traffic, averaging 21 per cent per annum, and with this and the general rate of European economic expansion in mind, Masefield forecast in 1955 an annual increase for the years 1956 to 1963 of between 15 and 20 per cent, with a corresponding rise in required capacity of over 100 per cent.[69] That he was wrong again is hardly relevant; in the 1950s it was beyond the capacity even of experts to make meaningful forecasts about market growth in such a turbulent business as air transport. It was bad luck for BEA that when the Vanguard entered service in 1960–61 the world air travel market was in relative depression. Annual growth had fallen from 14 per cent in 1959, when there had been widespread complaints about the lack of tickets in BEA's summer season, to 8 per cent in 1961. At the same time the corporation's capacity had expanded by 26 per cent, the largest increase since its foundation. Flying against competition from the Caravelle, the Vanguard began operations under the worst possible circumstances, with disappointingly low load factors. Instead of flying high-density routes at low cost, BEA was forced to utilise its capacity by offering concessionary fares.[70]

Thirdly, the evolution of both the Vanguard and Trident programmes exposed the inadequacies of civil aircraft procurement in Britain. BEA's first talks on the Trident were with Vickers-Armstrong, with whom they had already built up an excellent association. It soon became apparent that Vickers was not prepared to build an aircraft small enough to meet requirements. The company had taken the Vanguard contract, despite misgivings about a second-generation turbo-prop, largely to keep their Weybridge plant in operation, and they eventually lost around £18 million on the order. When designs were being sought for the jet, Vickers saw another unmarketable aircraft in the making and withdrew. After some exploratory exchanges with Bristols, the choice of manufacturer fell on the special company which de Havilland set up with Hunting and Fairey, and in the summer of 1958 it finally got the go-ahead from the government.[71] Like Vickers, de Havilland had found the BEA specification too small, and submitted initial proposals that were 'directed at a wider market than the purely short-haul field in which BEA is exclusively interested'. Unlike Vickers, however, they allowed themselves to be persuaded and eventually tailored their design exactly to the corporation's needs.[72]

V

It would be easy to place the blame for the shortcomings of the Vanguard and Trident programmes on the much-maligned British aircraft industry. Certainly the manufacturers received vast amounts of public money which they seemed to fritter away on one half-baked project after another.[73] A long list of aircraft can be cited which were conceived without sufficient thought for their commercial viability, although it has recently been pointed out that this 'failure to look with due economic sense at new techniques' was not restricted to the aircraft industry but was probably symptomatic of much of British industry in the post-war period.[74]

However, this article has sought to lay some of the responsibility elsewhere. Instead of using its substantial power, as owner and overseer of BEA and BOAC, to encourage the emergence of manufacturers big enough to take on the American aircraft builders, the post-war Labour government contented itself with the creation of the air corporations as a captive market for the many individual airframe makers which were then allowed to carry on their precarious existence into the 1950s.[75] Furthermore, by dividing the 'chosen instrument' into two (initially three) geographically specialised airlines, the government weakened Britain's civil aviation challenge at the outset and created in BEA an oddity in an industry characterised by conformity.

BEA prided itself on its expertise in international short-haul services and it was undoubtedly successful in terms of airline economics. But if this was to be the only yardstick for assessing its performance, then the statutory requirement that it buy British aircraft might have been dispensed with. It could have bought the best available aircraft 'off the shelf' like its early rival KLM and possibly spared the British taxpayer eight years of losses between 1947 and 1954.

Instead, the success of its procurement activity in stimulating the British aircraft industry should be seen as of equal importance to its flying operations, and, judged by this standard, the verdict on BEA is muted at best. Its role in sponsoring new types was based on the assumption that aircraft built to BEA specifications would also command an interest in the world market. This was unlikely since BEA did not consider for purchase foreign types in competition with the British-made product and therefore did not set standards that would appeal to other airlines. Even the Viscount appears to have owed as much to the design input of overseas customers as it did to BEA's instructions to Vickers.[76] Moreover, BEA consistently ordered aircraft that were too small. It did so in the reasonable belief that small aircraft, operated at sufficiently high frequencies, were the key to making short-haul services profitable and the only way to avoid over-capacity. Unfortunately for the manufacturers, small aircraft were less attractive to airlines not encumbered with BEA's limited operating range. By forcing companies like Vickers and de Havilland to meet a narrow set of technical criteria, BEA actually made it less probable that their aircraft would find a market anywhere else in the world. It kept their production runs short, by American standards, and thus deprived them of the benefits of economies of scale. Far from encouraging British aircraft manufacturing, as Lord Douglas and Peter Masefield wished and Labour's 1946 legislation had half-heartedly intended, the close relationship that BEA built up with its suppliers in the development of its aircraft actually reduced their chances of international sales.

Notes

1 The author would like to thank the Nuffield Foundation for providing the financial support for this research, and also Mr R. A. R. Wilson, who was of great assistance in introducing him to the British Airways archives.

2 The political origins of the nationalisation programme are surveyed in Sir Norman Chester, *The Nationalisation of British Industry 1945–1951* (1975), pp. 1–8.

3 By the end of the Second World War the railways were in desperate need of investment and reorganisation, see D. H. Aldcroft, *British Transport Since 1914* (Newton Abbot, 1975), p. 71; T. R. Gourvish, *British Railways 1948–1973: a Business History* (Cambridge, 1986), pp. 1–29.

4 Sidney Pollard, *The Development of the British Economy 1914–1967*, 2nd edn (London, 1979), p. 388. Also H. A. Clegg, 'Nationalised Industry', in G. D. N. Worswick and P. H. Ady, *The British Economy 1945–1950* (Oxford, 1952), pp. 424–7.

5 In fact, Imperial Airways' four predecessors had already received £382,635 in subsidies by the time it was set up in 1924. PRO, AIR/20, 4850, Report on British Air Transport Development, 31 August 1944. For the details of BOAC's foundation, see the official *The History of BOAC 1939–1974*, by Winston Bray, pp. 1–11.

6 BSAA had the unenviable task of developing services to Latin America. After a series of disasters with the Tudor aircraft, it was taken over by BOAC in 1949. Chester, *Nationalisation*, p. 456.

7 Derek H. Aldcroft, *The British Economy Volume 1: Years of Turmoil 1920–1951* (Brighton, 1986), p. 203.

8 See Derek H. Aldcroft, 'Britain's internal airways: the pioneer stage of the 1930s', in his *Studies in British Transport History 1870–1970* (Newton Abbot, 1974), pp. 208–25.

9 Aldcroft, *British Transport*, p. 57. In 1933 the Chairman of Imperial Airways wrote a memorandum in which the airline's remaining European services (London–Paris and London–Cologne) were described as 'a shop window' important only for the maintenance of British prestige in Europe. Sir Eric Geddes, 'Future of Civil Air Communication of the Empire', p. 7. PRO, AVIA 2/636.

10 Peter Fearon, 'The growth of aviation in Bri-

tain', *Journal of Contemporary History*, XX (1985), pp. 31–2. See also his 'The British airframe industry and the state 1918–1935', *Economic History Review*, XXVII (1974), pp. 249–51.

11 *Report of the Committee of Inquiry into Civil Aviation*, March 1938, HMSO, Cmd 5685 ('The Cadman Report'), p. 10.

12 BOAC's wartime operations are described in Bray, *History*, pp. 12–53.

13 Future Capital and Organisational Structure of BOAC, Knollys to Street, 19 June 1944. PRO, AVIA 2/2686.

14 Minute, 26 June 1944. PRO, AIR 2/6937.

15 See Derek H. Aldcroft, 'The Railways and Air Transport 1933–39', in *Studies*, pp. 226–42.

16 Railway View of Post-War Operation of Internal and External Air Services, 1944. PRO, AVIA 2/2462. See also 'British Railway Companies Plans for Air Transport', Submission to the Government, June and August 1944. RAF Museum, Hendon, Box 253.

17 Britain did not make transport aircraft during the war. In 1942 it was recognised that planning for a new generation of airliners would have to start immediately if the United States were not to dominate civil aviation after the war. To meet this need, the government set up a committee headed by Lord Brabazon of Tara to work out a list of new aircraft priorities. Its report was given in stages between August 1943 and November 1945, and recommended development of five basic types.

18 See War Cabinet Meeting Minutes, 24 January 1945, WM(45)8, where Swinton's plan, set forth in Memorandum WP(45)38, was approved. Notable dissenters were the Lord Privy Seal (Beaverbrook) and the Minister of Information (Brendan Bracken), both of whom feared that the award of monopoly rights to BOAC would strangle competition and impede the efficient development of British air transport. See also PRO, AIR 19/414, Memorandum, 5 March 1945, WP(45)137, Organisation of Civil Airlines, and WP(45)136. Bracken strongly opposed the participation of surface interests in the monopoly on the grounds that this would produce a cartel which would keep prices high.

19 'British Air Transport', HMSO, March 1945, Cmd. 6605.

20 See the series in PRO, AIR 19/197, Civil Aviation Post-War Planning, which began in 1943, and the later discussions in PRO, AIR 19/201. Also informative is the Committee on Post-War Air Transport, CAB 87/62.

21 Memorandum by Minister for Civil Aviation (Viscount Swinton), Lord President's Committee, LP(45)101, 10 May 1945, PRO, AVIA 2/2760.

22 Restated, because the 'buy British' provision had already been applied to Imperial Airways. 'British Air Transport', paragraph 41.

23 *Ibid.*, paragraphs 31, 23.

24 *Ibid.*, paragraph 16.

25 *Ibid.*, paragraphs 17–21. BSAA was to be owned largely by shipping interests.

26 'The Cadman Report', p. 6.

27 In 1947–48 BEA lost over £2 million on a total domestic revenue of £1·13 million. In 1961–62 the internal routes were still losing money: operating revenue was £11·3 million, expenditure was £12·7 million. *BEA Annual Report and Accounts*, 1947–48, 1961–62.

28 Cabinet Papers, PRO, CAB 129/CP(46)37. Lord Stansgate, Secretary of State for Air, favoured a single airline. 'The spur of competition would', he claimed, 'come from American and foreign airlines.' But he was opposed by the Minister of Civil Aviation (Lord Winster) and overruled in Cabinet. Chester, *Nationalisation*, p. 405.

29 Report to Minister of Civil Aviation for period to 31 March 1947, p. 9. *BEA Board Papers*, 15 (hereafter *BP*).

30 Aide-mémoire on BEA accommodation. *BP*, 1, 1 August 1946.

31 'End of the beginning', *Flight Magazine*, 17 April 1947, p. 351.

32 BEA's unit costs, measured as pence per CTM, came down from 83·6 in 1947 to 41·0 in 1956. *BEA Annual Report and Accounts*, 1946–47, 1955–56.

33 Lord Douglas to Harold Watkinson (Minister of Transport and Civil Aviation), CH/123, 31 January 1956, *BP*, 102.

34 The Act created the Air Transport Licensing Board (ATLB) with powers to license new carriers. BEA and BOAC lost their exclusive rights on scheduled services and it was now possible for another airline to run a parallel service in competition with them.

35 Load factor is the percentage relationship between capacity provided and load carried, i.e. an aircraft with three-quarters of its seats filled is operating at a load factor of 75 per cent.

36 See Peter G. Masefield, 'Problems of short-haul airline operations', *Shell Aviation News*, June 1954; Peter W. Brooks, 'Problems of short-haul air transport', *Journal of the Royal Aeronautical Society* (June 1951), pp. 442–4.

37 Stephen F. Wheatcroft, 'Ten economic lessons from short-haul airline operations', *Journal of the Royal Aeronautical Society* (April 1961), pp. 221–35.

38 Sales and Purchase of British Civil Aircraft in Germany, 4 February 1953. PRO, BT 245/344.

39 The common criticism that cross-subsidisation involves the overcharging and misallocation of resources hardly applies in the case of BEA because international fares were controlled by IATA. See Richard Pryke, *Public Enterprises in Practice* (1971), p. 402.

40 A pool is a formal arrangement between airlines jointly to plan the capacity on any given route and share the revenue according to a pre-arranged quota. See the Corporation's justification for pool agreements in 'BEA's commercial agreements with other countries', XG.1069, 24 January 1961, *BP*, 159.

41 'Wasted Seats in Air Transport: an examination of the importance of load factor', Lecture by A. H. Milward to the *Institute of Transport*, 14 February 1966, p. 21.

42 Lord Douglas of Kirtleside, 'The Progress of European Air Transport 1946–1961: with Particular Reference to BEA', *Lecture to the Royal Aeronautical Society*, 16 November 1961.

43 See the discussion in A. W. J. Thompson and L. C. Hunter, *The Nationalized Transport Industries* (1973), p. 50.

44 The Elizabethan was actually developed by the small Airspeed Company, which was taken over by de Havilland before the aircraft went into production.

45 Conversation between the author and Sir Peter Masefield, 2 July 1985.

46 Fearon, *The British Airframe Industry*, pp. 249–50.

47 *BEA Annual Report and Accounts, 1952–1953*, p. 41. The savings in maintenance costs alone to be gained by operating a one-type fleet, i.e. Viscounts only, were estimated to be in the region of £300,000. Memo, Masefield, Aircraft Development Situation, CX(52)12, 18 June 1952, *BP*, 63.

48 In 1955–56 the Viscount earned for BEA £1·13 million profit on £9·67 million total traffic revenue. The Elizabethan made a loss of £558,000 on a revenue of £5·98 million, although these figures included the writing-off of that aircraft's exceptional development and modification costs. *BEA Annual Report 1955–56*, Appendix 7.

49 Chris Harlow, *Innovation and Productivity under Nationalisation* (1977), p. 23.

. 50 For the Viscount's strengths, see the authoritative history of civil aircraft manufacture by Ronald Miller and David Sawers, *The Technical Development of Modern Aviation* (London, 1968), pp. 25–6, 43.

51 Peter G. Masefield, 'Operating experience with turbo-prop aircraft: BEA's results with the operation of the Vickers-Armstrongs Viscount with some thoughts on future possibilities', *Institute of the Aeronautical Sciences/Royal Aeronautical Society*, 5th Anglo-American Conference, Los Angeles, 20 June 1955.

52 Masefield, 'BEA's forward plans and future aircraft programme', CX(55)5, 9 September 1955, *BP*, 97.

53 'Reconsideration of pure jet aircraft for BEA',

P&D Report M/73, R. C. Morgan, June 1956. 'RAF Museum, Hendon, Box 241.

54 Douglas to Watkinson, CH/1044, 23 August 1957; also memorandum by the Chairman, 'BEA's jet transport aircraft requirements', *BP*, 119.

55 Special Board Room Chart, A.CH/56, J. J. Scarlett. 16 February 1961, *BP*, 159.

56 BEA Trident Engineering History, 1956–67, RAF Museum, Hendon, Box 239.

57 Morgan, *Reconsideration of Pure Jet Aircraft*, p. 6.

58 Charles Gardiner, *British Aircraft Corporation* (1981), p. 21.

59 Douglas to Watkinson, CH/955, 22 July 1959, *BP*, 143.

60 The Trident lost £1·06 million in 1964–65 on a revenue of £6·75 million — before capitalised costs of introduction were deducted. In 1965–66 it lost £711,000 on £17·04 million. In 1966–67 it made a small surplus of £90,000 on £25·47 million. By comparison the Viscount made £0·5 million on a revenue of £18·13 million. *BEA Annual Reports*, 1964–67, Appendix 7.

61 BEA was obliged to take the BAC 1-11 in place of the Boeing 737, and in 1968 after the government had rejected development of the BAC 2-11. the 'stretched' Trident 3 in place of the Boeing 727. The acceptance of the latter led to the payment of substantial compensation by the government to BEA. See Thompson and Hunter. *Nationalized Transport*, pp. 61–6.

62 Douglas to Watkinson, 23 August 1957, *BP*, 119.

63 For an account of the 727's origins, see Harold Mansfield, *Billion Dollar Battle* (New York, 1965).

64 Harlow, *Innovation*, p. 15.

65 Peter W. Brooks, *The Modern Airliner: its Origins and Development* 2nd edn (Kansas. 1982). p. 122.

66 'British European Airways Vanguards'. memo, Milward, CX(58)19, 22 August 1958, *BP*, 132.

67 The Vanguard was delivered late, with the result that extra aircraft capacity had to be chartered in 1961 at a cost of around £1·36 million. Memo,

Milward, Budget 1961–62. CX(61)3, 21 April 1961, *BP*, 160.

68 Masefield, 'Outline of requirements by BEA', *BP*, 36, 29 July 1949.

69 Masefield, 'BEA's forward plans', *BP*, 97.

70 *ICAO* (International Civil Aviation Organisation), Digest of Statistics, 90, Traffic; Memo, Budget 1960–61, Milward, CX(60)4, 22 August 1960, *BP*, 152.

71 *Select Committee on the Nationalised Industries/BEA* (1967).

72 Memo by Chairman, 'BEA's future aircraft requirements', 26 July 1957, *BP*, 118.

73 The industry was supported by the government at a cost of £88 million between 1946 and 1958, of which barely a quarter was recovered. A further £50 million was invested between 1960 and 1967, also with little return. *Report of the Committee of Inquiry into the Aircraft Industry*, Cmd 2853. 1964–65, pp. 18–19. See also Arthur Reed, *Britain's Aircraft Industry: What Went Right? What Went Wrong?* (1973).

74 D. C. Coleman and Christine Macleod, 'Attitudes to new techniques: British businessmen 1800–1950'. *Economic History Review*, XXXIX (1986). p. 597. A similar view of the British aircraft industry is expressed by Correlli Barnett. who speaks of 'a disharmony between scientific genius and industrial backwardness'. *The Audit of War: the Illusion and Reality of Britain as a Great Nation* (1986). p. 168.

75 At the end of the Second World War there were twenty-seven airframe makers and eight aero-engine builders in Britain. In 1957 there were still fourteen airframe and five engine makers. For the details of the industry's troubles and eventual amalgamation. see K. Hartley, 'The mergers in the UK aircraft industry 1957–1960'. *Aeronautical Journal* (1965).

76 The legendary Vickers designer George Edwards admitted that it was not BEA but the Canadian airline TCA which turned the Viscount into an aircraft of the standard required by American airlines. Gardiner, *British Aircraft Corporation*, p. 66.

9 Nationalisation and the independent airlines in the United Kingdom, 1945–51*

B. K. HUMPHREYS

THE period of the 1945–51 Labour Government is crucial to a thorough under-standing of the post-war development of British air transport, for these years saw the establishment of the basic structure of the industry. The 'mixed' two-sector type of industry that had evolved by the end of 1951, comprising the two nationalized Corporations on the one hand and numerous privately-owned operators on the other, survived the next 20 years remarkably well, despite periodic attacks and reforms. It is important, therefore – above all at a time of yet another official review of British air transport – to examine in some detail the policies that led to the establish-ment of this particular type of system, especially as it could be persuasively argued that it is the structure of the industry that has been largely responsible for many of the pro-blems that British civil aviation regulatory authorities have had to face since the War. In this paper particular attention will be focused on the role of the small privately-owned airlines, the so-called 'Independents'.

THE SWINTON PLAN

Long before the end of the Second World War it had become quite obvious that when peace eventually arrived a new civil aviation policy would be required. Consequently, upon his appointment as the first Minister of Civil Aviation in October 1944, Viscount Swinton rapidly set about preparing the necessary blueprint. The document that emerged, known as the Swinton Plan, was presented to Parliament as a White Paper in March 1945.[1] Although published by the Coalition Government the Plan shows all the signs of being a Conservative brain-child. Before the war Tory policy, as evolved by Mr Kingsley Wood, had favoured the concentration of the nation's effort in the international field behind a single, publicly-owned airline, leaving most domestic and charter services to private enterprise.[2] The British Overseas Airways Corporation (BOAC) was therefore established in 1939 with the exclusive right to receive a State subsidy for overseas services. In the post-war world, however, the Government felt that a single 'chosen instrument' would be too unwieldy to

* This paper is based on a chapter from my doctoral dissertation, 'The Economics and Develop-ment of the British Independent Airlines Since 1945' (Institute for Transport Studies, University of Leeds, 1974). I would like to express gratitude to my supervisor, Professor K. M. Gwilliam, and to colleagues within the Civil Aviation Authority Economic Department, for useful help and advice. The views expressed in the paper are my own and do not necessarily reflect those of my current employer, the Civil Aviation Authority.

operate efficiently and instead proposed three new Corporations linked together by a common denominator, the participation of BOAC.

The underlying philosophy of the Swinton Plan is summarized in the White Paper as follows: "It is . . . the essence of the Government's plan that those interests concerned in transport by sea and by land should be brought into a real and effective partnership with the organizations which will be responsible for transport by air".[3] The same principle, together with that of regulated competition, has remained at the heart of Conservative policy throughout most of the post-war period. The Government proposed that the first of the three Corporations, essentially the existing BOAC, should be responsible for scheduled air services on the North Atlantic and Commonwealth routes, with extensions to China and the Far East. The airline was to be wholly State-owned, but allowance was made for the participation of shipping companies in subsidiaries and on certain routes where they could make a "useful contribution". The exact extent of any maritime participation, however, was never enunciated.

The second Corporation, expected to be the most profitable and in which the Government intended BOAC to have a substantial, though not a majority, shareholding, would serve the European and domestic routes. The Swinton Plan thus abandoned the pre-war rigid division between internal British and Continental services. The main shareholders, apart from BOAC, were to be the railway companies, short sea shipping lines, and travel agencies, although other pre-war operators were offered the chance of either sharing in the capital of the new Corporation or joining with it to form joint subsidiaries to run particular routes. In addition, the Government left the door ajar for the participation of outside carriers in the development of new routes, while no restrictions were placed on the operation of charter services.

The third Corporation was to be responsible for the development of routes to South America and owned primarily by the four British shipping companies engaged in the South American trade who, in January 1944, had joined together to form British Latin American Airlines Ltd. Again BOAC was to be a shareholder, but with a smaller interest than in either of the other two Corporations. The Swinton Plan provided for the Minister of Civil Aviation to "have a general control over broad aviation policy"; he would have the right of veto over appointments to the boards of the two non-nationalized airlines and would retain the power to appoint the directors of BOAC. The three Corporations would not be permitted to terminate a scheduled service without the Minister's permission.

Inevitably, the Swinton Plan was a compromise, a hotchpot of policies designed to satisfy as many pressure groups as possible. Mr Herbert Morrison aptly summarized the background to the Plan during the parliamentary debate on the 1946 Civil Aviation Act:

[Lord Swinton] said, "What can I do to get some scheme through this Cabinet of conflicting points of view?" He said, "I will have three corporations", and he had three. He had one with substantially, if not predominantly, a railway interest. He said to himself, "That will square the railway interests". He had another with a very strong shipping flavour about it, and he said, "That will square the shipping people, the Conservative believers in private enterprise". It was real political genius. . . . Finally, he produced a public-ownership corporation, the BOAC, and he said, "That is for the Socialists." . . . That was the Swinton Plan, one for the railways, one for shipping and one for the Socialists.[4]

Whether or not the proposals were "real political genius", certainly in practice many of them would have had to be radically modified. The Plan affords several examples of policy proposals that did not make economic sense, the inevitable result of trying to reconcile too many diverse pressures. This is particularly striking in the attitude taken towards the important question of subsidies. The White Paper stated that while the Government would be prepared to subsidize BOAC's Commonwealth routes, "[it] is the intention that the agreed schedule of services on the European routes and the Latin American Service should be operated without subsidy".[5] Similarly, challenged to say what would happen if the Corporations lost money, Sir Stafford Cripps, Minister for Aircraft Production, replied: "First of all the Corporation bears the loss. If this exceeds its reserves it will have to give up the service and somebody will take it on."[6]

It would appear, therefore, that the Government totally failed to appreciate a fact that was obvious to most people in the industry, namely that all the Corporations, even the European airline, would need subsidizing after the War, and indeed that in the short run the subsidies would have to be considerably greater than they had been before 1939. Who exactly was going to take on the routes that the Corporations abandoned, since almost every company of any size that had ever shown any interest in air transport had already been included in the Plan, was anyone's guess.[7] In short, the thinking behind the Swinton Plan was vague and lacked an appreciation of the immense changes that the Second World War had brought about in civil aviation.

LABOUR'S PLANS

Although the Labour Party was strongly represented in the Coalition Government, and indeed Sir Stafford Cripps held the post of Minister of Aircraft Production and often spoke in the Commons on behalf of Viscount Swinton, the principles embodied in the Swinton Plan were very different from those that had become associated with Labour. Social-democratic parties throughout the world had for some time been discussing the feasibility of 'internationalizing' air transport, as distinct from the pre-war pattern whereby each country established and protected its own airlines, often using them in the exercise of national power (Germany's Lufthansa probably being the most blatant example of this). The governments of France (in 1932) and Australia and New Zealand (in 1944) had all proposed the formation of a world authority to own and operate the main trunk air routes, while the Canadians had suggested not the complete internationalization of civil aviation, but an authority "to ensure that . . . international air routes and services are divided fairly and equitably between various member states".[8] It was against this background that the Labour Party published, in 1944, its blueprint for post-war civil air transport, 'Wings for Peace'.

'Wings for Peace', therefore, inevitably tended to be a rather idealistic document, very much in the mainstream of left-wing political thinking at the time. Labour saw it as "the only programme which can adequately safeguard the world's peace against the dangers that result from the use of civil aviation as an instrument of national policy". Basically, it made three proposals:

1. The establishment of a World Air Authority with wide-ranging functions, including the provision of various international services, such as weather reports, health control, etc.

2. The establishment of a unified World Airways, owned and operated by the World Air Authority, or, as a second-best solution, a system of Regional Air Unions.

3. The immediate internationalization of civil aviation in Europe while the ground was still particularly fertile for such a development.

Like its Conservative counterpart, 'Wings for Peace' had several shortcomings. For example, it failed to foresee, perhaps not unexpectedly, the appearance of the post-war phenomenon of third-world nationalism that was destined to play such an important part in international air transport. Similarly, it did not face up to the very real problems created by the close association between civil aviation and national defence, especially in relation to a country's aircraft-manufacturing potential. But in the short term the main problem revolved around the fact that the implementation of the type of policies contained in 'Wings for Peace' was quite beyond the control of any single government. It required the acquiescence of at least a large proportion of the industrialized world, and as the Chicago Conference of 1944 revealed, this was simply not forthcoming.

NATIONALIZATION

By the time that the Labour Government came to power in July 1945, it was widely accepted that a more practical solution to the problem of the future development of British civil aviation than that contained in 'Wings for Peace' had to be found, and not surprisingly thought tended to revolve around the already prepared Swinton Plan. Indeed, it was reliably reported that up to 24 October (Labour's policy proposals were published in the form of a White Paper in December) the Cabinet intended to adopt the Swinton Plan with only one modification – that the shipping and travel interests, while participating in the two new Corporations, should do so as minority rather than majority shareholders. On that day, however, a group of Labour back-benchers threatened to organize a revolt in the parliamentary party, and the Government, fearing the kind of split in the ranks that had recently occurred over the National Insurance Bill, capitulated and proposed complete public ownership.[9] It is difficult to visualize how a Government apparently so committed to the internationalization of air transport and the public ownership of virtually all domestic inter-city public transport could have done anything but effectively exclude private enterprise from the mainstream of civil aviation development. On the other hand, the policy finally adopted did differ from normal Labour nationalization practice in two significant respects: there was no single, central body to administer air transport, and the question of the co-ordination of civil aviation with other modes of transport was almost totally ignored.

Labour's White Paper[10] followed Conservative policy in proposing the formation of three separate airlines, each with its own geographical area of responsibility. Thus, routes between Britain and other Commonwealth countries, the U.S.A., and the Far East were to be operated by the existing BOAC. British domestic services and routes to the Continent were given to a new company, British European Airways (BEA), formed by the amalgamation of the European division of BOAC and those independent airlines operating scheduled services within Britain. Finally, routes to South America were to be the responsibility of another new company, British South American Airways (BSAA), which eventually merged with BOAC during 1949 after a series of tragic accidents involving its Tudor IV aircraft. These three operators became Britain's 'chosen instruments'. They had the exclusive right to fly scheduled services, the only competition allowed being from foreign carriers on international routes. Those British private airlines not absorbed into BEA were permitted only to carry out such functions as charter flights, aircrew instruction and ambulance and rescue flying. The idealism of 'Wings for Peace', however, was not entirely abandoned; the White Paper opens with a pledge to work towards a single international owning and operating body, and continues: "The plan His Majesty's Government now present to Parliament is necessarily a national plan, but it has been so formed that it can be readily fitted into any future scheme of international organization".

The Civil Aviation Act received the Royal Assent in August 1946. BEA had been established in February of the same year as a Division of BOAC so that a nucleus organization could be built up by 1 August. On that date BEA took over the European services of 110 Wing, 46 Group, RAF, which had operated for a short time under the aegis of BOAC. Domestic air services, however, continued to be operated by a group of private airlines, the so-called Associated Airways Joint Committee (AAJC), under charter to the Corporation.[11] These airlines were eventually taken over by BEA in February 1947, for a purchase price of £550,000, of which £305,529 represented "the excess of the cost of the shares in the AAJC companies over the estimated value of the net tangible assets of those companies at the date of acquisition".[12] The eight carriers involved were:

Great Western and Southern Air Lines
Highland Airways
Isle of Man Air Services
North Eastern Airways
Railway Air Services
West Coast Air Services (ceased operations, June 1946)
Scottish Airways
Western Isles Airways.

In April BEA added Allied Airways to the list. This left Channel Islands Airways, a Jersey-registered company that began operations only in June 1945, as the sole remaining privately-owned scheduled British carrier. The states of Jersey and Guernsey rejected nationalization and insisted on preserving the identity of their 'own' airline. When, however, the British Government refused permission for Channel Islands Airways to operate to and from the mainland the Insular Authorities capitulated and the airline came under public ownership.[13]

Finally in this section mention should be made of the main Conservative criticism of the 1946 Act, voiced by Mr Lennox-Boyd, for to a large extent it foreshadowed later British civil aviation policy, both Tory and Labour:

First and foremost, we deplore the monopolistic feature of this proposal. No one is to be allowed to start a scheduled service. . . . We believe that there should be an executive council, an organization similar to that in operation in the United States where the Civil Aeronautics Board have contrived to give competition and service within the framework of a general Government supervision. We favour an independent tribunal to which any independent operator can apply in regard to routes at home and overseas. If the tribunal is satisfied that there is inadequate service, or no service at the moment, on a particular route and the tribunal is also satisfied as to the financial soundness of a proposal and technical ability of the people concerned, they would have the power to grant a licence to operate over that route.[14]

THE CHARTER COMPANIES

Thus, by 1946 both the main political parties had been forced to tone down their earlier civil aviation policies, although a large gap still separated them. The task now is to examine how the independent airlines in particular reacted to the new political and economic environment. It is important, first of all, to remember that the Second World War had an enormous effect on air transport development throughout the world. One commentator has estimated that "at the close of the hostilities we found ourselves probably fifty years further ahead in air transport techniques, in aeronautical knowledge, in the development of flying equipment and devices which could be adapted to commercial use, and in public acceptance of this new means of getting about the world than we would have been if the conflict had not taken place."[15]

The immediate post-war period was marked by the appearance of a very large number of small air charter companies, just as the end of the First World War had seen the mushrooming of private bus operators in and around London. During 1946 and 1947 hardly a week went by without the establishment of another airline; the small island of Jersey alone boasted well over a dozen registered charter companies at the time.[16] For the country as a whole it is very difficult to say with any certainty how many carriers were in existence, since no reliable estimate has ever been made. But during the period of the Labour Government the total probably came to well over 100, perhaps approaching 150. Certainly, a survey by *Flight* counted some 70 privately-owned airlines operating during April 1949.[17] The casualty rate, of course, was almost as high and Mr (now Sir) Peter Masefield's description of the pre-war British airlines "flitting like brief shadows across the scene"[18] applies even more to their post-war successors. This phenomenon was far from unique to Britain. France, for example, already had some 30 charter companies by the end of 1946,[19] while in the U.S.A. the Civil Aeronautics Administration later estimated that approximately 3,600 carriers had been established during the immediate post-war years.[20]

Two factors in particular favoured this rapid growth. Firstly, during the War large numbers of men had been taught how to fly aircraft and had become interested in the potential of air transport; most of them now suddenly found themselves in the labour market. Secondly, with the return of peace the Allied governments began to dispose of thousands of surplus aircraft at very low prices. Over 13,000 DC-3s had been built (including some 2,000 in Russia), 4,000 of which were sold off by the American Government alone at the end of the War. Similarly, between 1942 and 1946 almost 1,200 DC-4s had been built,[21] as well as thousands of bombers capable of conversion to civilian use. Mr Freddie Laker has claimed that it was possible to buy Halifax bombers from the Ministry of Supply for between £100 and £1,700 each, with spare engines selling for a little over £10 each.[22] Thus, the establishment of an air charter operation required relatively little initial capital and entrepreneurial skill. The difficult part was to *stay* in business.

Most of these airlines, of course, were small, almost 'one-man' affairs, although a few soon became relatively large and well-established, companies such as Airwork, Hunting Air Travel, Lancashire Aircraft Corporation (LAC), Scottish Airlines and Skyways. The Civil Aviation Act effectively limited their field of operation to various types of charter activity. In fact, the Independents were positively encouraged to seek this type of work: "We give to independent charter operators freedom of enterprise, and freedom of competition against these publicly-owned undertakings. . . . We genuinely desire that private enterprise should have a fair field in charter flying and good luck to it".[23] Given this encouragement and the current demand for air transport services, it is not surprising that for those airlines that managed to stave off bankruptcy the immediate post-war years proved to be a period not only of expansion but of near-boom. From the residue of work left for the Independents, ambitious operators were able to gradually rebuild a private sector in the industry, primarily by adapting themselves skilfully to the new situation and to new opportunities.

The reasons for the early success of the sector as a whole, despite individual failures, can probably best be seen by examining the type of work to which they turned.

Scheduled services at this time were usually characterized by an acute shortage of capacity, largely a reflection of the continuing war-time disruption of air services and the difficulty of obtaining new equipment. It was often necessary to book months in advance to fly to European destinations and a year in advance for South Africa and Australia. To a large extent this explains the amount of work given to the charter companies by the nationalized airlines. To give just two examples, Skyways operated BEA's once-weekly flight to Helsinki, while Scottish Airlines flew the same Corporation's Prestwick–Belfast, Renfrew–Belfast, and Aberdeen–Renfrew–London services.[24] According to its Annual Reports, BOAC spent £321,799 during 1946–7 on the 'charter of aircraft and crews', undoubtedly largely from the Independents, and a further £180,624 in 1947–8. The corresponding figures for BEA were £104,307 (August–March) and £173,651. There is also some evidence to suggest that the Government turned a blind eye to the open flouting of charter regulations by several companies, again no doubt because of the excess demand situation.

The nationalized Corporations were far from being the only customers for this type of charter work. A number of British airlines found a valuable market in providing services and advice to foreign companies and governments. Airwork, for example, had contracts for the technical management and operation of fleets of aircraft in Iran, Iraq, the Sudan, Ecuador, and Pakistan.[25] Scottish Airlines flew regular scheduled services for Icelandic Airways, KLM, Air France, Compagnie Belge des Transports Aériens, and Faroe Airways, in addition to providing all the equipment and technical assistance for a new carrier, Luxemburg Airlines. London Aero and Motor Services Ltd (LAMS) had subsidiaries operating in Australia and South Africa, and in January 1948 signed a contract with the Jewish Agency in Palestine for the establishment of Jewish National Airways.[26]

The Independents were not slow either in obtaining quite large-scale general charter contracts. For example, following a critical shortage of milk in Britain during the autumns of 1947 and 1948 the Ministry of Food chartered a large number of aircraft to supplement the shipping services in transporting extra supplies from Northern Ireland. The operation involved the movement of a daily average of 12,000 gallons in 1947 and 30,000 in 1948, employing 11 charter carriers. A further airlift was necessary in 1950.[27] Airwork gained a long-term contract to carry Muslim pilgrims between Mombasa and Jeddah. Hunting Air Travel signed an agreement with the Overseas Food Corporation (of the 'groundnuts scheme' fame) which involved the movement of some 2,000 passengers between London and East Africa during 1948–9.[28]

Most of the work mentioned so far, of course, tended to involve the larger private airlines. The smaller companies had to rely on the fairly buoyant, but less certain and probably more competitive general charter market, and it was mainly these carriers that faced financial difficulty and bankruptcy. But opportunities still existed for those with initiative. Olley Air Services, and later Solar Air Services, for instance, built up quite successful businesses flying passengers to all the major horse-race meetings and the Isle of Man T.T. races. A number of airlines developed close ties with shipping companies, flying crews and spares around the world. Two further events must also have aided the general expansion of the charter operators. One was the establishment in August 1946, of the British Air Charter Association (BACA) to act as spokesman and pressure group for the industry. The other was the opening of the Baltic Exchange air freight section in August 1947, making it easier to 'marry' cargo and aircraft and so obviate the common diseconomy that arises when one-way cargoes have to bear the cost of the return flight without pay-load.

Unfortunately, the honeymoon for the charter airlines proved to be short-lived. By the spring of 1948 most companies, especially the smaller ones, were beginning to feel the strain of a slack winter period. A major factor in this market downturn was the recovery of the national scheduled carriers from the immediate post-war chaos. Their use of the charter airlines' services began to decline markedly. It is significant that in May 1948, Ciro's Aviation became the first company to be prosecuted under the Civil Aviation Act for failing to furnish documents and information required by the Minister concerning flights to South Africa.[29] On the whole, therefore, the situation looked rather bleak for the Independents. They were saved by two developments during the second half of 1948. Probably the more significant in the long run was the decision by the Government to allow certain privately-owned airlines to operate scheduled services within Britain as 'associates' of BEA. But in the short run even more important was the Berlin Airlift, which created, in Mr Freddie Laker's words, the "launching pad for private operators".[30]

THE BERLIN AIRLIFT

The Berlin Airlift was not in fact the first operation of its kind in which the Independents had participated. During the autumn of 1947, for example, BOAC and several charter companies had carried out two major airlifts between India and Pakistan. The first, "up to that time the biggest air charter in the history of civil aviation", involved the carriage of 7,000 employees of the Pakistan Government and their families from Delhi to Karachi and 1,500 passengers in the reverse direction, as well as over 50 tons of food and medical supplies.[31] During the second operation, "the greatest civil air evacuation which has ever been attempted", a total of 35,000 persons was airlifted between the two newly independent States.[32] Altogether, the airlines flew well over 1,200,000 aircraft-miles and the two evacuations produced a gross revenue of £435,840 for the charter companies.[33] Similarly, in May 1948, Airwork secured a contract valued at £1,200,000 for the time charter of five DC-4s to the International Refugee Organisation for the carriage of displaced persons between Hamburg and Montreal.[34] But such operations almost pale into insignificance when compared with the Berlin Airlift.

The British civilian side of the Airlift, officially described as "the greatest and largest air supply operation ever attempted, or ever likely to be attempted again",[35] began in late July 1948. The Soviet Union finally lifted its blockade of Berlin early in May 1949, although civilian flights continued until August in order to build up strategic reserves in the city. At its peak 48 British civil aircraft of all types were involved, even including a few flying boats. The independent airlines were used to such an extent quite simply because there was no realistic alternative. Neither the R.A.F. nor the U.S.A.F., though doing the lion's share of the work, had the capability to perform the whole task without seriously impairing their world-wide operations, while the sole use of the Corporations would have caused severe disruption to their scheduled services, just beginning to recover from the wartime chaos. Altogether 25 British carriers took part in the Airlift, including BSAA and BOAC.[36]

TABLE I

The Berlin Airlift, Total Sorties and Tonnage

	Total sorties	Total tonnage
R.A.F.	65,857	394,509
U.S.A.F.	189,963	1,783,573
British civil	21,984	147,727
Total	277,804	2,325,809

Source: R. Rodrigo, *Berlin Airlift* (1960), 215.

It is difficult to over-estimate the importance of the Berlin Airlift, especially if viewed together with the change in Government policy towards the Independents that began in 1948. During the Airlift British airlines transported almost double the total tonnage of mail and cargo carried by all British civil aircraft on scheduled services over the previous 23 years.[37] Wheatcroft lists three ways in which the Airlift changed the status of the private companies. First, it gave them an accumulation of operating experience which would otherwise have taken them many years to acquire. Second, it persuaded the Government of the value of the privately-owned airlines as a military transport reserve, and indeed their later extensive use in the field of trooping can to some extent be seen as a direct outcome of the Berlin Airlift. Finally, it considerably increased the financial strength of the Independents since they were able, for the first time, to engage in a really large-scale transport operation.[38] Even those airlines not directly involved in the Airlift benefited from the general buoyancy of the charter market that resulted from an often acute shortage of large aircraft.

ASSOCIATE AGREEMENTS

In May 1948, the Government decided to allow the independent airlines to operate selected scheduled services for an experimental period of six months (later extended) as 'associates' of BEA. Such associate agreements were drawn up by the Corporation and defined exactly how the services were to be run. The main reason for this apparent *volte face* on the part of the Labour Government seems to have been a realization that BEA would not be in a position for some time to maintain all the domestic routes that had been taken over in 1946–7 and for which a demand apparently existed, without incurring very heavy losses. During this period of economic crisis, with huge amounts of capital needed to rebuild the economy and for the vast new public sector, any short-term means of tapping private risk capital must have appeared extremely tempting.[39] A clause in the 1946 Act had provided for the possibility of companies being made associates of one of the Corporations. The intention was probably to cover the need for one of the State airlines contracting for temporary or emergency operations. During the initial trial period associate services were restricted to seasonal routes, such as those to holiday resorts, and to short-distance ferry services. Cambrian Airways became the first Independent to be awarded a licence, for the route between Cardiff and Weston-super-Mare, abandoned by BEA as uneconomic. Altogether 20 charter companies received licences to operate 11 scheduled services and 13 inclusive tours.[40]

When Lord Pakenham (now Longford) succeeded Lord Nathan as Minister of Civil Aviation in June 1948, one of his earliest official actions was to appoint Marshal of the R.A.F. Lord Douglas of Kirtleside to undertake a thorough investigation into the operation of the associate agreements scheme. Lord Douglas eventually recommended that until BEA had established itself sufficiently to provide all the scheduled services for which there was a justifiable demand the private airlines should be allowed to continue to operate certain routes as associates of one of the Corporations. The Government accepted the report and announced that the Air Transport Advisory Council (ATAC), under the chairmanship of Lord Terrington, would consider each licence application and recommend acceptance or rejection, although the final decision had to rest with the Minister. Quite strict directives were laid down for the Council to follow, including the stipulation that licences should not be awarded for periods of more than two years.[41]

The ATAC had been established under the 1946 Act with two responsibilities: to consider any representation from the public about the services provided by the three nationalized Corporations and the charges made for them; and, secondly, to investigate any problem concerning air transport which the Minister might refer to it.[42] As there had been very few representations from the public, and none at all from the Minister, the Council had had little to do during the first two years of its existence. All that now changed. During 1949 it received a total of 231 applications for licences and finally recommended that 24 independent airlines should be allowed to operate 59 scheduled services (two were subsequently rejected by the Minister) and 26 inclusive tour programmes. The following year out of 177 applications the Council recommended the licensing of 80 scheduled services and 16 inclusive tour programmes, nearly all of which, like the previous year's, were for periods of just one year. This time the Minister rejected four of the proposed services.[43] The short duration of the licences, however, caused considerable dissatisfaction among the Independents, largely because of the difficulty of raising capital to finance the purchase of new equipment without greater

TABLE 2

Scheduled Services operated by all British Airlines, 1938–49 (000's)

| | Passenger-miles flown | Passengers carried | Passengers | Ton-miles flown | | |
				Mail	Freight	Total
1938	53,412	219·3	4,857	8,900	970	14,727
1945	322,769	259·6	31,298	6,075	17,518	54,891
1946	362,841	423·5	33,896	7,033	7,846	48,775
1947	441,140	586·5	40,605	8,240	10,201	59,046
1948	554,536	713·4	51,176	9,938	15,520	76,634
1949	613,383	917·2	55,901	10,563	18,081	84,545

Source: Ministry of Civil Aviation, *Civil Aviation Reports*, 1946–7 and 1948–9. No official statistics are available for charter traffic.

TABLE 3

Scheduled Services operated by British independent airlines, 1946–9 (000's)

| | Passenger-miles flown | Passengers carried | Passengers | Ton-miles flown | | |
				Mail	Freight	Total
1946	30,060	229·4	2,329	67	113	2,509
1947	1,987	14·2	149	8	14	171
1948	330	12·9	24	—	—	24
1949	5,965	59·1	463	—	209	672

Source: as for table 2.

security of tenure. As a result the Government decided in 1950 to increase the maximum period of licences to five years.[44]

Thus, from 1948 the basic principle of a State monopoly in British scheduled air transport ceased to exist in fact, although it continued as a legal concept for many more years. It was, furthermore, a Labour Government that first opened the door, albeit only slightly, to the participation of private operators in the provision of regular air services. The Government, of course, undoubtedly regarded the associate agreement device as a purely temporary solution to a difficult problem. Lord Pakenham warned the Independents that they would be unwise to consider the new opportunities opened for them as the thin end of a wedge. Three principles, he said, guided him in allowing the private sector to operate scheduled air services as associates of BEA:

> The first was that we must look to the time when the Corporations run all the internal scheduled services; secondly, that there is a limit to the burden that can be imposed on the taxpayer during the period while they [i.e. BEA] are cutting down their costs and actually developing their network; thirdly, that it would be wrong in the meanwhile to deny the public any facilities that can be offered under reasonable conditions by private companies. . . . (I believe that) nationalized air transport is the only conceivable form of air transport in this country.[45]

Over the next two years, however, Labour's new policy began to look more and more like a semi-permanent arrangement and when the Conservatives returned to power in 1951 it took on a different complexion and became the very "thin end of the wedge" about which Lord Pakenham had spoken.

DEPRESSION

The new scheduled services that the Independents were allowed to operate, of course, remained relatively few in number in the short term and it would be some time before they could make any positive contribution to the financial strength of the airlines concerned. In addition, as long as the Labour Party remained in power there would always be a major element of uncertainty about such services. A BACA report noted that "associate agreements are granted only with the approval of the Minister and are in no way permanent. They have helped the companies but the companies cannot depend upon a continuance of the agreements".[46] Meanwhile, the position of the private operators, especially those actively engaged in the general charter market, deteriorated markedly.

The downturn in the fortunes of the Independents had a number of causes. In December 1949, Hunting Air Travel lost its lucrative contract with the Overseas Food Corporation to BOAC under circumstances that led to protests from Hunting and BACA about unfair competition from the State airline.[47] Perishable fruit and flowers, which had once been the mainstay of the general air charter market, were by 1949 being carried almost exclusively by rail, partly because the airlines had tended to neglect this traffic during the Berlin Airlift and partly because the railways were increasingly able to compete in terms of both price and service by the use of refrigerated vans.[48] But with the ending of the airlift to Berlin the prime reason for the depression was over-capacity, forcing charter rates down to uneconomic levels and causing difficulties and bankruptcies among even the larger operators. An indication of the seriousness of the situation came in June 1950 when, following the termination of its contract with BOAC to operate a scheduled service to the Persian Gulf, the largest British independent airline, Skyways, went into voluntary liquidation.[49]

The smaller operators had usually, though far from always, managed to keep their heads above water during periods of relative prosperity. But in the event of a downturn in the charter market they were forced to resort to the only effective weapon at their disposal – price-cutting – with disastrous consequences for everyone in the industry. As Mr T. L. Logan, secretary of the Airbrokers' Association, said at the time:

Rates in any market fluctuate, but bear a mean relation to the current conditions. Aircraft operators can compete by the shading of their quotations or by offering better conditions, but the wholesale slashing of prices is not only suicide for the company quoting but causes needless depression for the market generally and eventual elimination even of the soundest operators.[50]

In other words, the private sector was now undergoing the long-overdue weeding-out of the smaller, less efficient carriers, together with some of the less secure larger airlines. The inability of the Independents to obtain sufficient work at economic rates was matched by their inability to acquire more modern, and therefore more efficient, equipment. Those that had managed to remain solvent since the War had usually been able to cover their prime costs and such overheads as salaries, hangars, and perhaps even depreciation of existing aircraft based on original cost. Unfortunately, in most cases the original cost had been artificially low, since the planes had been purchased very cheaply as surplus war-stock. Even those airlines making relatively healthy profits found it extremely difficult to accumulate sufficient reserves over a four- or five-year period to buy replacement aircraft at current prices unless they were backed by another company prepared to inject fresh capital. An operator of a Dakota (DC-3), which might have cost about £4,000 in 1945, would need £60,000 or so to replace it.[51] Fleet renewal had become a matter of some urgency to many airlines, partly because of the need to remain competitive in the world charter market and partly because the ex-bomber aircraft, with which many of them were equipped, were nearing the end of their operational life. The situation was made worse by the fact that the major scheduled airlines, the normal source of supply for charter operators, had replacement problems of their own and were releasing few second-hand aircraft onto the market. The American charter market, on the other hand, was booming and a number of British operators took advantage of the high prices being paid there for second-hand aircraft to sell out and leave the industry altogether during 1950–1.

The general economic situation in which the Independents found themselves is reflected in the experiences of numerous individual companies, many of which were to become famous in later years. For example, East Anglian Flying Services (Channel Airways) had been founded in 1946 by Squadron Leader R. L. (Jack) Jones. By 1951 business was so poor that Jones had to dismiss the entire staff with the exception of one boy and only kept the airline ticking over by carrying out pleasure flights.[52] Mr Harold Bamberg established Eagle Aviation in 1948 with a single Halifax bought for £500. After a period of flying fruit from Spain and Italy Bamberg acquired two more Halifaxes to take part in the Berlin Airlift. By the early 1950s, however, the general downturn in the charter market had caught up with him and he sold his entire fleet, reportedly saying that he did so as a personal protest against Labour's civil aviation policy.[53]

But probably the best-known aviation entrepreneur of the era is Mr Freddie Laker. A trained engineer, at the end of the war he worked for both BEA and LAMS. In 1947 he founded his own company, Aviation Traders, to buy and sell aircraft and spare parts. When the Allied airlift to Berlin began he bought 12 Halifaxes from BOAC for £42,000 (of which he borrowed £38,000 from a friend); half were operated on the Airlift and half used for spares. With the end of the Berlin emergency, during which he made a handsome profit, Laker correctly saw what was about to happen in the charter market. Unlike most of his contemporaries, therefore, he withdrew completely from air transport operations and instead began buying up some 6,000 surplus aircraft engines and 100 bombers, which he melted down and sold for scrap.[54] The wise investment of the profit was to prove an important factor in financing Laker's later aviation activities.

The charter market remained depressed throughout 1949 and into 1950, then began to pick up. In November 1950, Mr Eric Rylands, as chairman of BACA, commented: "It is becoming abundantly clear that if the independent operators are to survive, a proportion of their work must come either directly or indirectly from the Government".[55] This is exactly what had already begun to happen and was the major factor behind the 1950 recovery. The Korean War, which began in June, gave new opportunities to a number of carriers, as well as pushing up charter rates generally. More important, however, was the beginning of air trooping on a large scale, a development that was to provide the main source of income for the Independents over the next decade or so. In 1950 the Government spent a total of £250,000 on chartering aircraft from the privately-owned airlines; during 1951–2 contracts worth £4.5 million were placed.[56]

Thus, by the end of 1951, after six years of expansion and recession, optimism and gloom, a much slimmer, healthier independent airline industry emerged, one that had achieved a foothold in the operation of scheduled services, could look forward to large, profitable government contracts and, perhaps above all, saw the return to power of a Conservative Government committed "to restoring a wide measure of private enterprise in the air".[57] But the real importance of these six years lies in the fact that out of the political, economic and social disruption of post-war Britain emerged a civil aviation structure that, with its many imperfections and contradictions, was to last for the next 20 years.

NOTES

1. *British Air Transport* (1945, Cmd. 6605).
2. D. Corbett, *Politics and the Airlines* (1965), 105–6.
3. Cmd. 6605, 4.
4. Hansard, House of Commons Debates (hereafter H.C.), 24 Jan. 1946, vol. 418, col. 425.
5. Cmd. 6605, 8.
6. Quoted by J. Longhurst, *Nationalisation in Practice* (1950), 78.
7. *Ibid.*
8. J. C. Cooper, 'Some Historic Phases of British International Civil Aviation Policy', *International Affairs* (April 1947), 198; R. L. Thornton, *International Airlines and Politics* (1970), 126; H. A. Wassenbergh, *Post-War International Civil Aviation Policy and the Law of the Air* (1957), 76.
9. *Economist*, 10 Nov. 1945, 669 and 673; see also Hansard, H.C., 6 May 1946, vol. 422, col. 620.
10. *British Air Services* (1945, Cmd. 6712).
11. P. G. Masefield, 'Some Economic Factors in Air Transport Operation', *Journal of the Institute of Transport* (March 1951), 84–5; Ministry of Information, *Merchant Airmen* (1946), 31–3.
12. BEA Annual Report, 1946–7, 14.

280   THE JOURNAL OF TRANSPORT HISTORY

13. I. Scott-Hill and G. Behrend, *Channel Silver Wings* (1972), 8.

14. Hansard, H.C., 6 May 1946, vol. 422, col. 622.

15. J. H. Frederick, *Commercial Air Transportation* (1961), v.

16. G. Behrend, *Jersey Airlines* (1968), 11.

17. *Flight*, 28 April 1949, 504-6.

18. Masefield, *op. cit.*, 83.

19. J. W. Sundberg, *Air Charter* (1961), 25.

20. F. C. Thayer, *Air Transport Policy and National Security* (1965), 93.

21. R. Miller and D. Sawers, *The Technical Development of Modern Aviation* (1968), 103, 124, and 134.

22. F. A. Laker, 'Private Enterprise in British Air Transport', *Journal of the Royal Aeronautical Society* (1966), 332.

23. Mr Herbert Morrison, Hansard, H.C., 6 May 1946, vol. 422, col. 615.

24. *Aeroplane*, 17 Jan. 1947, 83, and 27 June 1947, 689.

25. *Ibid.*, 15 Aug. 1947, 193-5.

26. *Flight*, 8 Jan. 1948, 48, and 22 Jan. 1948, 90.

27. J. W. Swann, *40 Years of Air Transport in Northern Ireland* (1972), 37-8.

28. *Flight*, 10 Oct. 1947, 433, and 3 Nov. 1949, 581.

29. *Aeroplane*, 14 May 1948, 590.

30. Laker, *op. cit.*, 331.

31. BOAC, *Operation Pakistan* (1948), 1-3.

32. *Ibid.*, *Operation India* (1948[?]), 3-4.

33. BOAC Annual Report, 1947-8, 13.

34. *Aeroplane*, 28 May 1948, 649.

35. H.M.S.O., *Berlin Air Lift* (1949), 6.

36. Sir M. Wyatt, 'British Independent Aviation – past and future', *Journal of the Institute of Transport* (May 1963), 109; R. Rodrigo, *Berlin Airlift* (1960), 44.

37. J. W. F. Merer, 'The Berlin Air Lift', *Journal of the Royal Aeronautical Society* (July 1950), 519.

38. S. F. Wheatcroft, *Air Transport Policy* (1964), 33-4.

39. Corbett, *op. cit.*, 152-3.

40. Ministry of Civil Aviation, *Civil Aviation Report*, 1948-9, 23.

41. *Flight*, 3 Feb. 1949, 129; Hansard, House of Lords Debates (hereafter H.L.), 26 Jan. 1949, vol 160, cols. 350-4.

42. An Air Transport Licensing Authority had been established in 1938 to rationalize domestic air services, but had ceased to function following the outbreak of war (Ministry of Information, *op. cit.*, 30). It is interesting to note that while the ATAC acquired the licensing function almost by accident, its successor, the Air Transport Licensing Board, was principally a licensing body with an incidental consumer function under Section 4 of the 1960 Civil Aviation (Licensing) Act. The Civil Aviation Authority was established in 1972 and combines both functions in yet another way.

43. *Flight*, 4 Jan. 1952, 16-17.

44. *Ibid.*; ATAC Annual Report, 1951, 11-12.

45. Hansard, H.L., 2 Feb. 1949, vol. 160, col. 493.

46. BACA, *A Case for the Independent Air Transport Companies in the UK* (1950), 9.

47. *Economist*, 24 Dec. 1948, 1431-2; *Flight*, 3 Nov. 1948, 581.

48. *Economist*, 19 Jan. 1952, 174.

49. *Ibid.*, 17 June 1950, 1359; the airline continued to operate, on a much reduced scale, as Skyways (1950) Ltd, and was eventually acquired by Mr Eric Rylands' LAC in March 1952.

50. *Flight*, 20 Feb. 1950, 399.

51. *Economist*, 26 Feb. 1949, 381.

52. *Aeroplane*, 29 Sept. 1966, 5. Channel eventually went bankrupt in 1972.
53. J. Jackson, *The Sky Tramps* (1965), 78–9. Eagle closed down for the final time, after a chequered history, in 1968.
54. *Ibid.*, 77–8; TV interview, BBC 1, 8 Oct. 1972.
55. *Flight*, 9 Nov. 1950, 411.
56. Hansard, H.C., 16 July 1952, vol. 503, col. 2157; *Flight*, 16 March 1951, 322.
57. Mr Lennox-Boyd, *Flight*, 16 Nov. 1951, 631.

10 Trooping and the development of the British independent airlines*

B. K. HUMPHREYS

I

URING the 1950s and early 1960s trooping, or the carriage of military personnel and their families to overseas bases and back, played a vital part in the development of U.K. civil aviation, particularly for the private sector. Indeed, it is difficult to overestimate the importance of trooping for the privately-owned U.K. airlines, the so-called 'Independents', during this period.

The immediate post-war years saw the establishment of dozens of small charter airlines, despite the formation of the nationalized Air Corporations with a monopoly of scheduled air services. The charter carriers were supported at first by a general shortage of aircraft capacity and then by the demands of the Berlin Airlift. With the end of the Berlin Emergency, however, the air charter market became extremely depressed, with many operators going out of business. The long-term future of those that survived the short-term upheavals was guaranteed by two developments. Firstly, from 1948 the Government permitted certain independent airlines to operate scheduled services as 'associates' of one of the nationalized Corporations; this was an important political break-through for the Independents, but it would be many years before scheduled services could contribute significantly to the economic strength of the private sector. Far more important in the short and medium terms was the second development, the decision to award large-scale trooping contracts to the airlines.[1]

The first public recognition of the use of civil aircraft for trooping purposes appears to have occurred in August 1950, when Mr Arthur Henderson, Secretary of State for Air, referred in a speech at Plymouth to the use by the R.A.F. of the resources of the privately-owned airlines. He said that charter aircraft were already carrying Royal Auxiliary Air Force squadrons and other units to their training camps in different parts of the U.K. and Germany and he hoped that the scheme would eventually have a much wider application.[2] In a debate in the House of Commons the following May, Henderson elaborated on the scheme, pointing out that some £250,000 had been spent during the previous financial year on the charter of aircraft from both the nationalized and independent airlines. 'I think that it can be regarded as money well spent, not only because of the value of the service received, but also because it has

* The views expressed in this paper arise from work undertaken by the author in the course of his Ph.D research. They do not necessarily reflect the views of his present employer, the Civil Aviation Authority. The author would like to express his gratitude to colleagues within the C.A.A. and to his former supervisor, Professor K. M. Gwilliam, for useful comments.

helped to maintain a valuable and considerable potential represented by the civil aviation industry.'[3]

It must be remembered, of course, that at this stage the carriage of troops by air was still regarded very much as an experimental, marginal exercise; the overwhelming majority of servicemen continued to travel by sea. Nevertheless, not long after Henderson's statement in the House of Commons a number of sizeable trooping contracts were awarded by the Air Ministry to the charter airlines. In mid-1951, for example, Hunting Air Travel obtained what was claimed at the time to be the largest passenger contract ever awarded to an independent transport operator. The agreement provided for the carriage of military personnel and their families between the U.K. and Malta and Gibraltar, involving some 40–50 round trips per month to each destination.[4] Later in 1951 Airwork received an even larger contract, valued at over £1·25 million, for trooping operations between the U.K. and the Middle East.[5]

TABLE I

Trooping Operations by BIATA – Member Airlines, 1950/51–1965/66

Year	Passengers carried	Percentage of total BIATA operations	Passenger-miles performed (000s)	Percentage of total BIATA operations
1950/51	4,926	n.a.	n.a.	n.a.
1951/52	53,786	n.a.	109,120	n.a.
1952/53	88,285	n.a.	192,500	n.a.
1953/54	147,825	n.a.	315,607	n.a.
1954/55	214,594	n.a.	387,546	67
1955/56	204,700	n.a.	522,903	n.a.
1956/57	157,035	n.a.	516,302	n.a.
1957/58	137,821	10	462,604	66
1958/59	142,085	10	419,557	49
1959/60	119,584	8	419,346	50
1960/61	171,138	8	520,346	45
1961/62	314,734	12	564,387	40
1962/63	396,540	14	750,727	49
1963/64	425,362	13	847,893	46
1964/65	156,121	n.a.	646,618	n.a.
1965/66	184,068	n.a.	726,918	n.a.

Note: The table includes the majority of privately-owned airlines, but not all.
n.a.–not available.
Source: British Independent Air Transport Association Annual Reports.

The return to power of the Conservative Party in 1952, with their so-called 'New Deal' policy for civil aviation, gave an added fillip to the Independents' activities. Trooping was singled out as one of the areas of activity particularly well suited to private sector operation. Effectively, both BOAC and BEA were excluded from participation.[6] It is not surprising, therefore, that trooping rapidly established itself as an extremely important source of traffic and revenue for the U.K. independent airlines. By 1955 it accounted for 67 per cent of their total passenger miles (see table 1), and although this figure declined over the following years it remained on average well over 45 per cent until the mid-1960s. The growth in the relative importance of trooping during the early 1950s was matched by a corresponding fall in the amount of general charter traffic carried by the Independents. Government contracts increasingly provided the 'bread and butter' work, so that fewer airlines were forced to chase the low revenue/high risk *ad hoc* charter work. As a result much of this type of traffic was no longer carried by air.

II

There seems little doubt that throughout the 1950s most of the larger privately-owned U.K. airlines remained in business largely as a result of the security provided by trooping contracts. It is not difficult to see why trooping was so attractive to the airlines. It involved the provision of a round-the-year service, unlike holiday flights, with a guarantee that every seat would be filled, unlike scheduled services. In other words, there were no advertising costs, no sales effort, no load-factor problems, no peaks and no cancellations. Furthermore, trooping flights usually took place on weekdays, leaving aircraft free at week-ends for use on holiday charters. All of these attractions, of course, were in addition to the sheer size of the contracts, which were far larger than anything else available to the Independents at this time.

If the airlines' interest in trooping is understandable, the Government's attitude, particularly the strong preference for the Independents rather than the nationalized Corporations, the R.A.F. or the shipping companies, requires further explanation. The decision gradually to replace ships with aircraft was partly a matter of relative cost (see III below). But as with the preference for the airlines over the R.A.F., the country's possible future defence requirements also appear to have been taken into consideration. The strategic importance of civil air transport had been recognized for some time, not least in the United States. President Roosevelt, for example, described the airline industry as a 'reservoir' of men and machines always available for the defence effort.[7] His successor's Air Policy Commission noted in 1947: 'The airlines have a fleet of aircraft of great value to the military services as a reserve in time of war. As a potential military auxiliary the airlines must be kept strong and healthy.'[8]

A very similar attitude was to be found in the U.K., as is illustrated by the following statement by Sir James Barnes, Permanent Under-Secretary of State at the Air Ministry, to a House of Commons' Committee:

The basic reason (for air trooping) was the need to build up a substantial reserve of air transport resources. For example, when the Berlin air lift ceased, the charter companies were threatened with a very serious lack of business. It is also true that the cost of maintaining an air transport reserve of this character in the RAF would be very much greater than the arrangements we are now undertaking. What we have done is to take existing air transport capacity which, without wasting additional capital because it is already there, enables us to indulge in the experiments which we are now undertaking.[9]

The decision to employ primarily the Independents rather than BOAC and BEA may also have been influenced by strategic considerations, particularly after their success during the Berlin Airlift. However, it seems likely that other factors were also of some importance. In particular, trooping contracts were used by the Conservative Government as a means of supporting a fledgeling private sector, in other words as a type of indirect subsidy. This seems the only rational explanation for the exclusion of the nationalized Coroporations from participation in the major contracts, and their inclusion in the early 1960s when the Government felt that the Independents, supported by a much wider range of scheduled services, could stand on their own feet. Such support was perhaps rather ironic in view of the criticism frequently voiced by the privately-owned carriers throughout the 1950s that the State airlines were 'subsidized monopolies'.

Thus, although clear-cut evidence is obviously not available, it seems probable that the Independents received Government support both as a 'stop-gap' while they were establishing themselves on a viable basis and because of their potential strategic value as an air transport reserve. Such support can be regarded as a subsidy to the extent that the Independents received a near-monopoly of a particular area of work which they almost certainly would not have done in the absence of Government action. There is no reason to suppose that the Corporations would not have been willing to take part in what was clearly, at this time, a profitable activity, since by the early 1950s they certainly had suitable obsolescent aircraft available, which were often sold off to the independent carriers. Without trooping work the private sector would have experienced considerable difficulty in establishing an important, and relatively stable, position for itself in the U.K. air transport industry, despite the growth of substantial financial backing from several shipping companies. From the Government's point of view such a policy of indirect support had the added attraction that it cannot really be said to have seriously impaired the development of the State airlines. Finally, mention has already been made of the similarity of trooping developments in the U.S. and U.K. One American commentator has examined the role of the so-called U.S. supplementals (charter airlines) and concluded:

> Simply stated, the facts of the matter have never supported the political image of the supplemental airlines. Their economic history demonstrates they had become largely superfluous by 1947, were sustained only by the Berlin and Korean emergencies, both of which occurred before the U.S. had rebuilt its military strength, and are legal and economic anachronisms almost solely dependent upon Defence Department largesse.[10]

TABLE 2

Volume of Trooping Movements by Sea and Air, Selected Years (000s)

Year	Sea	Air	Total
1950/51	423	18·5	441·5
1954/55	616	172·5	788·5
1958/59	323·5	136·5	460
1959/60	298·5	134·5	433
1960/61	225	174	399
1961/62	115	284*	399
1965/66	5·5	n.a.	n.a.

* = Estimated. NB. These figures are not strictly comparable with those in table 1.

Sources: Select Committee on Estimates: 'Trooping', 1961/62, Evidence, p. 19, and 'The Movement of Service Personnel and Stores', 1966/67, para. 44.

TABLE 3

Expenditure on Troopships, Commercial Sea Passages and Chartered Trooping Aircraft, Selected Years (£000s)

Year	Sea	Air	Total
1954/55	10,560	4,549	15,109
1958/59	7,803	5,574	13,377
1959/60	7,555	3,966	11,521
1960/61	5,694	4,320	10,041
1961/62	4,565	5,478*	10,043
1965/66	1,026	n.a.	n.a.

* = Estimated
Sources: As for Table 2

III

The replacement of sea by air trooping was a gradual development spread throughout the 1950s and early-1960s. By 1951 a total of 21 ships with a combined tonnage of 204,000 gross tons were engaged in trooping operations, 16 owned by the Government and five chartered from private companies. Towards the end of the same year it was estimated that future overseas military commitments would require a trooping fleet of 13 ships. Over the years, except during emergencies, this number was gradually reduced, until by early 1960 the last of the government-owned vessels on long sea voyages was withdrawn. This left five chartered ships, plus three publicly-owned troopships operating between Harwich and the Hook of Holland, a combined tonnage of 92,000 gross tons.[11] The use of troopships was finally discontinued in 1962. Tables 2 and 3 give an indication of the size and time-scale of the transference of trooping operations from sea to air. By the mid-1960s only three classes of passengers were permitted to travel by sea: civilians employed by the Services, the families of Servicemen and senior officers of the equivalent rank of Major-General and above.[12]

In public at least, the main justification given for the increased use of air transport was that it saved both money and time and reduced the number of people in the 'pipeline' at any given moment. There does appear, however, to have been some disagreement over exactly when the financial savings first became evident. For example, as early as 1952 the Secretary of State for Air had claimed that it cost £4 less to fly a Serviceman to the Middle East than to send him by ship.[13] Similarly, Sir James Barnes told the Committee of Public Accounts in the same year: 'I have satisfied myself that in each case they (i.e. air charters as distinct from troopships) are actually cheaper as conditions are now without taking account of the saving of time'.[14] Another Air Ministry witness, on the other hand, later told the Select Committee on Estimates that the cost of air passages did not become generally less than that of sea passages until 1954/55.[15] The only published data available relates to 1960/61 (table 4), and there can have been absolutely no doubt about the financial and operational advantages of air trooping by then.

TABLE 4

Comparison of Costs and Timing of Sea and Air Trooping, 1960/61

Route (U.K. to:)	Approximate cost per passenger (£)			Journey duration (days)	
	Air charter (all categories of personnel)	Troopship		Air charter	Troopship
		(uniformed personnel)	(adult family members)		
Gibraltar	a	2·7 × a	1·2–2·0 × a	1	4
Malta	b	4·1 × b	1·7–2·7 × b	1	8
Cyprus	c	3·4 × c	1·4–2·3 × c	1	11
Aden	d	2·5 × d	1·5–2·5 × d	1	14
Singapore	e	2·1 × e	1·5–2·4 × e	1	23

Notes:

1. Letters substituted for confidential actual figures.

2. Cost per passenger by chartered aircraft includes the estimated cost of separate transportation of unaccompanied baggage.

3. Costs per passenger by troopship exclude the normal cost of messing for uniformed personnel and the cost of food for family members (which was recovered from latter group).

4. Troopship passages for children charged at ¼ to ½ the adult rate according to age.

Source: Select Committee on Estimates: 'Trooping', 1961/62, Evidence, p. 22.

Despite this apparent disagreement about precisely when trooping became cheaper by air than by sea (which may well have reflected differing costing methods), by the mid-1950s the cost advantage of air charters must have been apparent to all. Why then was substantial use still made of troopships? As late as 1959/60 they still accounted for some 69 per cent of total trooping movements. The reason again revolves around estimates of strategic requirements, this time of troopships. For most of the 1950s the maintenance of a sizeable troopship fleet was regarded as vital in case of war. Once this decision had been accepted, the short-term marginal cost of trooping by sea became far more attractive compared with air charter.

It was only with the decline in the envisaged strategic importance of such a reserve fleet, or the growing realization that aircraft would in future be of more significance than surface vessels, that air trooping was able to take over on a large scale. As a memorandum from the Treasury put it: 'So long as it is necessary to keep some troopships to meet possible operational requirements, it is obviously desirable to make the maximum use of them for normal trooping movements.'[16] A similar type of argument was to be used when trooping operations were transferred from the airlines to R.A.F. Transport Command.

IV

Despite their obvious usefulness for the independent operators, trooping contracts also brought problems, and it was not long before the airlines were complaining to the Government and seeking relief. The two principal complaints were the short duration and low revenue yield of most trooping agreements. The problems facing the Independents were strongly emphasized in the report of a civil aviation committee formed in April, 1957, by the Air League of the British Empire under the chairmanship of Sir Miles Thomas:

> The question of low yield from the business conducted by the independent companies is a dominant factor in their present situation. This, coupled with the insecurity of tenure resulting from the extremely short term of the contracts granted by the Government..., has prevented them from obtaining the finance necessary to re-equip their fleets. These at present consist almost entirely of obsolescent aircraft. Indeed, so meagre is the return from the principal source of the independents' revenue that the committee find it difficult to believe that the majority of these companies can continue to operate indefinitely on their present basis of earnings.[17]

To deal first with the question of low revenue yield, table 5 would certainly appear to support the view of the Air League's committee. In terms of revenue per load ton-mile, trooping produced the lowest income of any of the Independents' activities. But at the same time, of course, trooping was a particularly low-cost operation for the reasons already outlined, so that a low-revenue yield was not necessarily synonymous with low profitability. In any case, it is difficult to see what the Government could be expected to do, charged as they were with not only taking account of the airlines' strategic importance, but also with ensuring that taxpayers' money was wisely spent. There was certainly no shortage of bidders for trooping contracts, and if anything was to blame for the low rates paid it was competition among the carriers rather than Government parsimony.

THE BRITISH INDEPENDENT AIRLINES   53

TABLE 5
Sources of the Independents' Revenue, 1955/56

Type of service	Load ton-miles (millions)	Estimated typical revenue rate per load ton-mile (d)	Total revenue (£m)
Trooping	53·8	30	6·725
Charter and contract	35·3	36	5·300
Colonial coach	6·1	45	1·145
Normal international scheduled services	6·4	62	1·650
Vehicle-ferry	4·6	42	0·805
Domestic scheduled services	3·1	54	0·700
Inclusive-tours	2·5	35	0·365
Total	112	—	£17 million

Source: *Flight*, 6 December 1957, 868.

The criticism that contracts were of too short duration to give companies the security they needed to invest in more modern equipment appears to be more valid. Trooping contracts were usually awarded for a period of one year, with a customary (and invariably exercised) option of a further year. The Government was certainly not unaware of the problems this created, and indeed by the early 1960s the period covered by the average contract had increased to almost three years. From the Government's point of view, however, the advantages of short-term contracts were simply too large to give up, as the Estimates Committee reported in 1961/62:

> Your Committee would not expect any economy to result from committing the Air Ministry to longer contracts in the present state of the market. The Treasury do not expect any difficulty in obtaining tenders for contracts of the present length, and your Committee consider that longer contracts would offer no financial advantages and would curb the freedom of the Air Ministry to make new arrangements to meet the changing requirements of the Service departments.[18]

The Government was not, therefore, prepared to come to the Independents' help by awarding significantly longer contracts. But it was sufficiently concerned to attempt to help them more directly in obtaining modern equipment, if only because the lower operating costs of such aircraft would inevitably reduce the overall cost of trooping. Consequently, in 1955 three Britannias were ordered for delivery in 1957/58, with the intention of eventually handing them over to the charter companies. Once the advantages in operating aircraft of this type became evident, it was argued, the airlines would experience less difficulty in raising the necessary finance. Tenders were called for in 1957, with the option of buying the Britannias and obtaining a five-year contract or leasing them under a three-year agreement. The tenders against purchase were in fact very poor, but on the basis of leasing it was estimated that some £1.5 million would be saved annually on the Far East service alone compared with the previous Hermes contracts. Thus, the Government's action in placing orders for the Britannias appeared to be justified.[19]

Unfortunately, things turned out rather differently. Despite the previous complaints about the difficulty of raising capital to finance aircraft acquisition, a few of the larger Independents had in fact managed to purchase modern equipment. Some of these companies, on their own initiative, now quoted for the trooping contracts under consideration on the basis of using their own aircraft, and this resulted in an estimated saving of an additional £250,000 on the routes in question.[20] An example was the Far East trooping contract, awarded to Hunting-Clan, whose principal shareholder, British and Commonwealth Shipping, had financed the purchase of two Britannias. Similarly, Transair obtained the Mediterranean contract largely because it has previously ordered two Viscounts as a 'calculated risk'.[21] 'Since then we have not really been frightfully attracted by the idea of buying aircraft for contractors to buy off us or hire off us'.[22]

V

By the early 1960s the number of airlines engaged in trooping had shrunk dramatically, mainly as a result of the mergers that had taken place in the industry and the run-down of British overseas military bases. There were only three major contractors by 1961/62:[23]

Contract	Operator	Aircraft
U.K.–Singapore/Hong Kong	BUA	Britannia
U.K.–Aden/Nairobi/Cyprus	BUA	Britannia
U.K.–Gibraltar/Malta/North Africa	Cunard Eagle	DC-6
Medair (within the Mediterranean area)	Cunard Eagle	Viking
U.K.–North West Europe	Silver City	Hermes

An important development at this time was the introduction of air trooping to Germany. A trial one-year contract was awarded to Silver City in September 1960, involving about 50 flights (3,500 passengers) a month in each direction.[24] It is interesting to note the way in which Silver City worked out its tender for this contract. According to the airline's Chairman: 'The price at which we tendered for this particular contract was unduly depressed because in fact we had these aircraft as a residual of the past and we quoted a price which in fact did not contain any element of depreciation of the aircraft because we had no use for them sufficient to occupy the time.'[25] This type of marginal pricing was becoming more and more common in tendering for trooping work and was mainly responsible for the depressed, and worsening, revenue rates. The initial German experiment was successful and the following year a contract for the carriage of 11,000 passengers a month, using Viscount aircraft, was awarded to BUA.[26] This finally marked the end of sea trooping on a large scale.

The exclusion of the nationalized airlines from trooping work on the grounds that they had a near-monopoly of scheduled services could not be maintained after the passing of the 1960 Civil Aviation (Licensing) Act. In fact, the Corporations for some time had participated in small-scale *ad hoc* trooping operations that were normally arranged at short notice.[27] However, they wanted permission to carry large numbers of Servicemen and their families on scheduled services at reduced fares and to apply for long-term trooping contracts. At first the Government procrastinated and then referred the Corporation's application to the Air Transport Licensing Board. The ATLB eventually reported that it felt itself unable 'to come to any conclusion or to make any recommendations.'[28] In other words, the problem was rapidly dispatched back to its rightful place with the Government. Finally, in November 1964, the new Labour Minister of Aviation announced that the State airlines' request was to be granted.[29]

Both the Government and the Independents probably expected BOAC and BEA to move into charter trooping on a fairly large scale. Indeed, the Ministry of Defence admitted that it would welcome tenders from new entrants into the field, since by then the contracts were shared by just two airlines. But it later emerged that this was not what the Corporations had in mind at all. They were far more interested in filling up their empty scheduled service seats than in bidding for long-term charter contracts. BOAC stated that it 'had no surplus aircraft for charters', while BEA similarly argued that it did not want to expand its existing fleet for Service charter work.[30] In the event, the rates quoted for seats on scheduled services were not sufficiently competitive, so that the nationalized airlines failed to make any significant impact on the Independents' trooping market. In the first full year of the new scheme's operation, for example, BEA carried only 733 Service passengers at rebated fares, and total revenue earned barely exceeded £8,000.[31] Thus, the Independents on the whole maintained their monopoly of trooping work.

VI

The R.A.F., like the nationalized airlines, had always carried a small proportion of trooping traffic, amounting to some 4-6 per cent of the total by the beginning of the 1960s. The Independents had been worried for some time about the consequences of a possible increase in this percentage. As early as December 1957, the head of one airline mentioned in a speech that he viewed 'with apprehension' the large expansion of Transport Command that would take place with the introduction of 13 new Britannia aircraft.[32] But it was not until the mid-1960s that the R.A.F. began to carry a major part of the traffic. In evidence to the Estimates Committee in 1961 the Air Ministry stated that it had carried out a study of the comparative costs of making increased use for purely routine logistic purposes (i.e. trooping and/or freighting) of the R.A.F.'s Britannia units or of obtaining the same airlift capacity by chartering civil aircraft. The study concluded that charters were in fact more economical.[33]

Nevertheless, the Select Committee recommended 'that when the strength of Transport Command is increased, a higher proportion of its efforts than at present should be devoted to trooping or freighting.'[34] There was indeed a partial move in this direction, particularly following the order for five VC-10s for the R.A.F. in 1961.

By early 1963 Transport Command had already taken over the U.K.–Gibraltar/ Malta services from Cunard Eagle.[35] It appears that at least BUA, who earned some £4 million annually, 55 per cent of its total revenue, from trooping operations, saw the writing on the wall. The airline withdrew from one contract in order to use its VC-10s, previously employed on trooping for a while, on the new South American routes. BUA Chairman, Sir Myles Wyatt, commented in 1964: 'Trooping as a cut-price enterprise had been successful, but for a long time it has been a decreasing proportion of our business and we should like to decrease the proportion still further.'[36]

By the time that the Estimates Committee again investigated trooping, in 1966/67, the R.A.F.'s share of the market had risen to 13 per cent,[37] but this still left the operation as a whole very much in the hands of the civil airlines. The Ministry of Defence informed the Committee that it had established a Working Party to investigate whether Transport Command should undertake a larger proportion of the task. The conclusion reached was that a considerable expansion in air trooping by the R.A.F. was indeed desirable, with the result that the charter airlines would be excluded from virtually all Service movements except those to Germany and 25 per cent of those to the Far East. The estimated net saving that would result from the increased use of Transport Command in this way over the nine-year period, 1968/69 to 1976/77, would amount to some £4·4 million.[38]

Unfortunately, as the Select Committee was quick to point out, the Ministry's costing was defective in many respects. The most serious and revealing shortcoming was the assumption that most of the costs incurred by Transport Command for trooping would be incurred in any case, whether the R.A.F. undertook the work or not.[39] It is not surprising, therefore, that the Select Committee was highly critical of the Ministry of Defence's study: 'the decision largely to abandon trooping by charter in favour of Transport Command was of an order of magnitude too great to undertake without a study of all the relevant consequences and the full costing of Transport Command's operations should have been an important factor in this study'.[40] In complete contrast to its previous report on trooping, the Committee went on to recommend: 'that in considering the future ordering of aircraft for Transport Command . . . the possibility of making more use of the civil capacity of the charter companies and the Air Corporations, and of including them in future contingency plans, should be examined much more closely than hitherto'.[41]

By then, of course, the replacement of the airlines by the R.A.F. was virtually complete, and the process has never been fully reversed. The reasons for this development are complex and not completely clear. It may have partly reflected the changing strategy of defence planners, with increased emphasis being placed on the mobility of a U.K.-based military force rather than on overseas bases. It may have been felt that the need to transport such a force rapidly to trouble spots necessitated the expansion of the R.A.F.'s long-haul capacity. Equally, the fact that the Independents were now in a much stronger position, especially with the growth of their scheduled services and inclusive tour charters, may have been taken into account. However, a further factor also appears to have been of some importance, in fact it may well have been the vital factor in the decision to transfer trooping to the R.A.F., namely the purchase of military VC-10s. Unfortunately, it is extremely difficult to produce much in the way of 'proof', other than circumstantial evidence.

The R.A.F. ordered VC-10s in three separate batches of five, seven and three aircraft. The final purchase was a direct result of the attempt by BOAC to cancel its order for 30 Super VC-10s. Space does not permit a full description of this sorry episode here,[42] but the end result was that BOAC was ordered to take 17 Super VC-10s; to compensate the manufacturer, the British Aircraft Corporation (BAC), the R.A.F. was told to purchase three more VC-10s for its own use.[43] It is far more difficult to tie down the reasons for the previous R.A.F. VC-10 orders. However, it should be remembered that at the time the Government was actively engaged, against some opposition, in promoting a rationalization of the U.K. aircraft-manufacturing industry, and in particular the formation of BAC and Hawker Siddeley. In view of this fact, together with clear evidence of the pressure exerted on BOAC to buy the aircraft and of the doubtful financial position of Vickers and its successor, BAC,[44] it seems highly unlikely that the R.A.F.'s first two orders were placed for purely economic reasons.

Despite previous purchases of Britannias and Comets, the addition of VC-10s to Transport Command's fleet was in fact a major departure from the role it had been performing since the war. For once these aircraft had been ordered, work had to be found for them, which could only mean an increase in the R.A.F.'s trooping activities and a reduction in that of the Independents. As the Select Committee on Estimates remarked:

It is now unfortunately too late for any change in the Ministry's plan to expand Transport Command to be made. In a sense it was already too late for any other system of trooping to be adopted once the decision was taken to buy the new VC-10 for the Services in the numbers then fixed, since some peace-time use for a proportion of the new aircraft's flying time had to be found.[45]

VII

By 1966/67 the main trooping contracts and contractors were as follows:[46]

Contract	Operator	Aircraft
U.K.–Singapore/Hong Kong	British Eagle	Britannia
U.K.–Bahrain/Aden	BUA	VC-10
U.K.–Malta/North Africa and Medair	British Eagle	Viscount
U.K.–North West Europe	BUA	Viscount/BAC 1-11

With BUA gradually withdrawing from trooping, Eagle was left as the major operator in the field, until the R.A.F. took over. On its long-haul trooping commitments Eagle employed six or seven Britannias, plus one or two reserve aircraft kept for *ad hoc* requirements. The eventual withdrawal of Eagle's long-haul trooping contract was a major factor in the airline's bankruptcy in November 1968.[47] By the early 1970s the R.A.F. had taken over virtually all the shrinking long-haul trooping work, leaving a few short-haul contracts to the airlines. Today trooping accounts for a tiny proportion of the Independents' total output.

Thus, trooping was a major factor in the post-war growth of the U.K. independent airlines, probably as important in the 1950s and early-1960s as holiday charters are today. The transfer of trooping from the sea to the air and the use of the airlines rather than the R.A.F. were largely matters of cost, although political and strategic factors also played an important part. But the decision to exclude the nationalized Corporations must have been taken primarily for political reasons. It would appear that trooping was used as an indirect and politically relatively safe means of giving support to a fledgeling private sector in order to allow it to develop sufficiently to provide realistic competition against the publicly-owned carriers. In other words, an evaluation of the economic factors involved was of strictly limited importance.

The same is equally true of the decision to expand Transport Command in the 1960s and deprive the Independents of most of their trooping work. By then, however, the private sector was considerably stronger and more able to stand on its own feet, partly as a result of the 1960 Civil Aviation (Licensing) Act, but mainly because of the growth of short-haul inclusive tour and long-haul affinity group charters. Although the Independents still engage in trooping work, its relative importance is minimal.

NOTES

1. B. K. Humphreys, 'Nationalization and the independent airlines in the United Kingdom, 1945-51', *Journal of Transport History*, NS III no. 4, 265–81.

2. *Flight*, 17 August 1950, 204.

3. Hansard, House of Commons Debates, 6 May 1951, vol. 485, col. 252.

4. *Flight*, 17 August 1951, 207.

5. *Ibid,.* 9 November 1951, 585.

6. B. K. Humphreys, 'The economics and development of the British independent airlines since 1945' (unpublished Ph.D. thesis, Institute for Transport Studies, University of Leeds, 1974), Chapter 3.

7. Frederick C. Thayer, *Air Transport Policy and National Security* (Chapel Hill, 1965), 48.

8. S. F. Wheatcroft, *The Economics of European Air Transport* (1956), 203–4. See also M. E. Posner and J. F. Saganskey, 'Information, politics, and economic analysis: the regulatory decision process in the air freight cases'. *Public Policy*, Spring 1976, 302–5.

9. House of Commons Committee of Public Accounts 1951/52, Evidence, 348. It is interesting to note that even in 1969 the Edwards Committee commented: 'We take it . . . as axiomatic that a country with a strong and efficient air transport industry is strategically better placed than one without, even though it is not to be regarded or financed as part of the defence reserve.' (*British Air Transport in the Seventies*, Cmd. 4018), 12.

10. Thayer, *op. cit*, 98.

11. House of Commons Select Committee on Estimates, 'Trooping', 1961/62, Evidence, 1.

12. House of Commons Select Committee on Estimates, 'The movement of service personnel and stores', 1966/67, para. 46.

13. *Flight*, 5 December 1952, 692.

14. Committee of Public Accounts, *op. cit.*, 343.

15. Select Committee on Estimates, 'Trooping', *op. cit.*, para. 8.

16. *Ibid.*, Evidence, 76.

17. The Air League of the British Empire, *The Future of British Air Transport* (1957), 11.

18. Select Committee on Estimates, 'Trooping', *op. cit.*, para. 8.

19. Select Committee on Estimates, 'The movement of service personnel and stores', *op. cit.*, Evidence, Q. 1225.

20. *Ibid.*

21. *Flight*, 24 April 1959, 588, and 5 July 1957, 29.

22. B. Humphrey-Davies, Assistant Under-Secretary of State (Supply); Select Committee on Estimates, 'The movement of service personnel and stores', *op. cit.*

23. Select Committee on Estimates, 'Trooping', *op. cit.*, 23.

24. *Flight*, 23 September 1960, 522.

25. Select Committee on Estimates, 'Trooping', *op. cit.*, 58.

26. *Flight*, 13 July 1961, 62, and *Aeroplane*, 5 October 1961, 447.

27. Such work accounted for about 5 per cent of total air trooping activity by 1963: *Flight*, 4 April 1963, 456–7.

28. *Ibid.*, 26 September 1963, 532.

29. Select Committee on Estimates, 'The movement of service personnel and stores', *op. cit.*, para. 13.

30. *Ibid.*, para. 14.

31. *Ibid.*, para. 16.

32. *Flight*, 20 December 1957, 969. The number of R.A.F. Britannia aircraft later increased to 20.

33. Select Committee on Estimates, 'Trooping', *op. cit*, Evidence, 96.

34. *Ibid.*, para. 26.

35. *Flight*, 4 April 1963, 456–7.

36. *Ibid.*, 1 August 1963, 158, and 28 May 1964, 889; *Economist*, 28 November 1964, 1051.

37. Select Committee on Estimates, 'The movement of service personnel and stores', *op. cit.*, para. 10.

38. *Ibid.*, paras. 24 and 31.

39. *Ibid.*, paras. 32–4.

40. *Ibid.*, para. 36.

41. *Ibid.*, para. 42.

42. See Select Committee on Nationalized Industries, 'BOAC', 1963/64.

43. Hansard, *op. cit.*, 20 July 1964, vol. 699, cols. 39–49.

44. BOAC had been forced to increase its initial order for the VC-10 from 35 to 45 in 1960 because of the project's serious financial problems.

45. Select Committee on Estimates, 'The movement of service personnel and stores', *op. cit.*, para. 41.

46. *Ibid.*, Evidence, 1.

47. B. K. Humphreys, *op. cit.*, 112–16. Trooping accounted for 55 per cent of Eagle's total output in 1966 and 52 per cent in 1967. In evidence to the Select Committee on Estimates, Mr W. H. Hudson, Eagle's Commercial Director, said: 'When we consider these trooping tenders, they are always contested on what we would call a marginal basis; in other words, you add them on top of what you have got in other activities and they very rarely collect, because of the competitive nature of them, the full overhead allocation': 'The movement of service personnel and stores', *op. cit.*, Evidence, Q. 382.

11 Helicopter airlines in the United States, 1945–75

A. G. PETERS AND D. F. WOOD

THIS study concerns four helicopter airlines operating in the urban regions of New York, Chicago, Los Angeles, and San Francisco. It covers the period from 1945 to 1965 when the industry flourished, and the ten years after the ending of subsidies in 1965. The close of the Second World War made available trained pilots, equipment, and financial resources for the inception of helicopter airlines. Subsidies for development were obtained and when these were ended, somewhat prematurely, the subsidized lines reduced their operations or terminated them.

The idea of a helicopter dates back, as is well known, to Leonardo da Vinci in the fifteenth century.[1] The first helicopter flight was performed in 1907 by a Frenchman, Louis Breguet-Richert, although the machine was not controllable enough for free flight. Later that year another Frenchman, Paul Cornu, successfully flew his twin-rotor machine free of any ground attachment, but for less than a minute.[2] A noteworthy failure that same year was that of a Russian, Igor Sikorsky, whose twin-rotored machine could lift its own weight but not the weight of a pilot. After a second failure in 1910, Sikorsky abandoned helicopters and began building multi-engine airplanes.[3] In 1917 he emigrated to the United States, and later founded a successful seaplane manufacturing company.

A Spanish aeronautical engineer, Juan de la Cierva, developed a half-airplane, half-helicopter craft in 1923. Calling it the Autogyro, Cierva mounted four unpowered rotors on top of a stub-wing airplane fuselage. A short take-off run sent the rotors windmilling and the craft took off.[4] In the 1930s, Cierva perfected the autogyro, whilst dismissing the helicopter as a complicated, impractical machine. An American autogyro manufacturer, Kettget, and Eastern Airlines combined to win an airmail contract in Philadelphia in 1939. The single seat 225 horsepower Kettget KO-1 flew from the roof of the downtown Philadelphia Post Office to Camden Airport, six miles away. Eastern operated the service, five round trips a day, until the Second World War caused its cancellation.

Igor Sikorsky, who never lost interest in helicopters, developed and flew the first practical helicopter just before the Second World War. In 1940, the U.S. Congress appropriated $3,000,000 for the Army Air Corps to develop rotary-wing aircraft.[5] By 1943 helicopters were used in military operations, and by the end of the War some 4,000 Sikorsky helicopters were in military service. The role the War played in the development of conventional airline aviation is fairly well known, but it played an even more important part in the development of helicopter airlines since, before the War, helicopters were only experimental aircraft.

Military applications of the helicopter comprised artillery-spotting, search and rescue, carriage of troops and supplies, and submarine surveillance. Autogyros, which required a longer take-off and landing area than helicopters, dropped out of use. Technologically they were a 'cross' or compromise between helicopters and conventional airplanes, but they apparently produced more disadvantages than advantages.

The helicopter's most impressive attribute was its ability to operate in and out of small areas. In January 1944, a helicopter was used to rush blood plasma to a group of blast victims who could not be quickly reached by other types of transport. Describing the operation, the *New York Times* said: 'It was indeed routine for the strange rotary-winged machine which Igor Sikorsky has brought to practical flight, but it shows in striking fashion how the helicopter can make use of tiny landing areas in conditions of visibility which make other types of flying impossible.'[6]

The 'tiny landing areas' were in contrast to the needs of conventional aircraft. Even before the Second World War, there were differences of opinion in the United States about the desirable size of airports. At a regional meeting of the National Resources Board held in Omaha, Nebraska, in 1940, a discussion panel of representatives from ten states split when answering the question: 'In carrying out a long-term airport program, which would be more advisable in any one year: (a) completion of a small number of airports; or (b) completion of portions or units of a greater number of airports?'[7] At the same meeting, A. B. McMullen, then chief of the airports section of the U.S. Civil Aeronautics Authority, observed: 'The biggest job we have is telling them local airport people why their airports are not big enough'.[8]

Large conventional aircraft require large and expensive airports, and sites for them can usually be found only at some distance from a city's downtown area. From any given fund, large airports must mean fewer. To many people, it appeared that commercial aviation in the post-War period would follow the pattern just cited: large airports, few in number, and some distance from the city's centre. These large airports would accommodate larger commercial versions of wartime aircraft.

A small group of individuals, however, believed that the helicopter could be developed to complement the conventional airplane/airport system that has just been described. Initially their interest was in carrying mail, later they would carry passengers. Eventually their principal function would be to collect and distribute passengers who were also flying on major airlines. The remainder of this paper describes the four helicopter airlines which operated in the United States.

LOS ANGELES AIRWAYS

During the Second World War, Clarence M. Belinn, an experienced engineer and airline maintenance man, decided that the developing helicopter would be the vehicle to fulfil his dream for collection and distribution of mail over the vast and growing Los Angeles area. He recognized that it would be some time before the machine would be available commercially, and only after the War had ended. He formed a company, Los Angeles Airways (LAA), and 'to get his foot in the door' he filed two applications in 1944 with the U.S. Civil Aeronautics Board (CAB). One was to operate an integrated airplane and limousine service in the Los Angeles area until suitable helicopter equipment was available. This petition was denied. In 1947, the CAB approved the other application to serve as a true helicopter airline. Los Angeles Airways received a three-year Certificate of Public Convenience and Necessity and a subsidy grant to operate the world's first scheduled helicopter airline.[9]

There were many problems involved in being the first helicopter airline. The first was the lack of existing governmental safety regulations for helicopter operations. There were, for example, no minimum weather regulations, or operating altitudes for helicopters over congested areas. All regulations had been drawn up for conventional aircraft operations. There were no trained commercial helicopter crews, only ex-military personnel who were unfamiliar with the operational standards of an airline. On the other hand, if fixed-wing airline experience were to be the standard for employment, then the helicopter airline might not develop its unique advantages and it would become just another airline. With a small group of enthusiasts, Belinn worked to solve these problems.

On 1 October 1947, LAA inaugurated service from the roof of the downtown Los Angeles Post Office Annex to Los Angeles International Airport with Sikorsky S-51s. The S-51 provided seats for three plus the pilot. The LAA certificate and subsidy covered only mail service over four routes. These were: Segment 'A', the congested San Fernando Valley; Segment 'B', the San Gabriel Valley and most of the cities between Los Angeles and San Bernardino; Segment 'C', not opened until 1949, which covered the coastal area south of Los Angeles Airport through Whittier and Long Beach to Santa Ana; and Segment 'S', the shuttle between the Los Angeles Post Office and the airport.

LAA's new service was a success. Not only did the volume of mail far exceed the Post Office Department projections, but LAA was unable to carry all the mail tendered it.[10] To deal with the heavy volume, the company purchased four Sikorsky S-55 helicopters in 1955. These machines were the civilian version of an Army 10-passenger, two-man crew helicopter. The airline converted the aircraft to a seven-passenger,

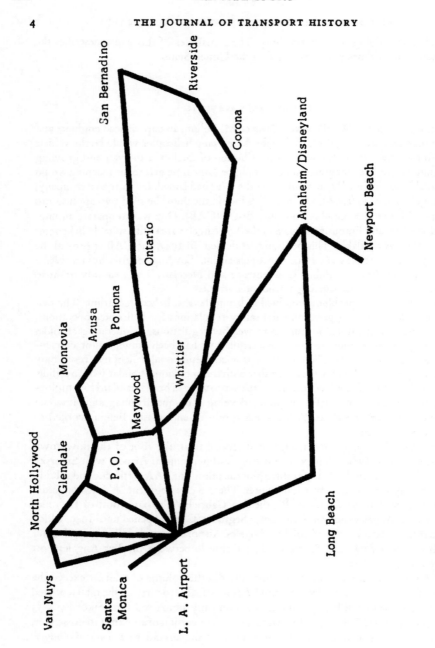

LOS ANGELES AIRWAYS
1960

10 Miles

single-pilot plus cargo, configuration. It cruised at 85 mph. The downtown Post Office shuttle operated 42 flights a day at its peak level of service.

While the growing airline did not carry passengers, there was space for them. LAA's mail service pattern had heavy traffic in the early morning out of the Los Angeles Airport to the suburbs and little, if any, traffic on the return. By midday the traffic was moderate in both directions. By evening the morning pattern was reversed with air mail posted after business hours being picked up in the suburbs and flown to Los Angeles International for connecting overnight flights to the North and East. Potential passenger traffic could operate in the reverse of the mail traffic since travellers in the outlying areas would want to go from home to the airport in the morning and from the airport towards home in the evening. Belinn, however, wanted to avoid carrying passengers. He felt that carrying people would require more employees and hence higher costs in an industry already plagued with high costs. Accordingly, when Los Angeles Airways did expand it attempted to develop more cargo business. It started Air Express service on all its routes except the Post Office shuttle.

The company met the demand of the ever-increasing mail volume, and under pressure from the government to expand into passenger business, eventually started passenger service in November 1954. While this meant merely allowing passengers on the mail and express flights, Los Angeles Airways found enough demand to warrant passenger- and baggage-only flights to popular close-in points such as Anaheim-Disneyland. By 1956 LAA had 72 daily flights, 17 of which carried passengers, to a total of 16 cities. Its seven-passenger S-55s had a direct operating cost of 29¢ per seat mile. Adding indirect costs, the total became about 50¢ per seat mile. LAA had hoped to bring this cost down to 8¢ per seat mile when its newly ordered twin-turbine Sikorsky S-61Ls arrived in 1960, but later the airline admitted it would be willing to settle for a figure closer to 16¢ per seat mile. In 1962, LAA finally began receiving its S-61Ls, 28-passenger craft adapted from Navy anti-submarine helicopters. With a crew of two pilots and a flight attendant, the S-61L could carry a full load of passengers, plus baggage, mail, and express loaded in its under-floor compartments, at 150 miles per hour. Business boomed as the giant helicopters were added to the fleet. LAA's passenger traffic more than doubled in 1963 over 1962.[12] LAA's passenger fare yield was 18¢ per mile, but subsidy was still necessary.

At this time, two other helicopter airlines, discussed below, were also receiving subsidies and operating in the New York and Chicago regions. Helicopter airline officials, manufacturers, and the CAB had all believed – or at least hoped – that subsidies would be necessary only for that 'generation' of airline helicopters and that markets would grow to the point where the next 'generation' of equipment would be on such a scale that it would reduce operating costs below revenue. The CAB had planned to continue subsidies on a diminishing scale, ending in 1970.[13]

However, in 1963, San Francisco Oakland Airlines (SFO), which had been organized in 1962 by five former Los Angeles Airways' executives, applied for a permanent helicopter airline certificate without an accompanying request for subsidy. In its certification hearings, SFO used Los Angeles Airways as an example of inefficiency. Los Angeles Airways, said SFO, was charging only 16·8¢ per seat mile, which cost 40·3¢ a seat mile to provide. Further, said SFO, LAA, to break even on both its S–61 and S–55 operations, needed 20·5 passengers, while LAA's average flight had only 8·6 seats available.[14] Other points brought out were equally unkind.

SFO got its certificate, but the damage had been done. Congressional cost cutters, eager to end helicopter airline subsidies, now gained a new weapon – an operating helicopter airline that did not need and did not want government funds. Within two years the congressional opponents of helicopter airline subsidies managed to convert a majority of their colleagues and in mid-1965 subsidy payments to the Los Angeles, New York, and Chicago helicopter airlines ceased. All three airlines were to find, however, that there was no substitute for subsidy.

Belinn signed agreements with United and American Airlines for guaranteed loans and the underwriting of certain flights. In exchange, LAA agreed to continue terminating the bulk of its flights at United's terminal at Los Angeles International Airport. LAA also agreed to route certain flights to American's airport terminal. The trunk airlines reasoned that they would gain additional passengers because of better connections to and from LAA's helicopter flights. The underwriting cost was viewed by these trunk airlines as a form of promotional expense.[15]

Los Angeles Airways, however, was still hit hard by the subsidy cutback. All of the non-passenger flights were discontinued. The last of the S–55s was withdrawn from service. Mail and express only heliports were dropped. The passenger business did grow rapidly and in 1967 and 1968 LAA added some later-model S–61Ls. The biggest growth area was Anaheim–Disneyland, where the major part of the traffic was not, as one might think, tourists to Disneyland, but businessmen living in the rapidly growing Orange County suburbs. By 1968 Anaheim had 60 flights daily and was boarding over 1,000 passengers each day.

In the late 1960s the trunk airlines slowly withdrew their support of LAA as their own cost problems developed. Tragedy struck in 1968 when, within one month, LAA suffered two fatal, but unrelated accidents. After a brief shutdown to determine the cause of the mishaps, LAA began service again, but with only a small fraction of its former patrons.

LAA also experienced other troubles in the late 1960s stemming from competition. Several commuter airlines using air taxi certificates and small, conventional aircraft like the 17-passenger DeHavilland Twin Otter able to operate into and out of short runways, were starting up at points near LAA heliports and draining some of the traffic to and from the Los Angeles International Airport.[16] By 1970 LAA had decided to join the competition to a certain extent by operating a pair of 17-passenger Twin Otter jet-props to Ontario and San Bernardino, two of its longer routes. Trouble struck again in the form of a six-month pilots' strike. Only three months after the strike ended, Los Angeles Airways ceased operations, in October 1970.

NEW YORK AIRWAYS

New York Airways (NYA) was incorporated in 1949. After receiving its certificate from the CAB it began scheduled mail-only service between the three major New York airports – La Guardia, New York International, and Newark – on 15 October 1952. Using Sikorsky S-55s, eight round trips per day were made between 7 a.m. and 3.45 p.m. In December, NYA extended its service to Westchester County and into Connecticut. Early in 1953, NYA began freight service, and using Los Angeles Airways' experience, started night operations. Schedules were increased to 16 flights daily.[17] In July 1953, NYA became the first helicopter airline in the world to operate scheduled passenger service. The service was so successful that passengers were being wait-listed for flights after the service was only a few weeks old.

The East Coast weather was never kind to NYA, and at one point the flight completion factor was only 29 per cent,[18] but despite the ever-present weather problems, the airline grew. The mid-1950s saw the start of air express service and a helicopter-plus-fixed-wing joint fare agreement signed with Northwest Airlines set a precedent. A Manhattan heliport at West 30th Street on the Hudson River was opened. NYA's load factor climbed to over 50 per cent.

NYA received the first S-58 helicopters from Sikorsky in 1956. The 12-passenger, two-pilot S-58s were the civilian version of a machine developed for the Navy. These 98 mph machines were put on the inter-airport shuttle. In 1958, NYA turned in its Sikorsky fleet for five Vertol V-44Bs. These twin-rotor, single-engine helicopters carried 15 passengers and a two-man crew at a cruising speed of 120 mph. Poor weather still caused cancellations of nearly 25 per cent of NYA's flights, and the airline still needed subsidy to operate.[19]

In the early 1960s New York Airways announced that it had developed plans for an economic helicopter airline operation. These plans had four important factors:

1. The purchase of the twin-rotor Vertol V-107, the *first* helicopter designed specifically for commercial use. This high speed (155 mph), high capacity (25 passenger) aircraft would be more productive than previous aircraft.
2. The V-107s would have twin-turbine engines permitting lower maintenance costs.
3. NYA was working with a British firm to install in the New York area a helicopter navigation system. This plus the twin-engine reliability of the 107s would place NYA's flight completions in the 97-98 per cent area of the conventional airlines.
4. NYA had made an agreement to provide direct service to populous mid-town Manhattan, with a roof-top heliport on the 59-story Pan Am Building.

It was none too soon, since the SFO helicopter certification hearings were giving publicity to the fact that NYA was the most costly helicopter airline. SFO showed that NYA's revenues covered only 36 per cent of its costs and its seat-mile costs were 60·38¢, more than 50 per cent higher than the two other subsidized helicopter airlines.[20]

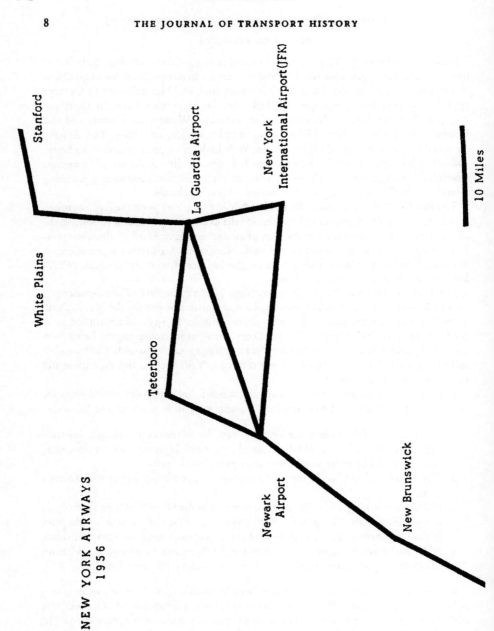

Federal subsidies ended for NYA in mid-1965. Two international carriers, Pan Am and TWA, agreed to underwrite some of NYA's flights. Service to the Pan Am Building Heliport was started in the same year and Pan Am purchased three V-107s and leased them to NYA. Pan Am Building traffic was impressive, 300,000 passengers in the first 12 months. In 1966 NYA achieved the highest load factor for a helicopter airline, 65 per cent, but its break-even load factor was even higher, an astronomical (and impossible) 225 per cent.[21] The underwriting airlines became alarmed at NYA's increasing inability to cover costs and, faced with cost problems of their own, started withdrawing support.

As losses mounted in the late 1970s, NYA tried substituting two Twin Otters for the costly helicopters between the three airports. Despite the use of STOL runways, the Otters suffered great delays in the congested New York air traffic lanes. Traffic dropped over 50 per cent.[22] In 1969, Pan Am and NYA entered into an agreement where Pan Am would buy 44 per cent of NYA stock with an option for more shares later. In exchange, Pan Am agreed to lease to NYA some hangar space and three Sikorsky S-61Ls.

By late 1970, with NYA's all S-61 fleet operating and the V-107s in mothballs, the firm advertised '30–30 service', 30 seats every 30 minutes. The result was a break-even load factor down to 55 per cent while the load factor was up to 48 per cent. Even better was its mechanical reliability factor – over 99 per cent. Flight completion factor, despite loss of the British Decca Navigation System which was suspended with the V-107s, was up to 91 per cent.[23] As at the time of writing (1975) NYA is still in business, operating at a scale somewhat less than its former peak and apparently on its way toward becoming a viable carrier.

CHICAGO HELICOPTER AIRWAYS

Chicago Helicopter Airways (CHA) was formed in 1946. It was initially known as Helicopter Air Service and organized to provide mail service within the Chicago area. It started service on 20 August 1949 with three daily flights to 34 suburban heliports along three routes, plus 18 daily shuttles from Midway Airport to the roof of the downtown general post office. Its first equipment was six Bell-47s, a two-seat helicopter. With one seat and other gear removed heavy mail loads could be carried in two specially-designed saddle boxes. Helicopter Air Service used the same operations programme as LAA had developed, namely four aircraft on the mail schedule, one on stand-by in case of mechanical trouble and one in the hangar for maintenance. While this assured reliable service, fleet utilization was low.

In 1956, HAS changed its name to Chicago Helicopter Airways, acquired three Sikorsky S-55s and started passenger service between the two major airports, O'Hare and Midway, with 16 flights a day. In 1957, CHA added Meigs Field, a small but convenient Chicago lakefront airport in the downtown area. Later in the year it received three 12-passenger S-58s to help handle the growing traffic and extended

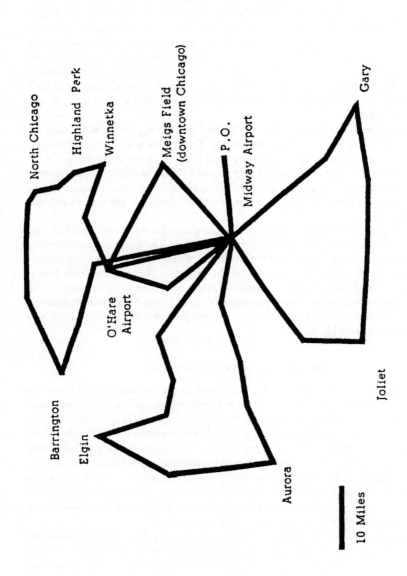

CHICAGO HELICOPTER AIRWAYS
1960

service to suburban heliports in Winnetka, Illinois, and Gary, Indiana. By 1958, CHA was carrying over 108,000 passengers, making it, in only two years, the largest passenger-carrying helicopter airline. The load factor was still low, only 37 per cent.

CHA ordered two more S-58s and traded in the last of its S-55s. It increased its daily flights from 86 to 103.[24] Four Bell-47s were retained for the mail-only routes. In 1959, CHA passenger loads increased to 90 per cent above 1958 figures and the load factor soared to 51 per cent despite an increase of flights to 158 daily. CHA received one more S-58 and ordered two more. The intra-airport traffic was booming with the coming of jets to O'Hare.

By 1960, CHA operated over 200 flights with eight S-58s hauling over 309,000 passengers, an increase of 34 per cent over 1959's 204,000. However, the major airlines began transferring more and more of their operations to O'Hare with the intention of eventually operating from only one airport. CHA suffered a fatal accident, the first ever in helicopter airline history. CHA still had, however, a 53 per cent load factor. Its costs were down to 30¢ per seat mile. CHA said it could break even on the O'Hare, Midway, Meigs triangle, but wanted to continue to develop the mail and suburban routes. The Gary and Winnetka routes suffered badly from directional imbalance. Big loads to the city in the morning and away from the city in the evening kept the load factor down around 35 per cent.

Throughout the early 1960s, CHA's traffic and overall business declined. In 1962, Midway Airport was shut down for all regular airline operations. CHA sold and leased some S-58s, took in maintenance and flight training contracts, and even performed 'traffic 'copter' services for law enforcement agencies and radio stations. It operated only 34 daily airline flights. After federal subsidies ended in mid-1965, CHA was unsuccessful in finding any trunk operators willing to underwrite its operations. On 1 January 1966, CHA ceased scheduled operations. (In 1969 it resumed limited service with 14 flights per day on a Monday–Friday schedule, but this was also unprofitable.) The firm is still alive, but performs non-airline helicopter services.

SAN FRANCISCO–OAKLAND HELICOPTER AIRLINES

San Francisco–Oakland Helicopter Airlines (SFO) was started by former executives from Los Angeles Airways. They observed in detail the turbine-powered Sikorsky S-62 which Los Angeles Airways had leased to give flight crews turbine experience before LAA took delivery of the S-61Ls. The S-62, a 10-passenger single-turbine craft, was amphibious and weighed under 12,500 pounds. The five decided that the S-62 was a low-cost helicopter with an important safety factor, water-landing capability, necessary for operating in an area such as San Francisco.[25]

Incorporated in January 1961, SFO began flying two S-62s under an Air Taxi Certificate on 1 June 1961, between its namesake airports and heliports in downtown Oakland and San Francisco. A third heliport was opened in Berkeley. The San Francisco area was ideal for helicopter operations. It had the geographic barriers of

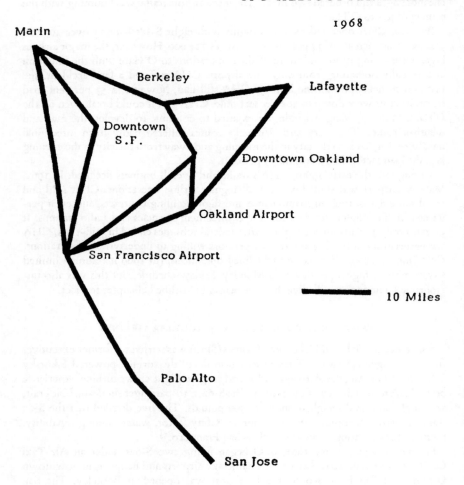

SFO HELICOPTER AIRLINES

1968

the Bay and the hills. These created narrow traffic corridors that would be as heavily travelled as Los Angeles' in the years to come. And it had two competing airports, like Chicago. The SFO management planned to operate SFO with the low cost levels of LAA, but with fare yields similar to NYA. Relatively high fares could compete with taxi fares because of the circuitous routing required by the geographic barriers.

The firm hoped to show that an adequate, if only slightly profitable, operation could be developed using the S-62 without subsidy. Having proved that, SFO would apply to the CAB for a permanent certificate in contrast to the temporary certificates of the subsidized carriers. The permanent certificate would permit large-scale financing and allow SFO to buy Sikorsky S-61s.

SFO's traffic grew well in the first years of operation, but defects in the new S-62s kept both costs and flight cancellations high. The directional imbalance of traffic was much higher than anticipated. Oakland Airport, although the biggest revenue point on SFO's system, put pressure on airlines to add new jet service at Oakland. This airport competition hurt SFO since it reduced the number of travellers who had to travel between the two airports.

In 1962 SFO, operating three S-62s with 100 flights a day, carried 104,000 passengers, and with a 34 per cent load factor after less than two years of operation, was the second largest passenger carrier in the industry, second only to NYA. It applied to the CAB for a permanent certificate.

During the CAB's 1963 hearings, SFO demonstrated that it was the most efficient helicopter operator with an aircraft utilization of 5 hours 27 minutes revenue hours per aircraft per day. This compared with the other carriers' average of less than 3 hours per day. SFO pointed out that while its load factor was low it was growing. Even if the other operators could get their load factors to an impossible 100 per cent, they still could not make a profit. SFO, on the other hand, needed only a little over 50 per cent to break even.[26]

In late 1963, the CAB granted SFO its permanent certificate. Its mail service, begun 12 months earlier on an interim basis, became a permanent part of SFO operations. No special mail routes were started; SFO received straight mail pay with no subsidy, and it carried the mail only on regular passenger flights. In 1964, SFO added another heliport (in Marin County), Air Express service, and a fourth S-62. Traffic increased moderately and the company cut its annual loss to $187,000, or half the loss of 1963.

SFO acquired a fixed-wing overhaul and repair company. This operation was promptly put on a profitable basis and helped cut the overall company losses. Moreover, by merging the helicopter maintenance with the fixed-wing operation SFO gained access to specialized shops and repair facilities that it could not otherwise have afforded.[27]

In 1965, SFO signed loan and assistance agreements with TWA and American Airlines guaranteeing a $9,000 monthly profit if certain cost levels were held. It opened new service to Contra Costa County heliport and to the Palo Alto and San José airports. It acquired three second-hand amphibious Sikorsky S-61Ns, each seating

26 passengers. The new fleet required a cut in service to 88 daily flights to keep capacity in line with traffic.

Under a federal demonstration grant, SFO also operated a pair of turbine-powered, British-built hovercraft in San Francisco Bay between the San Francisco and Oakland airports and between a hoverport in downtown San Francisco and the Oakland Airport. The project found the air cushion machine was operationally feasible, but its small size made it vulnerable to high wind and waves. Its operating costs were similar to the S-62.[28]

SFO continued to do well. Its load factor went up to 39 per cent in 1967 while break-even declined to 49 per cent. The flight completion factor hit a new high of 97·6 per cent. A fourth S-61 was acquired. The S-61s were improving service and business increased. The fixed-wing maintenance service prospered because of the U.S. involvement in South-East Asia, and this heavy volume of military maintenance gave SFO its first year of profit in 1967.

However, the war tapered down, and so did the maintenance business. SFO's employees began unionizing while, at the same time, a sluggish economy reduced patronage. The firm changed management. Several routes were dropped and the maintenance business was discontinued. These cutbacks were not enough, and on 1 August 1970, the firm placed itself in voluntary bankruptcy. Under court guidance, SFO cut its service back to two routes, disposed of several helicopters, and continued in operation (see addendum).

SUMMARY

So the era of the helicopter airlines virtually came to an end. The maps show the four airlines' most extensive routes. Two of the airlines ceased operations, whilst the other two continue on very limited routes. The surviving operations are in the New York and San Francisco regions and the reason for their survival may be that the respective areas they serve contain many water barriers to conventional surface transport.

Why did the helicopter airline experiment not succeed? The answer is the extremely high cost of operating helicopters and helicopter airlines. Helicopters are expensive to buy; their limited market keeps production costs per unit high. They are also expensive to operate: the lowest seat-mile cost the subsidized operators could claim was 30¢.[29] In reality, this figure was nearly doubled because of the acute imbalance of airport traffic - i.e. in the morning there was traffic to airports but nothing in return; the evenings reversed the pattern.

Why were subsidies ended? Helicopter airline passengers had high incomes; it was difficult to justify taxing the masses for their benefit. One congressional critic of the subsidy program said: 'I don't think there should be a general tax on 999 people in a thousand who do not use them so that one person, being among the most affluent in this society, can use them.'[30] The limited number of helicopter airlines resulted in an inadequate geographic political base to 'lobby' for additional federal subsidies.

This article was written to describe a brief episode in transport history. It depended upon conventional airline markets, because the helicopter ride was but one short leg at either end of a long air journey. Taking the helicopter ride was dependent upon the decision to take the long trunk journey; the reverse does not hold. In the post-war United States a particular combination developed of airline aircraft, air navigation aides, airports, and ground transportation links to reach these airports. Had a different 'mix' of these four developed, the helicopter airline's usefulness might have altered. If there had been a larger market for helicopter airline aircraft, the average cost of building each helicopter would have been less.[31]

How would the story have ended if subsidies had been continued? Presumably, all four helicopter airlines would still be in operation. The proposed 1970 cut-off date for the subsidy programme would probably have been unfortunate. All airline business was then in the doldrums. Many of the trunk and international carriers were suffering from financial problems and it is unlikely that they could have aided the helicopter airlines. Businesses whose employees flew tightened up on employee travel expenditures, and this would have hit helicopter airline travel especially hard. It should be remembered that 1970 was the year that the SFO went into bankruptcy. So perhaps the story would have ended in much the same way. Like supersonic transport, the airline helicopter represents an exciting technological development whose commercial market has not yet come.

NOTES

1. Richard G. Hubler, *Straight Up* (New York, 1961), 14–15.
2. Charles Gablehouse, *Helicopters and Autogyros* (New York, 1967), 12–13.
3. *Ibid.*, 14.
4. *Ibid.*, 35–41.
5. Charles L. Morris, *Pioneering The Helicopter* (New York, 1945), 27.
6. Cited in Morris, *op. cit.*, 151.
7. *Proceedings, North Central Regional Aviation Planning Conference* (held at Omaha, Nebraska, 23–4 March 1940, sponsored by The Omaha Office of the U.S. Natural Resources Planning Board), 68–9.
8. *Ibid.*, 60.
9. Los Angeles Airways Traffic Manual (Los Angeles Airways, 1956), 1001: 1–2.
10. *Ibid.*, 1001: 9.
11. Hubler, *op. cit.*, 148.
12. Civil Aeronautics Board, *Handbook of Airline Statistics* (Washington: Government Printing Office, 1971), 148.
13. *New York Times*, 26 January 1965, 1.
14. San Francisco-Oakland Helicopter Airlines, *Application before the Civil Aeronautics Board Docket 12029, et al.*, 1963, Exhibit SFO 212 (h), 1.
15. Arthur G. Tobey, Vice-President, Operations, SFO Helicopter Airlines in a personal interview, 15, 20 November 1972.
16. This type of aircraft is called STOL for Short Take Off and Landing.

17. Hubler, *op. cit.*, 161.

18. *Ibid.*, 163.

19. New York Airways, *1959 Annual Report*, 8.

20. San Francisco-Oakland Helicopter Airlines, *op. cit.* 212.

21. New York Airways, *1971 Annual Report*, 3-4.

22. Martin Schnebel of New York Airways in a personal interview, 14 November 1972 and 2 April 1972.

23. New York Airways, *1971 Annual Report*, 1.

24. Chicago Helicopter Airways, *1958 Annual Report*, 3-5.

25. San Francisco-Oakland Helicopter Airlines, *Annual Report 1961*, 3.

26. SFO Application, *op. cit.*, Exhibit SFO 211, 3.

27. Arthur Tobey, personal interview, 16 November 1972.

28. John L. Lambert, *Air Cushion Vehicle Mass Transportation Demonstration Project* (Washington: U.S. Department of Housing and Urban Development, 1967), 71-2.

29. *New York Times*, 10 March 1965, 81.

30. Statement of Senator William Proxmire, cited in *New York Times*, 12 March 1965, 66.

31. See David S. Lawrence: 'Airports Again: Access or Avoidance?', *Traffic Quarterly* (January 1970), 5-20, for a presentation of the viewpoint that resources would be better spent for helicopter rather than conventional aircraft systems.

ADDENDUM

In 1976, after a strike by mechanics, the San Francisco Helicopter operation announced its intention to go out of business. As of the writing of this addendum (November 1976) its helicopter operations have ceased.

12 A short history of London's airports

P. W. BROOKS

L ONDON's airports—that is to say, aerodromes which have been used by scheduled air services since the start of civil aviation in 1919—have had an eventful history. The following account is concerned primarily with the nine aerodromes near London which have handled scheduled commercial services during these 38 years.[1] It does not seek to record the history of all London's aerodromes, of which there have been something like seventy within 25 miles of Hyde Park Corner. Less than a third of this number remain in operation today, and only two, London Airport (at Heathrow) and Croydon, are used by scheduled airlines. A third, Gatwick, is now undergoing extensive development and is expected to replace Croydon and to be again handling scheduled traffic from 1958.

The radius of 25 miles taken as defining the London area has no special significance except as an approximate, if somewhat arbitrary, boundary to the London "commuting area". It happens, however, to include all the important airports which have served London to date. There are several aerodromes outside this radius—Stansted, Luton, White Waltham, Blackbushe, Farnborough, and West Malling—which are usually regarded as part of London's complex of aerodromes. Of these, Blackbushe has been used for scheduled operations by some private operators in recent years (notably the Hunting-Clan and Airwork "Safari" services) but it remains primarily an alternate for flights diverted from London Airport. Luton is believed to have also been used for a few scheduled operations between the wars.

THE BEGINNINGS

Commercial air transport did not start in this country until 25 August 1919, when the official ban on international civil flying imposed during the First World War was finally lifted. The first scheduled flying in the London area had, however, taken place nearly eight years earlier.

In September 1911 an experimental air mail service was run for $2\frac{1}{2}$ weeks between Hendon aerodrome and a field at Windsor, both points being within our defined "London area". The purpose of this service, which was operated by the Grahame-White Aviation Co. Ltd, using two Bleriot monoplanes and a Farman biplane, was to commemorate the coronation of King George V, to raise money for charity, and to demonstrate the possibilities of the aeroplane as a means of transport. It succeeded admirably in these objectives and also qualified Hendon as the precursor of all London's airports. In addition, Hendon shares with Brooklands the distinction of being the oldest and most famous of London's original aerodromes. With Farnborough, Leysdown (in the Isle of Sheppey), and Larkhill (on Salisbury Plain), these two were among the five "nurseries" of British aviation.

Hendon featured, late in 1918, in the first scheduled transport flying undertaken by the newly formed Royal Air Force. At the end of the war, a communications flight at Hendon was expanded into a squadron and then into a wing, No. 86 (Communication) Wing. From January to September 1919, this R.A.F. unit operated a scheduled service to Paris with Airco D.H.4 and 4A and Handley Page 0/400 aircraft to provide rapid transport for delegates and mails to the Peace Conference. The service ran initially from Hendon, but the London terminal was shifted in May 1919 to Kenley R.A.F. station, on the high ground near Caterham in Surrey. Kenley continued to be used until the service closed down at the end of the summer.

Hendon had associations with scheduled commercial air transport as soon as this began towards the end of that same summer of 1919. As works aerodrome of the Aircraft Manufacturing Company Ltd, parent organization of Aircraft Transport and Travel Ltd—Britain's first airline—Hendon was the base but not the operating terminal for the first civilian scheduled services. Later, from 7 October 1919, a weekly scheduled service was operated from Hendon to Amsterdam (clearing customs at Hounslow) by another company, British Aerial Transport Co. Ltd, but this service ceased by the end of the year and was therefore hardly sufficient to qualify the famous aerodrome as one of London's airports. Neither Hendon nor Kenley, although they have survived as R.A.F. stations, has been used again for scheduled services. It was recently announced that Hendon is soon to be finally closed as an aerodrome.[2]

HOUNSLOW HEATH (1919–20)

Beneath the approach funnel of "28 Left", one of the two parallel main runways at London Airport today, lies an area of rough grass which 38 years ago was London's first civil airport. Hounslow Heath had at one time been a cavalry training ground which was brought into regular use as a Royal Flying Corps aerodrome in 1914. Before that, it had been used as an aerodrome as early as 1910. A detached flight of No. 1 (Communication) Squadron was stationed at Hounslow at the end of the war. At the beginning of May 1919, the Controller-General of Civil Aviation at the Air Ministry, which was then responsible for both civil and military aviation, acquired Hounslow from the R.A.F. as the London Terminal Aerodrome. For its day, Hounslow was a large aerodrome; it provided a maximum run of about 3,500 ft. One of the hangars on the north side of the landing area was converted into a customs shed, and the airport came into formal use on 25 August 1919, when the first service of the pioneer airline, Aircraft Transport and Travel Ltd, left for Paris.

A. T. & T. had been formed specifically for air transport operations on 5 October 1916 by George Holt Thomas, the founder of the Aircraft Manufacturing Company

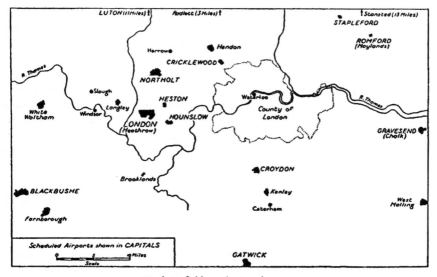

Civil Airfields in the London Area

Ltd, one of the largest firms in the aircraft industry at that time. The pioneer airline could not, however, start operations until the wartime ban on international civil flying had been lifted.

Two A. T. & T. flights were made to Paris on the first day; one was by a D.H.4A flown by Lieut. E. H. Lawford carrying one passenger and the other by a D.H.16 piloted by Major C. Patterson with four passengers. There was also a "proving flight" to Paris the same day by a Handley Page o/400 of the rival company, Handley Page Transport Ltd, which departed from its home aerodrome of Cricklewood but landed at Hounslow to clear customs. The o/400 was flown by Major E. L. Foot and carried eleven journalists as passengers.

The A. T. & T. flights on 25 August were historic as the start of the first daily scheduled international commercial air service in the world. From this date A. T. & T. ran a regular scheduled service between London and Paris, which was maintained for 16 months until 17 December 1920, when the company was forced to close down by financial difficulties. The A. T. & T. service operated from Hounslow until the spring of 1920, when the London terminal was moved to Croydon. The Handley Page flight on 25 August was followed by regular services to Paris (started on 2 September 1919) and to Brussels (started on 23 September).

Hounslow Heath was also used by French-operated services. It reverted, however, to the War Office in March 1920 and was not used again as an aerodrome.

CRICKLEWOOD (1919–21)

The Handley Page services mentioned above were the start of operations by Handley Page Transport Ltd, a subsidiary of the famous aircraft manufacturing company. These ran, with interruptions, on several routes between London and the Continent until March 1924, when the company was absorbed into the Government-sponsored Imperial Airways Ltd. The Handley Page services were based on their parent company's aerodrome beside its factory at Cricklewood. At first, as with the "proving flight" on 25 August 1919, the aircraft landed at Hounslow to clear customs. Later, customs facilities were provided at Cricklewood and the services operated direct from there. The Handley Page 0/400, 0/7, 0/10, and 0/11 aircraft continued to use their home aerodrome until May 1921, when operations were moved to Croydon, which by then had been in use as London's chief airport for more than a year.

Cricklewood continued as Handley Page's works aerodrome until the company opened a new and larger one at Radlett in 1929.

CROYDON (1920–39, 1945–   )

Croydon became London's official airport on 29 March 1920, when the landing area of the R.A.F. aerodrome of Waddon was taken over by the Controller-General of Civil Aviation. The new airport combined facilities from two previous aerodromes which dated from 1915. The terminal area, on Plough Lane, consisted of the buildings of the old Wallington aerodrome to the west, and the buildings and landing area (2,900 ft by 2,700 ft) of Waddon to the east. The strange agglomeration of temporary wartime buildings and hangars continued to serve as London's main air terminal until 1928.

On 1 April 1924 the four surviving pioneer British airlines—Handley Page Transport Ltd, the Instone Air Line, the Daimler Airway, and the British Marine Air Navigation Co. Ltd—were combined into the Government-sponsored Imperial Airways Ltd.[3] Imperials based themselves at Croydon, following the example of three of the constituent companies. The formation of a national airline company soon injected a new urgency into the development of British air transport. On the aircraft side, Imperial Airways stimulated progress by a decision to standardize as soon as possible on three-engined aircraft. This policy led to the development of the De Havilland Hercules and Armstrong-Whitworth Argosy, which played a big part in the expansion of British air routes in the late 1920s. At the same time, it became obvious that greatly extended base facilities would be required. In 1925, therefore, work started, at an estimated total cost of £267,000, on an ambitious scheme to develop Croydon Airport. A fine new terminal area was developed on the east side of the aerodrome alongside Purley Way, and Plough Lane was closed, the old buildings were demolished, and the landing area was extended to include that of the old Wallington aerodrome. At the same time, additional land was incorporated, increasing the landing area to 4,350 ft by 4,050 ft.

The dimensions of the enlarged Croydon were more than adequate for the aircraft of the day. As a contracting state to the International Civil Air Navigation Convention of 1926, Britain accepted fixed take-off requirements for its civil aircraft. This restriction on take-off and landing distances was reiterated in 1931, when the requirement was still that to obtain a Certificate of Airworthiness civil aircraft should be able, on take-off, to reach a height of 66 ft (20 metres) within a distance of 656 ft (200 metres) at full load in still air conditions. This so-called "I.C.A.N. screen" still represented the official requirement in 1936; but by then the development of high-performance monoplanes, particularly types like the American Douglas DC-2 and DC-3, had shown that some relaxation in take-off requirements was necessary to permit the operation of these much more economic and efficient aircraft. The effect of the "I.C.A.N. screen" on the aerodrome requirements of the aircraft using London's airports up to the mid-1930s is illustrated opposite. Thereafter, longer take-off and landing runs gradually came to be accepted, and by 1939 it was clear that a radical extension of existing airports would soon be necessary.

The development of radio and lighting aids at this time was making it possible to maintain scheduled operations in increasingly adverse weather conditions. It was soon appreciated that, even with the earlier performance standards, larger landing areas were necessary for landings in low visibilities. The newer types required even more space. By the mid-1930s, the Air Ministry's previous requirement for a Class A airport, which was for a maximum run of at least 2,400 ft, was seen to be inadequate, and the Ministry was suggesting that, for bad-weather operations, a "fog landing strip" of 4,200–4,500 ft was desirable. At the same time, the growing size and weight of transport aeroplanes was causing increasing problems with grass surfaces, particularly in winter. This was to lead logically in due course to the adoption of hard-surfaced runways.

The permanent buildings put up at Croydon in 1926–8 still stand today. In their time, they were the finest of their kind in the world and included a main terminal building, large hangars, and a hotel. The new buildings were opened by Lady Maud Hoare, wife of the Secretary of State for Air, on 2 May 1928. Croydon continued in use as London's major airport until 1939, but with the emergence in the early 1930s of independent air transport companies operating in parallel with Imperial Airways, it ceased to be the only aerodrome used for scheduled flying. On the outbreak of war in 1939 the civil operators evacuated Croydon, and it reverted to being an R.A.F. station. It remained so until 1945, although towards the end of the European War scheduled services to the Continent were again operated from Croydon by No. 110 Wing. R.A.F. Internal air services by the surviving civilian Air-Sea Group of companies also returned to using their old London terminal at this time.

The Government stated on 20 December 1945 that Northolt and Croydon would be London's airports for European and domestic air services in the immediate post-war

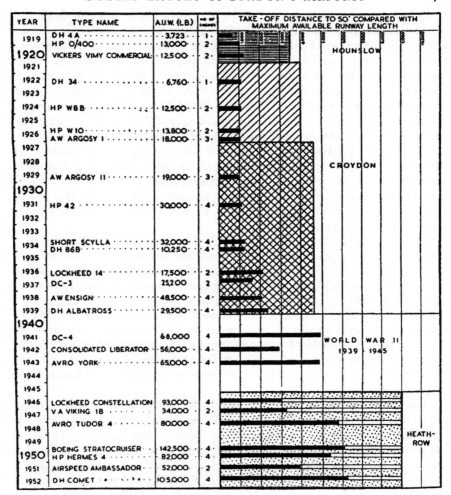

Take-off Distances and Runway Lengths

period. But the continued use of Croydon by the majority of domestic services was short-lived. Scheduled activity was cut to a low level soon after the formation of the new national airline corporation, British European Airways, on 1 August 1946. B.E.A. took over the services of No. 110 Wing immediately and those of the Air-Sea companies on 1 February 1947 and concentrated its operations on Northolt. Since that time Croydon, with its limited grass landing area, has survived as a scheduled airport only because of the operations of a number of small private companies. It has recently been announced that this famous old aerodrome is to be finally closed in 1958 when the new airport at Gatwick is due to open.

ROMFORD (1932–4)

The Essex bus operator, Edward Hillman, was probably the most significant figure in the re-emergence of private airlines in the United Kingdom in the early 1930s. From 1924 until 1932 there had been very little British air transport activity outside the operations of the Government's "chosen instrument", Imperial Airways. During the summer of 1932, however, several small companies opened scheduled services within the British Isles. Of these, that started by Hillman between Maylands aerodrome (near Romford) and Clacton, using De Havilland Puss Moths and later Fox Moths, was particularly important. The following year, using the new De Havilland Dragons (designed to his special requirements), Hillman added a daily service to Margate and on 1 April 1933 a twice-daily service to Paris—the latter in direct competition with Imperial Airways' Handley Page H.P.42s operating out of Croydon.

Maylands was strictly limited in size—its landing area measured only 2,550 ft by 1,095 ft. It therefore soon became too small for Hillman, and he moved away. The aerodrome was used thereafter intermittently for club flying until 1939.

HESTON (1933–9)

Heston Air Park, as it was originally called, was opened in 1929 by Airwork Ltd, as a centre for civil flying. At first this took the form of private, instructional, and club flying, together with a certain amount of charter work, but with the reappearance of independent scheduled operators in the 1930s Heston soon came into use as an airport. The first airline to use Heston was Spartan Airlines, which opened a regular twice-daily service to Cowes, in the Isle of Wight, on 14 April 1933. The service was operated with Spartan Cruisers. As with most of these early services, it ran only during the summer months.

Heston expanded rapidly as an airport and was soon second in importance only to Croydon. It was purchased by the Air Ministry in 1937 and was progressively developed until it had facilities comparable to those at Croydon itself; its landing area was only slightly smaller, having been enlarged until it measured 3,540 ft by 2,700 ft. As at Croydon, an instrument landing system and high-intensity lighting were installed.

When British Airways Ltd, the United Kingdom's largest privately owned airline, moved to Heston in 1938, the airport was confirmed as London's second airport. Its period of use in this role was, however, short, and after the war Heston did not continue as an aerodrome because of the development of the nearby site at Heathrow as London's new major airport.

STAPLEFORD (1934–6)

Hillman moved his base from Romford to Stapleford (sometimes called Stapleford Abbott, Abridge, or "Essex Airport") in 1934. The landing area was considerably larger than that at Maylands, measuring 3,780 ft by 2,790 ft.

In November 1934 Hillman's Airways Ltd gained a mail contract from the Post Office for services ⁓ Belfast and Glasgow, operated by way of Liverpool and the Isle of Man. Stapleford was used as the London terminal. Although Edward Hillman died on 31 December 1934, his company continued its operations from Stapleford until it became one of the constituent companies of the new private airline, British Airways Ltd. Hillman's first combined with Spartan Airlines and United Airways on 1 October 1935. This union was followed on 21 October 1935 by a further amalgamation with British Continental Airways of Croydon to produce British Airways Ltd. The De Havilland Rapides and D.H.86s of British Airways used Stapleford until the company moved to Gatwick in 1936. In 1940 British Airways was itself to be amalgamated with Imperial Airways to form B.O.A.C.

Other operators, including Air Dispatch Ltd, ran services from Stapleford during 1935, but when Hillman's ceased to be the main users the aerodrome closed down as an airport and reverted to private flying. It was later used by an R.A.F. Flying School (No. 21 E. & R.F.T.S.) and, as "Stapleford Tawney", was taken over by the R.A.F. during the war. A period of disuse followed the end of the war, but Stapleford is now once again a club–flying aerodrome and is the home of the aircraft manufacturers, Edgar Percival Aircraft Ltd.

GATWICK (1936–9, 1948–54)

Gatwick originated as an aerodrome in 1931, but it was only in 1936, when the owners, Airports Ltd, opened a new terminal building of advanced design connected by pedestrian tunnel with the airport's own railway station on the London–Brighton line, that the site qualified as a major London airport suitable for scheduled services. The landing area measured 3,180 ft by 2,210 ft.

British Airways moved its operations to Gatwick soon after the airport was opened, and for a time it looked as if it was destined to achieve general acceptance, with its easy rail access, as the best-sited of London's airports. However, as so often happened with London's aerodromes before the days of runways, the site soon proved troublesome because of flooding of the landing area during the winter. As a result, on 29 May 1938 British Airways moved their main base to Heston. The base had previously been partly accommodated at Gatwick and partly at Croydon. Gatwick did not recover before the war from this desertion by its most important user. It remained, however, in limited use as an airport up to 1939, when it was requisitioned by the R.A.F.

The owners of Gatwick, Airports Ltd, also opened an aerodrome at Gravesend (Chalk) in 1933. This aerodrome just comes within our defined "London area" and is believed to have been used at one time for a small number of scheduled services. These were not on a sufficient scale, however, to qualify this aerodrome as one of London's airports.

After the war Gatwick became a base for charter operators and for limited scheduled services by B.E.A. and certain private companies, but, following the public inquiry of 1954, the Government announced its intention of developing the site as London's second airport.[4] The necessary development work on buildings and runway is now in progress, and Gatwick is scheduled to come into use in its new and very much enlarged form (it will have a main runway 7,000 ft long) in 1958.

NORTHOLT (1946–54)

Originally opened as a Royal Flying Corps aerodrome in 1915, Northolt was used for civil purposes for a time after the First World War. It soon reverted to R.A.F.use, however, and in the later 1930s became one of the most important sector stations in No. 11 Group, Fighter Command. As such, it played an important part in the Battle of Britain and subsequently in the more offensive fighter operations staged in the years which followed. In 1943, with the formation of Transport Command with its head-quarters at Harrow, nearby Northolt came progressively into intensive use as London's main transport terminal. By the end of the war, it had two runways (of 5,520 ft and 4,800 ft) and temporary buildings suited to the handling of passengers and freight. As a result it stepped naturally into the role of London's civil airport.

Northolt became officially London's Airport on 4 February 1946. It remained the capital's most important airport until 1950, although the new London Airport at Heathrow, which was also opened early in 1946, was soon in use by the Avro Lancastrians of the short-lived British South American Airways Corporation. B.S.A.A. had been formed as a national airline corporation along with British European Airways by the Civil Aviation Act of 1946. B.S.A.A. had its maintenance base at Langley, the aerodrome of Hawker Aircraft Ltd, near Slough, but it operated its services from London Airport. B.E.A. established its headquarters beside Northolt Airport and built up its engineering base in the old R.F.C. hangars there. This corporation maintained most of its London services from Northolt until 30 October 1954. During these years Northolt handled nearly five million passengers and came to be accepted as London's short-haul terminal, handling domestic and European services, while London Airport catered for the long hauls. In due course, as progress with the development of Heathrow permitted, B.E.A. transferred its engineering and other operating facilities to the new airport. B.E.A.'s operations for some years after the war relied on the "interim" Vickers Viking and war-surplus American Douglas DC-3s. The Vikings were progressively replaced in 1952 and 1953 by more modern aircraft, the Airspeed Elizabethan and Vickers Viscount, and these new types were maintained and operated from the start of their careers from the new airport.

Since 1954, when it ceased to be a civil airport, Northolt has reverted to R.A.F. transport and communications use and has been used again by the Fairey Aviation Co. Ltd for the final assembly and testing of some of that company's products, as it was for many years between the wars. Because the headquarters of the United States Air Force in Great Britain is near by, Northolt is also used as a communications aerodrome by the Americans.

LONDON AIRPORT (1946–)

Planned as a transport aerodrome for the R.A.F. in the later years of the Second World War, Heathrow included the site of the pre-war Great West Aerodrome (also called Heathrow or Harmondsworth) which was used and owned by Faireys. It had originally been opened by them in 1930. The pre-war aerodrome had been grass-covered, but a pattern of runways was essential by the time Heathrow's development for the R.A.F. got under way in 1944. A system of three runways (the longest of 9,000 ft) was in use by the time the airport was opened and named "The London Airport" by the Minister of Civil Aviation, Lord Winster, on 25 March 1946.

Runways at post-war civil airports have to be long enough to meet new performance requirements far more exacting than those which applied in 1939. The International Civil Aviation Organization, formed under the United Nations after the war, soon defined internationally agreed standards which required that mainline transport aircraft should be operated in such a manner that an engine failure can be experienced at any stage of a flight without causing an accident. This means that runways have to be long enough for the aeroplane to be able to climb away safely after an engine failure or, if the engine fails early in the run, to abandon its take-off and stop before the end of the runway. These requirements have meant that London Airport, like other main terminals for long-distance services, requires runways approaching 10,000 ft in length, as well as elaborate radio, radar, and lighting aids. The introduction of large jet transports during the next three years may increase the length requirement to about 12,000 ft.

London Airport has steadily developed since its opening in 1946. A busy terminal area has been built in the centre of the airport, reached by a tunnel passing beneath the surrounding pattern of runways. Both B.O.A.C. and B.E.A. have developed great engineering bases on the east side of the airport. Although in 1957 the so-called Central Area buildings are handling only short-haul passenger and freight services, it is intended that eventually all operations shall be from this area and further traffic buildings are planned to make this possible. Until these are available, the long-haul services will continue to use the temporary buildings along the Bath Road on the north side of the airport. In earlier years these formed the only terminal facility.

London Airport is still developing rapidly. Today it handles services by forty airlines. During 1956 three million passengers passed through the airport, and this figure will probably continue to grow for the next few years at something like the rate of

15 per cent per annum which has been the average annual air traffic growth since the war. Present estimates suggest that the airport will be saturated by the traffic it will have to handle by the middle 1960s at the latest. Before that, a large part of London's short-haul air traffic will probably be flowing through Gatwick. Soon afterwards, in the later 1960s, a third airport will be required to serve London. Thus London will follow the pattern of air transport development in the United States, where in 1956 New York already had three airports, handling twelve million passengers per annum. It is still not possible to say where London's third airport will be. There are, however, indications that Southend may be the most attractive of the various alternatives.

No mention has been made in this account of helicopter air stations. However, in conclusion these should, perhaps, have a reference. Probably the first scheduled passenger helicopter service in the world was operated in 1950 with a Sikorsky S.51 from a sports ground at Barnes to the British Industries Fair at Castle Bromwich in Birmingham. This service ran for only a few days. To B.E.A. goes the credit for starting shortly afterwards the first regular scheduled passenger helicopter service which was maintained for a reasonable period. This service operated between Cardiff and Liverpool from 1 June 1950 to 31 March 1951. B.E.A. first ran helicopter services from Northolt and London Airports in 1951. The corporation also operated in 1954 a helicopter freight service between Gatwick and London Airport. Finally, on 25 July 1955 B.E.A. opened a scheduled airport-to-city-centre passenger helicopter service between London Airport and an air station on the South Bank of the Thames near the Waterloo Air Terminal which ran until 31 May 1956. The South Bank site was the first true helicopter air station to be established for scheduled services in the London area. As the first of a new type of London air terminal—which is, however, due to be closed in the near future—it is a fitting landmark at which to end this brief history.

NOTES

1. This article is mainly based on information already printed in various sources but not hitherto brought together. The following in particular have been consulted: *Flight* (from 1909); *The Aeroplane* (from 1911); *Reports on the Progress of Civil Aviation* (H.M.S.O., from 1919); *The Air Pilot* (H.M.S.O., from 1919); G. Holt Thomas, *Aerial Transport* (1920); *The Approach towards a System of Imperial Air Communications* (H.M.S.O., 1926); A. E. W. Salt, *Imperial Air Routes* (1930); A. J. Jackson, "Beginnings of British Air Transport", *Air Review*, VII (1945), Part 1, 30–4, Part 2, 56–9, Part 3, 52–6; J. Stroud, *Famous Airports of the World* (1956).

2. An exhibition "Flying at Hendon", commemorating the aerodrome's history, was held at Church Farm House Museum, Hendon, in the summer of 1956.

3. See A. J. Quin-Harkin, "Imperial Airways, 1924–40", *Journal of Transport History*, I (1953–4), 197.

4. Cmd. 9215 (1954).

For Product Safety Concerns and Information please contact our EU
representative GPSR@taylorandfrancis.com Taylor & Francis Verlag GmbH,
Kaufingerstraße 24, 80331 München, Germany

Batch number: 08158427

Printed by Printforce, the Netherlands